the world of automobiles

An Illustrated Encyclopedia of the Motor Car

COLUMBIA HOUSE/New York

Consultant Editor: Tom Northey
Executive Editor: Ian Ward
Editorial Director: Brian Innes
Assistant Editors: Laurie Caddell
Mike Winfield
Art Editor: David Goodman
Art Assistant: John Heritage
Picture Research: Evan Davies
Mirco Decet
Cover Design: Harry W. Fass
Production Manager: Warren Bright

contributors
WILLIAM BODDY: Minerva
Morgan
DAVID BURGESS WISE: Merz
Métallurgique
Meyer
Moon
Mors
LAURIE CADDELL: Moretti
PAUL DARKE: Morris
TONY DRON: MIRA
GRAHAM GAULD: Michelotti
JOHN JAMES: Mirrors
BRYAN JONES: Mitsubishi
Moskvich
MIKE KETTLEWELL: Mexican Grand Prix
Monaco Grand Prix
TOM NORTHEY: MG
ROBERT PEMBERTON: Military Vehicles
L. J. K. SETRIGHT: Miller
MIKE TWITE: Mercury
Merlyn
Mille Miglia
Milton
Moll

Monaco
Monica
Monte Carlo Rally
Monteverdi
Montlhéry
Monza

Picture acknowledgments
Page 1321: *; *; *; *; *—**1322:** National Motor Museum—**1323:** *: *; *—**1324:** *; *—**1325:** Ford—**1326:** National Motor Museum—**1327:** National Motor Museum; Suddeutscher Verlag—**1328:** *; National Motor Museum; *—**1329:** National Motor Museum—**1330:** National Motor Museum—**1331:** London Art Tech—**1332:** London Art Tech—**1333:** *; National Motor Museum; National Motor Museum—**1334:** *—**1335:** National Motor Museum; *—**1336:** N. Bruce; National Motor Museum—**1337:** *; *—**1338:** National Motor Museum; *—**1339:** *—**1340:** *; *—**1341:** BLMC—**1342:** *; Quattroruote; *; G. Gauld; Triumph—**1343:** Quattroruote; National Motor Museum; G. Gauld—**1344:** G. Gauld; *; *; Quattroruote; *; *—**1345:** National Motor Museum; I.G.D.A.—**1346:** National Motor Museum—**1347:** National Motor Museum—**1348:** National Motor Museum—**1348-9:** National Motor Museum—**1350:** National Motor Museum—**1351:** *; *; Quattroruote; *;—**1352:** I.G.D.A.; B. H. Vanderveen Collection—**1353:** B. H. Vanderveen Collection; I.G.D.A.—**1354:** P. Tilley—**1355:** *—**1356:** *; *; Quattroruote; *; *—**1357:** *; Quattroruote; *; *—**1358:** *; Quattroruote; *; Keystone—**1359:** Quattroruote—**1360:** *; Quattroruote; *—**1361:** Quattroruote—**1362:** London Art Tech—**1363:** National Motor Museum; Indianapolis—**1364:** Quattroruote; Quattroruote; C. Posthumus—**1365:** Indianapolis; National Motor Museum—**1366:** National Motor Museum—**1367:** Indianapolis—**1368:** Quattroruote; National Motor Museum; National Motor Museum—**1369:** National Motor Museum; Quattroruote; Quattroruote; Quattroruote—**1370:** National Motor Museum; G. Goddard—**1371:** Mira—**1372:** Mira—**1373:** Mira—**1374:** Mira—**1375:** L. J. Caddell Orbis; P. Revere—**1376:** P. Revere—**1377:** Quattroruote—**1378:** Quattroruote—**1379:** Quattroruote; Quattroruote; Colt; L. J. Caddell Orbis—**1380:** C. Posthumus—**1381:** Tosi; Quattroruote; London Art Tech—**1382:** Quattroruote; Société de Bains de Mer—**1383:** Quattroruote—**1384:** Quattroruote; G. Goddard—**1385:** G. Goddard—**1386:** C. Lawrence; Spencer Smith; Spencer Smith; Spencer Smith—**1387:** Spencer Smith—**1388:** L. J. Caddell/Orbis—**1389:** Quattroruote—**1390:** Quattroruote—**1390-1:** Quattroruote—**1391:** Quattroruote—**1392:** Quattroruote—**1393:** Quattroruote; Spencer Smith—**1394:** Spencer Smith—**1395:** Quattroruote; Spencer Smith—**1396:** C. Posthumus—**1397:** M. L. Rosenthal—**1398:** Quattroruote—**1399:** Quattroruote—**1400:** Quattroruote—**1401:** National Motor Museum—**1402:** Autocar; National Motor Museum—**1403:** Autocar—**1404:** National Motor Museum; Quattroruote—**1405:** Zagari—**1406:** Moretti—**1407:** Moretti—**1408:** Moretti—**1409:** Quattroruote; Quattroruote; National Motor Museum; National Motor Museum; Boschetti—**1410:** National Motor Museum—**1411:** National Motor Museum—**1412:** Marka; National Motor Museum—**1413:** Belli; Belli; L. J. Caddell—**1414:** National Motor Museum—**1415:** Cherrett; A. Morland; A. Morland—**1416:** National Motor Museum; National Motor Museum (I)—**1417:** Classic Car—**1418:** Boschetti; National Motor Museum—**1419:** L. J. Caddell/Orbis—**1420:** BLMC—**1421:** National Motor Museum (I); National Motor Museum—**1422:** Quattroruote; National Motor Museum (I); National Motor Museum—**1423:** National Motor Museum (I); National Motor Museum—**1424:** Quattroruote; National Motor Museum; National Motor Museum—**1425:** Cherrett—**1426:** National Motor Museum; National Motor Museum; J. Spencer Smith—**1427:** N. Bruce—**1428:** National Motor Museum—**1429:** Quattroruote; Di Santo—**1430:** Quattroruote—**1431:** British Leyland; National Motor Museum—**1432:** National Motor Museum—**1433:** National Motor Museum—**1434:** London Art Tech—**1435:** D. Barker; National Motor Museum—**1436:** National Motor Museum—**1437:** Allardyce—**1438-9:** National Motor Museum—**1439:** Quattroruote—**1440:** National Motor Museum—**cover:** London Art Tech

Contents

		Page
AT WORK AND PLAY	Military Vehicles: Warfare on Wheels	1345
CARS OF TODAY	Mercury Cougar XR7	1325
	MG BGT V8	1341
	Monica	1388
	Morgan Plus 8	1419
	Morris Marina	1420
	Moskvich	1440
THE GREAT CARS	Mercury: Ford's Messenger of the Gods	1321
	Métallurgique: The Luxury Market Their Forte	1328
	MG: A Great Sporting Name	1333
	Minerva: Goddess of Automobiles	1368
	Mitsubishi: A Small Part of an Empire	1377
	Monica: An Anglo-French Alliance	1386
	Monteverdi: Luxury Motor Cars With Swiss Precision	1393
	Moon: "The Car of Comfort With a Reserve of Speed"	1401
	Moretti: Purpose-Built Town Cars and Rebodied Fiats	1405
	Morgan: An Ageless Thoroughbred	1409
	Morris: Purpose Built for the Masses	1421
	Mors: The Gateway to Life	1432
	Moskvich: The Son of Moscow	1437
HOW IT WORKS	Mirrors: An All-Round View From the Driving Position	1375
THE MOTOR INDUSTRY	Michelotti: A Triumph in Design	1342
	MIRA: A Proving Ground for Design	1371
WHO'S WHO	Merz: Germany's Iron Man of Motor Racing	1327
	Meyer: The First Triple Indy Winner	1330
	Milton: Outstanding Despite Handicap	1367
	Moll: The Grand Prix Race Ace From Algeria	1380
WORLD OF SPEED	Merlyn: Wizards of the Race Track	1326
	Mexican Grand Prix: Grand Prix Racing South of the Border	1331
	Mille Miglia	1355
	Miller: The Arch American Racer	1361
	Monaco Grand Prix: Road Racing on the Riviera	1381
	Monaco: The High-Street GP Circuit	1385
	Monte Carlo Rally: Through the Snow to the Sun	1389
	Montlhéry: Four Famous Motor Race Circuits in One	1396
	Monza: Home of the Italian Grand Prix	1398

FORD'S MESSENGER OF THE GODS

Above: Mercury—the fleet-footed, winged-sandled messenger of the gods, and the name given to the new car concern created by the Ford Motor Company in 1938

MERCURY WAS AN IDEAL NAME for a motor car because Mercury was a Roman god with winged sandals who was the messenger of the gods. Several British and American companies used the name in the early days of motoring, but when the Ford Motor Company of the USA was looking for a new *marque* identification, the name of Mercury was available and they quickly settled on it for their new brand name.

The first Mercury, which appeared on 4 November 1938, was in effect a Ford with a different body, becoming one of the fore-runners of today's much despised 'badge engineering' techniques where near-identical cars are sold under different *marque* names. In price the new Mercury fell between the existing Ford V8 and the Lincoln, so that Ford now had cars in over 90 per cent of American price categories. The Mercury 8 as it was called featured the Ford box-section, cruciform braced chassis with rigid axles front and rear, suspended on transverse leaf springs and double-acting hydraulic dampers. Four-wheel hydraulically operated drum brakes were fitted all round and power came from an enlarged version of the Ford V8 side-valve 3.9-litre engine, which gave 95 bhp at 3600 rpm. Power was taken via a three-speed gearbox

through a torque tube drive to the rear axle. The four-door sedan body of the standard model was the first Ford product to be styled from a clay model within the company's own studios. The body was quite pleasant by 1938 standards, its resemblance to the post-war Standard Vanguard being most marked. As well as the sedan there was a two-door convertible with an electrically operated roof and leather upholstery as standard equipment.

Ford could do no wrong in 1939, as they were out-selling General Motors by 2 to 1 and the Mercury was enthusiastically received despite its similarity to the Ford line. Over 65,000 Mercury's were registered in 1939, although in the first model year the cars were actually known as Ford-Mercurys. The Ford name was dropped for 1940 when the only major change was a new four-door convertible version which was not very popular. A column gear change and sealed-beam headlamps were also introduced in 1940.

The Ford factories were still producing cars in 1942 although the USA had entered the war in 1941. The Mercury models were restyled once again, the front end being drastically revised with a low, wide grille. The power output of the Ford 'flathead' was up to a

Below: 1939 Mercury four-door sedan

Bottom: 1946 Mercury Sportman

Top: 1949 Mercury club coupé

Above: Mercury Monterey Sun Valley

claimed 100 bhp and for the first time a semi-automatic transmission was available.

Car production came to a halt in early 1942 and the factories switched to war production, building tanks, amphibious machines, jeeps and even B24 bombers for the US and allied services.

Edsel Ford, who had played a large part in introducing the Lincoln and Mercury names to the Ford range died during the war and in September 1945 Henry Ford II became President of Ford. He immediately set in motion plans to divorce Lincoln and Mercury from Ford operations, setting up the Lincoln-Mercury Division of the Ford Motor Company. Work began on new factories in Los Angeles and Metuchen, New Jersey, and the St Louis factory was switched entirely to Lincoln and Mercury products.

The 1946 models were very similar to the cars that had been in production in 1942 with the exception of a new convertible called the Sportsman which had wood panelled bodywork like the station wagon. Yet another grille restyling job was carried out and nearly 90,000 Mercurys were sold in 1946. With demand running well ahead of production there was little need for change in the years that followed and the Mercury range was unchanged in 1947 and 1948.

The first really new Mercury since 1938 was announced in late 1948. The chassis remained much as before except that coil-spring independent front suspension was introduced and a hypoid rear axle fitted. The faithful V8 engine was increased in size to $4\frac{1}{4}$ litres and the power output was increased to 110 bhp. The three-speed gearbox was retained but an innovation was the availability of a Borg Warner overdrive of the type which was engaged by depressing the throttle pedal.

By 1950 the one-millionth Mercury had been built and it was now necessary to build a new factory at Wayne, Michigan to keep up with demand. A slightly modified Mercury Sport Coupé was added to the range in 1950 and a total of 320,000 cars were delivered during the year.

By 1953 the range had swollen to eight different models and Mercury started to give models individual names; one new name was the Monterey, a model which stayed with the company until 1974, along with several other alliterative names.

In 1954 Ford's new V8 overhead-valve engine was introduced, this $4\frac{1}{4}$-litre engine giving 161 bhp in its Mercury form. The rest of the design changed little, the emphasis being on body styling to attract customers. One example of this was the Monterey Sun Valley, a coupé with the front half of the roof made from transparent plastic. It did not last long because buyers fried under the greenhouse roof. Mercury entered the dream-car field in 1954 with the XM800, which was simply a styling job in glassfibre on a standard chassis.

Mercury had offered little for the motor-racing enthusiast because their cars were just cheap, basic, unexciting transportation, but veteran mechanic Bill Stroppe had achieved some success in the Mobil Economy run and had persuaded Lincoln to give him cars for the Pan-American Road Race. His cars finished first, second, third and fourth in 1952 and 1953, earning Stroppe a contract with the Lincoln-Mercury Division. When Chevrolet began winning Stock-Car races in the early 1950s and promoting motor racing in a big way, both the Ford and Lincoln-Mercury Divisions retaliated with racing programmes. Stroppe ran the team for Lincoln-Mercury using Mercury cars, winning several races on the West Coast himself in 1955, but Ford were far more successful, largely because they put more finance into their effort.

The 1955 production Mercurys were considerably modified; the wheelbase was increased to 119 inches and two new versions of the ohv V8 were introduced, both of 5 litres capacity, one with a 7.5:1 compression ratio giving 188 bhp and the other with 8.5:1 compression ratio giving 198 bhp. Another restyling job undertaken, with a big wrap-around windscreen, hooded headlamps and a full-width grille/bumper design. A new model was added to the range, the Montclair, to bring Mercury up to ten different models. In 1955 Mercury production was raised to its highest ever level of 434,911 cars.

Detroit's greatest styling excesses were perpetrated in the late 1950s, the Mercurys of the 1956 to 1959 model years, ranking as some of the ugliest ever made.

Below: the Mercury Cougar, a car with a strong luxury/sports personality, added a new dimension to the American motoring scene in 1967. It was one of the new breed of compact cars very popular in the USA at that time. Outstanding performance was provided by powertrain combinations featuring either 289 cubic inch V8 engines, with two or four-choke carburation, or a 390 cubic inch V8, with four-choke carburation

Significantly, Mercury sales began to tail off at the start of this period with 1956 sales down to 327,943 cars. More new cars were announced for 1956 but they were largely adaptations of the 1955 models. The cheaper Medalist range was added to the Monterey and Montclair ranges and an optional 260 hp version of the V8 engine was available in 1956.

On the production side the 1957 cars showed the influence of the XM Turnpike Cruiser of 1956, for the cars were longer, lower and wider, the wheelbase now up to 122 inches and the standard engine being a 6-litre 290 bhp V8. Despite the new styling, sales slumped again to 263,245, little more than half of the 1955 production. However, the 3-millionth Mercury

was eventually produced during the year 1957.

In 1958 Ford launched the new Edsel *marque* which was designed to fit between the Ford and Mercury price brackets. A new division, the Mercury-Edsel-Lincoln Division was formed and Mercury announced an additional range of cars, the Park Lane series which were built on a new 125 in wheelbase chassis. The horsepower race was still on with a vengeance despite the so-called ban on advertising, giving a claimed 400 bhp. A new three-speed automatic transmission made its appearance, a feature which was specified by most drivers.

Although the new Edsel was supposed to hit at General Motors' sales, it took a large bite out of Mercury sales which crashed to a modest 132,271 during the 1958 season.

The Edsel was a complete failure and was dropped in 1959, so the division was renamed the Lincoln-Mercury Division and great efforts were made to improve the Mercury range. The Monterey and Montclair models used a 126 in wheelbase while the Park Lane used a 128 in wheelbase chassis. Overall styling remained largely unchanged, but dual-headlamp systems were now almost universal. The range was now huge, with many permutations available on the basic chassis, while engines ranged from the 5-litre 210 bhp V8 of the Medalist to the 7.2-litre 345 bhp V8s of the Park Lane. Sales in 1959 improved to 161,237.

The American motor industry was beginning to panic in the late 1950s at the inroads made into the US market by imported cars, most notably the Volkswagen. Prior to this, the US manufacturers had felt that imports were little more than a pinprick, but suddenly the imports were heading for a 10 per cent market share and 10 per cent of 5 million cars was a little more than Detroit could bear. So the big three makers hurriedly designed and built their so-called Compact cars, which, although fairly small by US

standards, were still big compared with the European cars which were invading the market. Ford brought out the Falcon and Mercury produced an almost identical car called the Comet. This was a very conventional car on a 114 in wheelbase powered by a 2.3-litre straight-six cylinder engine giving 114 bhp. The Comet was an immediate success with 100,000 sold within six months of its announcement, helping to push Mercury sales back up to a healthy 317,055 for

1960, firmly establishing the 'Compact' concept.

For 1961 Mercury decided to capitalise on the Comet successes by offering another economy range, the Meteor 600 and 800 series powered by 3.6-litre 135 bhp straight-six engines developed from the Comet unit. However, the Comet still took the lion's share of sales in 1961, racking up 197,263 sales against the 120,088 of all other Mercury models put together.

The 1962 range followed the clean cut, uncluttered style of the previous year's cars and more sporty models were being produced with four-speed manual gearboxes, separate bucket seats, and a variety of optional engines. Sales improved slightly to 321,817.

Ford had decided in the early 1960s that a return to factory racing participation would be advantageous and they gradually began to build up their involvement in practically every branch of the sport, especially in Europe with rally cars, saloon-car racing and even single-seater racing with especial emphasis on Indianapolis. Mercury were not left out although their task was to concentrate on stock-car racing through Bill Stroppe once again.

By mid-1963 the Mercury Marauder had been announced; this was a high performance car fitted with a 7-litre V8 giving options of 415 or 425 bhp. This car formed the basis of Parnelli Jones' successful racers.

In 1964 Ford invented the 'Pony car' with their Mustang, a medium-sized, sporty looking car with performance potential which took America's youth market by storm. Rival manufacturers quickly reacted by bringing out their own 'pony cars' but it was some while later before Mercury brought out their Cougar,

Above left: the Mercury Cougar XR7 two-door hardtop of 1969

Top: the convertible version of the 1969 Mercury Cougar

Above: another 1969 model, this is the Cyclone CJ two-door fastback

Above left: the Mercury Cougar XR7 two-door hardtop of 1971. It captured the imagination of the Americans with its sporting image and good performance

Above right: a front view of the 1971 Mercury Comet four-door sedan. It was available with a choice of either six or eight cylinders

a somewhat up-market version of the Mustang with a rather different body, although it, too, was a two-door hardtop. The Mustang went on to achieve success in the Trans-Am series for medium-sized saloons of up to 5 litres in capacity but Mercury did not enter their similar Cougar.

By 1967 the Comet was still in production but the accent had swung away from economy and the wheelbase had increased by 2 in to 116 in. Not too many owners specified the straight-six engine as most buyers wanted good acceleration. A whole new range of models had come in including such models as the Capri (a two-door coupé having no connections with Ford of Britain's Capri), the Caliente, the Cyclone GT, the Villager station wagon, the S55 convertible, the Monterey, the Montclair, the Park Lane, the Brougham, the Marquis and the Colony Park. By careful manipulation between Ford and Mercury it was possible to offer a seemingly endless series of cars, although very often there was little to choose between them in specification.

By 1970 Detroit was again worried about the threat of foreign imports and Ford announced the Maverick, a sub-compact, 2-door coupé powered by a straight-six 2.7-litre engine giving 105 bhp in standard trim. Mercury did not follow suit immediately but eventually the Comet range was completely revised to follow the Maverick lines, but was available as a two-door coupé and a four-door saloon as well. The same engine was used, although in standard trim it gave only 82 bhp, and the cheapest version, the 2-door coupé, cost 2193 dollars in 1972.

Mercury also attracted some attention in the performance-car market with the Cyclone GT and Spoiler, the latter model having an aerofoil mounted on the boot lid. The standard engine for the Spoiler was a 370 bhp version of the 7-litre V8 which gave the car a top speed of around 120 mph. An optional engine was a 375 bhp version of the same unit.

By 1972 the US motor industry was in a state of panic over the safety and pollution laws which were promising to be more stringent than anticipated. Most manufacturers found it difficult to make their big V8s comply with the pollution tests, so gradually the

bigger engines began to fade from catalogues and power outputs dropped drastically as engines were 'de-toxed' to cope with the regulations. The necessity to cope with crash tests on all models caused manufacturers to trim their model ranges considerably, while all convertible models were soon abandoned as the US manufacturers felt they could not be made to comply with the regulations. However, the 1972/3 Mercury range was still quite extensive for they had the Comet, the Montego, the Cougar, the Monterey, the Marquis and the Colony Park station wagon. But the Marauder, Cyclone and Brougham ranges had been dropped as had all the convertible models except the Cougar.

In 1973 the fuel crisis arrived and with it yet more demands for smaller cars. The Mercury Comet sold well during late 1973 and through much of 1974 while the bigger cars would hardly sell at all. To cash in on the new boom in smaller cars, Ford instigated a crash programme to bring out new small cars. The Ford Mustang 11 was a much smaller car than its predecessor and in late 1974 Ford announced their Ford Granada and the equivalent Mercury Monarch. Neither car had any relation to the British Ford Granada as they were fairly unsophisticated semi-compact cars weighing around $1\frac{1}{2}$ tons and available with either the straight-six or V8 engines. The cars were not particularly attractive to look at partly because of the massive bumpers.

With the arrival of the Monarch, Mercury decided to drop one of their biggest cars, the Monterey, a name which had been with Mercury for many years. However, the loss of the Monterey was just another sign that Detroit felt the day of the $2\frac{1}{2}$-ton car had ended.

Mercury, like most other American manufacturers, has never gone in for designs with advanced engineering features, preferring the annual styling change on a simple, uncomplicated, reliable chassis. As a subsidiary of the Ford Motor Company, Mercury has never really established its own identity, largely for financial reasons, and still labours under the stigma of being a Ford with a different badge. However, if Mercury has never produced an exciting car neither has it built a really bad one. MT

COUGAR XR7

The Mercury Cougar was introduced in 1967 as an up-market variation on the Ford Mustang 'Pony-Car' theme. While the Mustang underwent several changes during which it became somewhat smaller, the Cougar took the other route and gradually got larger and slower.

By 1975, the Cougar XR7 was one of the dying breed of American fuel-gulping land cruisers. The 1975 Cougars are powered by either 5752 cc or 7539 cc V8 engines.

In 5762 cc (163 bhp) form, the car has a top speed of 115 mph and returns 12.3 miles per gallon. In the larger 220 bhp form, the car has a top speed of 121 mph and returns just 11.8 miles per gallon.

The suspension for the Cougar is of the independent type by wishbones, lower trailing links, coil springs, an anti-roll bar and telescopic dampers at the front, while the rear is of the rigid type by an axle, lower trailing radius arms, upper oblique torque arms, coil springs and telescopic dampers. Heavy-duty suspension is optional, complete with a rear anti-roll bar.

Naturally, there is a power-assisted steering with 3.99 turns from lock to lock, and there is also a servo-assisted braking system utilising discs at the front and drums at the rear.

The Cougar XR7 is only available as a 2-door coupé, although there is still ample room for five people.

A large range of extras are available and include air-conditioning, electric windows, a tilting steering wheel and a limited-slip differential. Various final-drive ratios can also be specified.

ENGINE Front-mounted, water-cooled V8. 101.6 mm (4 in) bore × 88.8 mm (3.50 in) stroke = 5752 cc (351 cu in) (163 bhp), or 110.7 mm (4.36 in) bore × 97.8 mm (3.85 in) stroke = 7539 cc (460 cu in) (220 bhp). Maximum power 163 bhp at 4200 rpm, or 220 bhp at 4000 rpm; maximum torque 278 lb ft at 2000 rpm (163 bhp), or 355 lb ft at 2600 rpm.

Cast-iron cylinder block and heads. Compression ratio 8.2:1 (163 bhp), or 8:1 (220 bhp). 5 main bearings. 2 valves per cylinder operated, via pushrods and rockers, by a single camshaft at the centre of the V. 1 Motorcraft downdraught twin-barrel carburettor (163 bhp), or 1 Motorcraft downdraught four-barrel carburettor (220 bhp).

TRANSMISSION Torque converter and three-speed automatic gearbox. Maximum ratio of converter at stall 2.09 (163 bhp), or 2.16 (220 bhp). Ratios for 163 bhp (220 bhp in brackets) 1st 2.400 (2.460), 2nd 1.470 (1.460), 3rd 1 (1), rev 2 (2.180:1). Hypoid-bevel final drive. Ratio 2.750, 3.250 optional for both cars. Limited-slip differential optional.

CHASSIS Perimeter frame.

SUSPENSION Front—independent by wishbones, lower trailing links, coil springs, an anti-roll bar and telescopic dampers. Rear—non-independent by a rigid axle, lower trailing radius arms, upper oblique torque arms, coil springs and telescopic dampers.

STEERING Servo-assisted recirculating ball. Turns from lock to lock 3.99.

BRAKES Servo-assisted front discs and rear drums.

WHEELS 5½ in × 14 steel.

TYRES HR78 × 14.

DIMENSIONS AND WEIGHT Wheelbase 114 in; track—front and rear 63.40 in; length 215.50; width 78.60 in; height 52.40 in; ground clearance 4.48 in; dry weight 4247 lb (163 bhp), or 4540 lb (220 bhp); turning circle between walls 42.4 ft; fuel tank capacity 18.3 gals.

BODY Coupé 2-door, 5 seats.

PERFORMANCE Maximum speed 115 mph (163 bhp), or 121 mph (220 bhp); fuel consumption 12.3 mpg (163 bhp), or 11.8 mpg (220 bhp).

MANY SMALL BRITISH racing-car constructors started up in the early 1960s, most of them trying to cash in on the new 'cheap' Formula Junior which started in 1958. A large majority of the firms soon fell by the wayside, but one which has stayed the course is Merlyn.

Started in 1960 by Clive Maskrey and Selwyn Hayward the company was named Colchester Racing Developments with premises at Little Bentley, Colchester, Essex. Their first car was a Formula Junior car, the Mk 1 which was conventional by the standards of the day, although it was mid-engined at a time when some of the more experienced constructors were still sticking to front-mounted engines.

As many drivers were attracted to the new Formula Junior, Merlyn had no difficulty in finding customers in the early days, despite the lack of experience of its constructors. No great success came the way of Merlyn in the first couple of years in Britain but the make was much more successful in the United States where a number of cars were sold. Belgian André Pilette, the former Grand Prix driver, bought a Merlyn which he used to win the 1962 Belgian Formula Junior Championship and he planned an abortive Formula One car based on the FJ Merlyn, using a 1½-litre Ford engine.

The company was sufficiently encouraged by the successes of its Formula Junior cars to go into the sports-car market with the Mk 4. The Mk 4A version was designed for international racing so it was made to comply with the Appendix 'C' sports-car regulations which demanded certain minimum dimensions to allow a passenger to be carried and to give space for luggage. The engine bay at the rear was designed to take a variety of engines including the 1100 cc version of the Ford Anglia unit, tuned to give 100 bhp by Cosworth, but the Coventry Climax 1998 cc single overhead-camshaft unit could also be specified. For international racing these engines were mated to a five-speed Hewland/Volkswagen gearbox but for British club racing Merlyn brought out the Mk 4T which was supplied with an unmodified engine and four-speed gearbox.

By 1963 the Formula Junior car was becoming quite refined, particular attention being paid to the aerodynamics of the car. In order to create the minimum amount of drag the front suspension coil springs and dampers were placed horizontally above the chassis out of the airstream, being operated by rods from the lower suspension arms. The works supported drivers for 1963 were Roy Pike and Jonathan Williams who put up some good drives without ever really coming near to dominating the Formula, which was becoming extremely competitive.

For 1964 the Mk 6 sports car and Mk 7 single-seater were announced; the Mk 6 was simply an improved Mk 4 to enable larger engines to be fitted and the single-seater was designed to be used in both Formula Two and Formula Three. Quite a fair number of the single-seater were sold and, although F2 was dominated by the Brabhams, several good places were obtained. One of the most consistent Merlyn drivers was Chris Irwin who notched up several good wins.

In 1965 the Mk 8 sports car was introduced but this gained little success on the sales front and only a couple of cars were built. The company concentrated on producing customer Formula Three cars in 1965 and 1966, the Mk 9 and 9A models, but there was little in the way of success and the company faded out of the limelight to some extent.

Then in 1967 came Formula Ford, which changed the firm's fortunes. They introduced the Mk 11 for FF and it was an immediate favourite with drivers both in Britain and in the USA. The greatest success came

WIZARDS OF THE RACE TRACK

Although they have raced in other formulae, Merlyn's speciality is Formula Ford

from the young Australian Tim Schenken who carefully prepared a Mk 11 with a Chris Steele engine and won his first ten races in the car with consumate ease.

In 1968 Merlyn built a Formula Two car, the Mk 12, powered by the Cosworth FVA engine; it was chosen by the Bob Gerard team to race in the European Championship but it was conspicuously unsuccessful and Merlyn soon abandoned F2.

The Mk 14 F3 car was quite a successful machine and in 1969 and 1970 the Merlyn was undoubtedly one of the top cars in both FF and F3. A notable driver of the FF Mk 11A was Emerson Fittipaldi who drove one to several victories when he first arrived in England in 1969, before switching to F3. His Merlyn was purchased by Colin Vandervell for the 1970 season, a wise buy as it transpired, for the son of the late Tony Vandervell, of Vanwall fame, scored no less than 29 victories in FF and picked up the Les Leston Formula Ford Championship.

This success persuaded Merlyn to move into other formulae in 1970, notably the American Formula B, (the Mk 15) which is similar to Europe's Formula Atlantic, and F100 (the Mk 16) for cheap sports cars. There were few sales made to America for Formula B, while Formula F100 proved to be a great flop in Britain so very few sales were made.

Although cars for various categories have been offered since 1971, Merlyn production has been concentrated almost entirely on Formula Ford, gradual improvements being made each year. In 1974, the then current Mk 25 sold for around £2200 complete, or at around £1600 less engine and gearbox.

Many prominent drivers have bought Merlyn FF cars and obtained success. Bob Arnott won the 1972 Townsend Thoreson Championship in a Mk 20, the American David Loring put in many good drives, and Tim Brise drove entertainingly in a highly modified Merlyn in which the radiators were placed at the side of the chassis. MT

Above: although Merlyn are best known for their highly successful Formula Ford cars, they have, from time to time, built cars for other formulae. This is the Merlyn F3 car of H. M. Bennett competing in the Brunton hill-climb of 1963

Germany's iron man
of motor racing

EVEN IN AN ERA of larger-than-life racing drivers, Otto Merz stood out from his contemporaries. Not simply because he was physically a giant, but also because of his phenomenal strength—he was reputed to be able to drive six-inch nails into a plank of wood with his fists, and when, during the 1929 Ulster Tourist Trophy, a damaged front wing impeded his Mercedes, he ripped it off with his bare hands.

But Merz, who was born in 1889 at Cannstatt, had another claim to fame. Following a period as a mechanic with Mercedes (whose factory was, after all, in his home town) in which he rode with Willy Poege, 'the gentleman driver', Merz became a chauffeur in the service of the Archduke Franz Ferdinand of Austria. He was driving the car which was following the Gräf und Stift carrying Franz Ferdinand and his morganatic wife Sophie Chotek when they were shot by the assassin Gavrilo Princip at Sarajevo. And it was Merz who carried the dying Archduke into a nearby house; after which, having lost his employer, he returned to Mercedes.

After the war, he joined the Mercedes racing department, and began to score successes in local events. Merz first came to the attention of the international motor-racing public in 1924, when he secured first place at both the Solitude and Klausen hill-climbs. In 1925, he won the race on the narrow, winding, Solitude Ring, a tortuous circuit of closed public roads which circled the Schloss Solitude near Stuttgart at the wheel of a 2-litre, four-cylinder Mercedes; not content with this feat, he repeated it the following year, averaging a hair-raising 57.29 mph in his new, Porsche-designed, Mercedes 2-litre straight-eight, a car which was hardly renowned for good handling (the model had already caused Count Louis Zborowski's death at Monza).

Then, in 1927, the new Nürburgring circuit in the Eifel mountains was officially opened; the first German Grand Prix was held that July over a distance of 316 miles, resulting in a victory for Merz's Mercedes.

But the following year the German GP acquired full international status. If 1927 had seen the Mercedes pitted against a motley selection of stripped touring cars (including a brace of Hanomags with 499 cc single-cylinder engines), 1928 saw them ranged against a formidable array of foreign vehicles, including 2.3-litre Type 35B Bugattis, and top drivers like Chiron, Varzi and Nuvolari. On top of this, the weather was swelteringly hot, and the drivers were rapidly overcome by heat exhaustion. Mercedes driver Christian Werner collapsed, and his car was taken over by Walb, who had crashed at Wehrseifen; then Caracciola flaked out and Werner, re-

Above: Otto Merz—Germany's 'strong man' of motor racing—hurls his Mercédès up Klausen Hill during 1924

covered, took over *his* Mercedes, which eventually won. As Walb had taken third place, Werner had the confusing distinction of featuring as joint winner and joint third place.

But the savage heat had not beaten Otto Merz, who drove the entire distance single-handed, to come in second, the steering wheel of his Mercedes sticky with blood from his hands, chafed raw by his gruelling drive.

The 1929 Ulster TT saw the Mercedes of Merz/Caracciola finish 13th and this partnership also contested the 1931 French Grand Prix, in which year Merz took fifth place in the German GP at the Nürburgring.

Merz had an enforced break from racing in 1932, for that year Mercedes-Benz decided to forsake motorsport because of Germany's finan-

cial crisis (though it was only a temporary abandonment); but the driver Manfred von Brauchitsch made a gallant freelance effort in winning the Avusrennen in an antiquated SSK Mercedes endowed with a streamlined cigar-shaped body developed in the Zeppelin wind-tunnel by the aerodynamicist von Koenig-Fachsenfeld. The car was thus endowed with a greater speed potential than either the Alfas or the Bugattis, lapped at 125 mph in practice (beating Caracciola's existing record for the circuit), and won the race at over 120 mph.

A repeat performance was planned for 1933, with Merz as driver, but a few days before the race, practising on the track in heavy rain, Otto Merz overturned the big car and was killed instantly. DBW

THE LUXURY MARKET THEIR FORTÉ

Métallurgique were long established as makers of locomotives and rolling stock before turning their attention to the manufacture of luxury cars

LA SOCIETE ANONYME LA MÉTALLURGIQUE had long been established as manufacturers of locomotives and rolling-stock at their factory at La Sambre, Belgium, when they first ventured into car manufacture in 1898. They must have felt that the horseless carriage had a future, for two years later they established a special car factory at Marchienne-au-Pont.

Two years later, there was a change to shaft drive, while in 1905 more modern vehicles with steel chassis frames, shaft drive, high-tension ignition and the option of a dynamo to supply an electric lighting outfit were introduced. That they were built on Mercédès lines was not entirely coincidental, for Ernst Lehmann, who had become Métallurgique's chief engineer in 1903, was an ex-Daimler man.

The cars were well built and fast; like all Belgian cars of that era, they had to sell in export markets to survive. Métallurgiques became very popular in Britain, which, indeed, eventually took most of the production from Marchienne-au-Pont.

In 1906 a massive 10-litre 60/80 sporting car was added to the range; after World War I one of these cars was fitted with a 21-litre Maybach aero-engine, reputedly by Ernest Eldridge, in which form it is still running, the ancient transmission coping admirably with the extra power and torque.

Up to 1907, Métallurgiques had a flat-fronted radiator similar to that of the Mercédès; then they acquired a handsome vee-fronted cooler that became their trademark, and which they guarded zealously against other manufacturers who tried to copy its square-cut elegance, threatening them with legal proceedings if they continued the practice.

Right: although the Belgians no longer make cars, they were once a force to be reckoned with in European motor manufacturing. This is a poster depicting a 1913 Métallurgique. The company was once one of Belgium's most important car makers

Below: a 1907 Métallurgique two-seater. It was fitted with a 10-litre, four-cylinder engine which developed 100 bhp and gave the car a top speed of 160 kph

'The imitation of this distinctive radiator by other manufacturers,' proclaimed the marque's English agent, Warwick Wright, 'can only be described as an attempt to filch the good name of Métallurgique cars for their own productions.'

The last of the two-cylinder Métallurgiques, a 12/14 hp model, appeared in 1908; it was supplanted the following year by a new 12/14 four-cylinder model built in Germany by the Bergmann Elektrizitätswerke AG of Berlin.

Recalled Guy Lee-Evans, who worked for Métallurgique Ltd, who took over the British concession in 1911: 'Métallurgique of London sent an inspector to Halle (Berlin) to watch production. These chassis came to Cricklewood works and after testing they went to low-priced coachbuilders for open two and four-seater bodies. Belgian chassis were marked MM and the German ones BM. The Bergmann-Métallurgiques were good cars, but owing to the Continental duties and transport expenses they were too highly priced to sell readily against the good English cars. Also, it may be that some agents knew about the German chassis, and avoided them for political reasons.'

However, Bergmann-Métallurgiques continued to

be produced after the war, though by that time they were built entirely from German components, unlike the earlier cars, which had a fair Belgian content.

In any case, it was the luxury market that was really Métallurgique's forte, and the Belgian-built cars were almost exclusively shipped to Britain already equipped with Vanden Plas coachwork of surpassing elegance. Take the 38/90 Berline de Voyage which the company's Regent Street showrooms supplied to a lady who planned a Continental tour in that fateful summer of 1914: all the interior cabinets were of the finest inlaid woodwork and contained glass and cutlery. There was also a silver-plated washbasin with water laid on from a tank, all enclosed in a cabinet. A London silversmith made a mascot for the radiator in the form of a solid silver statuette of Siegfried about six inches high, in full armour. The chain mail was made up of separate links; the cost was 50 guineas.

Unlike just about every other Edwardian luxury car maker, Métallurgique never built a six-cylinder model only big fours, relying on superior engineering for smoothness of running.

Commented Wilfred Gordon Aston, motoring journalist and Métallurgique owner, in 1912: 'Not only are their engines quiet and docile to a high degree, but the use of the highest grade materials has enabled such a lightening of the reciprocatory parts to be made that the engines, without having to be over-developed to this end, are capable of giving a really enormous output of power, in relation to the comparatively small cylinder dimensions'.

He subsequently commented: 'It seemed as though those four busy cylinders (of his 15/20 Métallurgique), my passenger and myself, made the most contented of parties. The remote hum from under the bonnet seemed to damp all conversation as mile after mile was covered in what is next to perfect silence. To drive long and fast through the night is to realise that cunningly designed machinery has something in it not far short of a soul'.

In view of such comments, it is hardly surprising that Métallurgiques did well in the contemporary sporting trials (though their ventures into racing, such as the 1907 Kaiserpreis, Tourist Trophy and Coupe de Liederkerke, were hardly as successful).

Oscar Cüpper, who became managing director of the London branch of the business, was one of the firm's most able competition drivers, and put up outstanding performances in the Prince Henry Trials, for example. One of the 1910 5.7-litre Prince Henry cars (which had F-head engines) subsequently attained 105 mph on Brooklands.

In 1914 the *Badminton Magazine* reported: 'In the Grand Prix of Russia a semi-speed, semi-reliability Trial was run over what are probably the vilest roads in Europe, and in addition through abominable weather . . . a 15/20 Métallurgique, driven by Duray, the former De Dietrich racing driver, won the prize for reliability, and obtained third prize for speed. Considering that this car was one of the smallest in the competition and was the identical one which had previously won first prize in the Tour de France, this result must be admitted to be a very fine performance indeed'.

The same year a 26/60 Métallurgique was driven 2600 miles from St Petersburg to London, without any involuntary stops except for tyres and refuelling, inside seven days.

In fact, the sole Achilles Heel of these splendid cars seems to have been the clutch, in which brass shoes were expanded inside a drum by threaded screws. 'It was troublesome if badly adjusted,' recalled Mr Lee-

Evans, 'and brought in a good deal of work to the repair shops at Cricklewood'.

The 5-litre 26/60 was continued after the war, with the addition of Adex four-wheel brakes (a *sine qua non* of Belgian luxury cars of the era), but the traditional export markets had been closed by tariffs like the $33\frac{1}{3}$ per cent import duty imposed on cars brought into England. Métallurgique had survived the occupation better than some of its contemporaries, having managed to conceal jigs and spares from the Germans, so that the 15/20 and 20/40 models could also be put back into production without too much difficulty. The 15 hp model was dropped in 1922, the same year that a new 12 hp model was announced. This was a modern design with an 1882 cc engine equipped with pushrod overhead valves and four-wheel brakes, and was the firm's mainstay for the next five years. Its designer was Paul Bastien.

But in 1927 the Minerva-Imperia consortium took over Métallurgique, killed it off and divided the spoils, the factory going to Minerva and the machine tools to Impéria. And M Bastien emigrated to America, where he designed the 'Safety' Stutz Vertical Eight. DBW

Above: Métallurgique was a Belgian locomotive and rolling-stock manufacturer which ventured into car production in 1898. The company continued to make cars until 1927. Pictured are two 1913 Métallurgique models, the lower one being the four-cylinder, 5-litre 26/60 version which became regarded as the company's most famous model

The first triple Indy winner

Left: Louis Meyer, one of only four men ever to have won the Indy 500 three times, and the first to do so. He later formed the Meyer-Drake engine company

IN THE LONG HISTORY of the Indianapolis Motor Speedway, only four men have ever won the celebrated 500-mile race three times—Louis Meyer, Wilbur Shaw, Mauri Rose and A. J. Foyt. The first man to achieve the coveted treble was Louis Meyer, born in 1904.

Meyer was a comparatively unknown mechanic from California who helped racing driver Frank Elliott prepare a straight-eight Miller for the 1926 Indy 500 by reducing the stroke to bring the swept volume within the $91\frac{1}{2}$ cu in limit for the race. The Miller was, indeed, a car of ill-omen, for it was the 'death car' in which Jimmy Murphy had crashed fatally at a meeting at Syracuse, NY, in 1924, and when it was resold to Fred 'Fritz' Holliday of the Holliday Steel Company in 1927, its new owner renamed the racer 'Jynx Special'. Meyer, who had hoped to drive the car in the 1927 '500', went with the deal, acting as mechanic for the Miller's new driver, Wilbur Shaw.

During the race, Meyer drove 40 laps while Shaw rested, and managed to take the car from seventh to sixth place.

The following year, Meyer got his first big break. Wilbur Shaw was negotiating to drive a new Miller Special in the Indy for Phil Shafer, who was promoting a new type of automatic fuel pump. However, when tests proved that the pump was less efficient than the conventional handpump, Shafer put the car on the market. Shaw could not afford to buy it, but Meyer persuaded Alden Sampson to buy him the car, fitted it with a hand fuel pump, started 13th in the race, took the lead in the 181st lap and won by 45 seconds at an average speed of 99.5 mph.

That same season Meyer also took first place in a 200-mile race on the Altoona $1\frac{1}{4}$-mile board speedway at 117.02 mph in his Stutz-Miller, and was placed in sufficient events throughout the season to ensure him the American Championship, which he also won in 1929 and 1933.

Meyer was beaten into second place at Indianapolis in 1929 by Ray Keech, who drove the Simplex Piston Ring Special Miller—in which Keech was killed a fortnight later while leading the 200-mile event at Altoona. Meyer won the season's second Altoona 200-miler at 110 mph.

The 1931 Indianapolis 500 saw Meyer up against strong opposition; he could manage no better than fourth place in the event, which was dominated almost from the start by Billy Arnold. Racing was sharply cut back during the Depression, and Meyer was forced to move into dirt-track racing.

After a couple of years in the doldrums, the US racing scene recovered, and in 1933 Meyer was entered for the Indianapolis at the wheel of a Tydol Special Miller. Thanks to good pit work, he was able to take the lead on the 129th lap, and from then on he was unassailable, drawing a little further away from the rest of the pack each lap. With two laps to go, he was confident enough to be able to slow down and pull alongside Shaw's car, four laps behind to shout: 'Are you going to make it?' through cupped hands. And to wait for Shaw's reply!

Despite this voluntary slackening of the pace, Meyer's time for the event was a record, for he won at an average of 104.16 mph, a victory which was to ensure his place in the exclusive 'Hundred-Mile-an-Hour Club' a couple of years later (the club was for those drivers who had averaged over 100 mph in the Indy 500).

He was also one of the top ten drivers who, in 1935, formed Champion Drivers Inc, a promotional group intended to boost racing at the tail-end of the Depression, but which proved an expensive mistake as adverse weather conditions caused repeated cancellations of races.

Meyer had another successful season in 1936, however, which started with a second place in the 200-mile event on the tricky Ascot track in California and culminated in his victory in the Indy 500 with his Ring Free Special Miller at an average of 109.1 mph. He also won on the board track at Altoona.

Meyer was all set to take his fourth Indianapolis victory in 1939 when, battling for the lead with Wilbur Shaw just four laps from the end, he overcooked things on the North Bend and spun off. He was unhurt, but it was his last race. His Bowes Seal Fast Special went to Rex Mays the following season, while Meyer reverted to his original status as a mechanic—but on a more ambitious scale.

In 1946 he and Dale Drake bought the Offenhauser engine plant, which was the successor to Harry Miller's company—and for the next 18 years the Meyer-Drake Engineering Company provided the power for every Indianapolis winner, until Jim Clark and his Lotus-Ford created motoring history by winning the 500.

By that time Meyer himself was part of the Ford racing organisation, having accepted a 1964 offer to take over the assembly and help with the development of the Ford racing V8, which powered four Indy winners during the five years that Meyer worked with them. DBW

GRAND PRIX RACING SOUTH OF THE BORDER

Although the history of the Mexican Grand Prix is short, it is nevertheless packed with incident and drama—both on and off the track

THE MEXICAN GRAND PRIX was held from 1962 until 1970, all but the first qualifying for the Formula One World Championship. Held late in the year it was usually the final round of the championship and at the end of a particularly closely fought season—such as in 1964 or 1968—the destination of the championship was in the balance until the finish of the race. Ironically, the beginning and end of the Mexican Grand Prix series coincided with the deaths of Mexico's two greatest racing drivers, the Rodriguez brothers. The younger of the two, Ricardo, was killed practising for the first race in 1962; Pedro Rodriguez was killed in Germany in July 1971 and shortly after this tragedy the projected end-of-season date was cancelled.

The state-owned Autodromo Magdalena Mixhuca, opened in 1962, was in many ways ahead of its time. A flat, artificial road circuit measuring exactly 5 km (3.107 miles), it was laid out in a municipal sports ground beyond the eastern suburbs of Mexico City (the Olympic Games were held there in 1968) and incorporated both fast and slow corners plus one long and several short straights. The long, bumpy banked corner which led on to the main/pits straight was controversial. The pits themselves put their European counterparts to shame. Extremely roomy, each pit had running water, electricity, a work bench and a lockable gate. The facilities also included a permanent control/ press tower plus covered grandstands.

The chief problem of the autodrome was its height. Mexico City, built on an old dried-up lake, is 7500 ft above sea level. The altitude rendered both men and machinery short of power; barometric pressure was 22.8 in instead of the sea level normal of 29.9 in. At each race teams had difficulty running their engines to the conditions and, coupled with the usual high temperatures, this also resulted in overheating.

All the leading Formula One teams were invited to participate in the inaugural Mexican Grand Prix on 4 November 1962, four weeks following the United States Grand Prix and eight weeks before the South African Grand Prix. Works teams from Lotus, McLaren, Cooper and Brabham appeared plus private entries ranging from Rob Walker's and Bowmaker's to hopeful amateur owner/drivers.

The crowd's darling, 20-year-old Ricardo Rodriguez, who had borrowed a Lotus 24-Climax from Rob Walker as his usual team, Ferrari, was absent, crashed and died in practice. Although some reports suggested Ricardo was trying too hard, his elder brother, Pedro, maintained that the rear suspension broke. Talking to the American press some time later he said, 'There was evidence that the rear suspension of the car had broken first, thus throwing the car into a spin that sent it whirling along the guard-rail, disintegrating as it went'. Before the race Licenciado Adolfo Lopez-Mateos, the President of Mexico, who was a friend of Rodriguez' father, read a eulogy for the dead driver and led the spectators in silent tribute.

The start of the race was chaotic. Jim Clark's pole-position Lotus 25-Climax refused to fire up on the line; a mechanic changed the battery and still the car remained silent; eventually mechanics push-started the car, although this was contrary to the regulations. By this time, however, the other cars on the grid were overheating badly, John Surtees' Lotus 24-Climax burning its transistor ignition unit and Walt Hansgen's Lotus 18-Climax bursting an oil line. Clark's team-mate, Trevor Taylor, led initially, only for Clark to take it over on lap 3. Clark was disqualified after 10 laps (although his car was leaking oil anyway and unlikely to last the full 60), but he was given permission to take over Taylor's car. A slick pit stop cost 10 seconds and dropped the Lotus to third behind Bruce McLaren's Cooper and Jack Brabham's Brabham. McLaren's car blew its engine after half-distance and it became a mere formality for Clark to overtake Brabham's slightly ailing machine to win.

In 1963 the race was the penultimate round in the World Championship series and, although the title had already been won by Clark who had amassed sufficient points by September's Italian Grand Prix, a representative entry was secured. Clark underlined his superiority with a start-to-finish victory, lapping all but the second and third finishers. But it was a different,

Above: Graham Hill's BRM leads a group of cars during the 1964 Mexican GP. This event was one of the most interesting in the history of GP racing. It was the last race of the 1964 season and the World Championship depended upon its outcome. Three drivers, Clark, Hill and Surtees, were vying for the title. During the race, however, Clark's engine seized, Hill was rammed off the track and victory went to the Brabham of Dan Gurney. Surtees finished second, thus gaining enough points to take the world title

more exciting story in 1964. Mexico was the final round in the series and three drivers were in with a chance: the favourites were Graham Hill and Jim Clark, while fellow Briton John Surtees had a mathematical chance.

In terrific form, as ever, Clark urged his Lotus 33-Climax in front and began to increase his lead; Hill's BRM P261 was a strong third and so long as he could keep this position the title was his, even if Clark did win. However, Lorenzo Bandini's Ferrari 1512 was attacking Hill furiously and shortly before half-distance the Italian collided with Hill at the slowest corner of the circuit. Hill spun into the guardrail, bent the BRM's exhausts and seemingly lost all chance of the championship. Into the closing minutes the scene seemed set for a Clark victory, but an oil line had broken on the leading Lotus and it slowed dramatically as it crossed the line with a lap to go. With Clark grinding to a halt, the championship seemed back in Hill's court; even though Hill was out of contention so far as the race was concerned the title was his so long as Surtees's Ferrari was placed worse than second. Surtees was, in fact, holding fourth place, but with Clark's departure he became third and as a result of frantic pit signals his team-mate Bandini was ordered to slow on the final lap to let Surtees slip through into second place and take the title. The championship was literally decided in the closing seconds of the race. Who won the race? In the drama Dan Gurney's victory in a Brabham went almost unnoticed by motor-racing enthusiasts.

In 1965 the very last race under the 1½-litre Grand Prix formula saw the first victory ever for a Japanese machine when Richie Ginther's Honda RA272 led from start to finish, easily outdistancing fellow American Dan Gurney's Brabham BT11-Climax. The 1966 race, the first under the 3-litre formula, witnessed a dogged and determined drive by John Surtees (Cooper T81-Maserati) who beat that year's World Champion Jack Brabham (Brabham BT20-Repco). The following year it was Jim Clark's turn to win in the Ford-engined Lotus 49, despite a fumbled start.

In 1968 there was another cliff-hanger finish to the World Championship. Denny Hulme had a slender chance of taking the crown, but a rear damper broke early in the race and his McLaren M7A-Ford crashed into the guardrail and caught alight briefly. It was between Graham Hill (Lotus 49B-Ford) and Jackie Stewart (Matra MS10-Ford). Stewart led briefly in the early stages, but the on-form Hill overtook him and won both the race and the championship, his rival suffering chronic engine problems and dropping to a lowly seventh.

This race marked the beginning of the end for the Mexican Grand Prix. Up until this year military police had been used to keep the enthusiastic crowds under control, but, for fear of rekindling recent student riots, unarmed police and marshals were substituted. They failed, for by the end of the race some parts of the track were literally lined by the crowd. In 1969, when Denny Hulme won in his McLaren M7A-Ford, the situation was not quite as bad, but in 1970 the race was in jeopardy even before the start. This was delayed for over an hour while police, officials and drivers pleaded with spectators to move back. A record crowd of over 200,000 could not be adequately contained and eventually the organisers persuaded the drivers to participate, everyone fearing that if the race was not held there would be a riot and bloodshed. That there was no loss of life—with spectators lining the track and others throwing bottles on to it—was a miracle, but in the end the race ran its true course with Jacky Ickx and Clay Regazzoni scoring a fine 1–2 result for Ferrari.

The Mexicans were at first refused permission to include the Grand Prix on the 1971 World Championship list. Eventually, however, an agreement was made with the Fédération Internationale de l'Automobile whereby a bond of several thousand pounds was deposited in a Swiss bank as a guarantee of the Mexicans' good faith that crowd-control would be tightened. In early July, Pedro Rodriguez, who had become a hero in Mexico just like his brother a decade before, was killed in a sports-car race in Germany. This was sufficient to cause the cancellation of the race, and it has not been run since. MK

Above: John Surtees drives his Cooper-Maserati to victory in the 1966 Mexican Grand Prix. Mexico must hold very pleasant memories for Surtees, for it was here in 1964 that he won the World Championship. His victory in the 1966 event must have tasted sweet too, because earlier in the season he had quit Ferrari, after a row with the team manager, to join the struggling Cooper team. Also in the picture is Jack Brabham who drove his car to second place

A GREAT SPORTING NAME

When the term 'sports car' is mentioned
it is difficult not to think of the MG

Right: as the number
plate indicates, this is
MG number one.
Although the MG Car
Company was not
officially formed until
1928, Cecil Kimber,
Managing Director of
Morris Garages, had
built several bodies
based on Morris chassis,
beginning in 1923.
These 'Kimber Specials'
were known as MGs
(the abbreviation of
Morris Garages)

Far right: an early
example of Morris
Garages advertising;
this shows the 1926
MG saloon, which was
based on the Morris
Oxford 14/28 model

OF ALL THE GREAT SPORTING NAMES associated with
motor racing, perhaps that of MG has been the most
easily approachable and the most attainable of all. Just
the initials of the firm have established MG throughout
the world as being synonymous with good and safe
performance cars in which people of all ages may
expect to find those qualities which go together in a
motor car to enable it to bear the label of 'sports car'.

By 1928, the MG Car Company had been formed,
and in 1929 the works was moved to Abingdon,
Oxfordshire, now recognised by many enthusiasts all
over the world as the spiritual home of Morris Garages
sports cars. On 21 July 1930, the MG Car Company
Limited had been registered with one Cecil Kimber as
its first managing director.

The first special-bodied motor car produced by
Kimber was on a Morris Cowley chassis. Bought
from the main Morris works in suitably stripped form,
the chassis was clothed in an open 'Chummy'-type
body by Carbodies of Coventry. By 1923, Kimber had
entered one of his special-bodied cars in the London–
Land's End Trial and had done well enough to be
amongst the prize winners. The car was also in the
newspaper columns, as the trial type of contest was a
peculiarly British type of event which placed a
premium on the all-round performance of a motor car
rather than on just speed and acceleration.

Although it could not be said that customers formed
queues outside the small premises of Morris Garages,
there was, nevertheless, sufficient interest being
manifested for Kimber to press on with his plans. He
ordered six special bodies from the coachbuilding
concern of Charles Raworth of Oxford and these
Cowley-chassied specials are thought by many people
to be the first recognisable MG sports cars. According
to some historians, a gentleman by the name of

Oliver Arkell ordered a 'yellow sports car' from
Kimber on 11 August 1923, and this was duly registered on 16 August. Priced originally at £300, this was
subsequently raised to £350 and it took Kimber almost
a year to sell six of his special cars. Furthermore, as
well as having to contend with other companies,
Kimber was also bedevilled by the introduction of
the Morris Motors Chummy at a price of £215—
effectively killing interest in his own products.

Undaunted, Kimber still pursued his own way and
the first MG ever advertised was based on a 14/28
Morris Oxford chassis and named the MG Vee-Front
Saloon. By early 1924, Kimber had been shown a
modified 14/28 Morris fitted with a body not dissimilar
to that offered on the famous 30/98 Vauxhall. By
March, a similar car had been built for a young MG
salesman and when a famous Trials driver of that
time, Billy Cooper, expressed an interest in buying an
MG, he was quickly persuaded into purchasing a
similarly bodied vehicle. The fact that Cooper assisted
the Brooklands timekeeper fairly regularly and therefore always parked his car near the start line at Brooklands was yet another factor in the growing reputation
of the small MG operation. Still based on a standard
Morris chassis, the MG was already displaying signs of
Kimber's almost intuitive genius for making minor
modifications which transformed what was basically
a humdrum vehicle into something much more potent
and attractive. Simply by lengthening the chassis,
Kimber not only improved the roadholding and the
handling of the vehicle but also improved the aesthetic
appeal of the car, thus attracting the more discriminat-

Above: the 1932 MG Midget J2 was powered by a four-cylinder, 36 bhp, 847 cc engine. Its shape was later to be echoed in a number of other MG models. This car was recognised as a motoring classic from the very first day of its introduction

ing enthusiast. As a result of modifications to springs, steering rake and dampers, and giving the vehicle a higher final-drive ratio, Kimber was steadily moving towards the point where he would have to build a car from scratch in order to put all his ideas and principles into action.

There were to be many battles fought before that happy day would come, though, and Kimber was forced to carry on with an empirical approach to the whole business of producing a sports car. Perhaps the marque's first road test in the 25 May 1925, edition of *Autocar* helped him towards his goal, and certainly the interest expressed by *Motor* and *Motor Sport* magazines also contributed to the growing reputation of MG. This in turn was leading to production problems as the working conditions at the original Alfred Lane, Oxford, factory became intolerable.

However, there were other parts of the William Morris empire on the expansion trail as well so that Kimber was able to hire some space in a recently purchased Morris radiator factory at Bainton Road. By now, the still-evolving MG Company had a work force of about 50 people, and it was gradually taking shape as a motor-car production outfit of its own.

A revised Morris chassis, produced in September 1926, offered Kimber some problems as it was much heavier than its predecessor and, in order to bring it into line with MG engineering philosophy, much had to be done to it. For instance, flatter springs had to be fitted, a Marles steering assembly replaced the original Morris steering, Hartford dampers were fitted to the rear and a higher final-drive ratio was incorporated into the specification. Re-designed brakes were also fitted, and the balloon-tyred wheels were attached to the car by 5-stud wheel hubs.

Also, by this time, it was standard MG practice to polish combustion chambers as well as the induction and exhaust ports, and stronger valve springs were being fitted as an aid to performance and reliability. Despite these efforts, when *Motor* came to road test the 14/40, it was found to be no faster than its pre-

decessor, with poorer acceleration but with improved roadholding owing to the chassis modifications. Even so, production continued to rise, but Kimber found himself forced to move when the radiator people decided that they needed more of their own factory's room. With some trepidation, Kimber approached William Morris. He outlined his problem and plans and then put forward the bold answer to many of his major worries: that Morris should allow him to build his own factory exclusively for the manufacture of MG cars. So it was that Morris advanced £10,000 for the building of a plant at Edmund Road, Cowley, near Oxford, and Kimber took yet another step towards a form of self-sufficiency.

Because of factory building problems, the Motor Show of 1927 was not a success for MG. Pressure of work had denied them the time to go about their business of modifying and up-dating their motor cars, with the net result that there was little of note ready for the annual event, although Kimber did manage to put together an MG Featherweight Fabric Saloon which featured Kimber's modified Morris Oxford chassis and a fabric body by Gordon England. No success by any means, it was some time before the factory was able to sell the car.

Overall, however, MG was still progressing. By July 1927, Morris Garages had been registered as a Limited Company which, by November, was accepting responsibility for the Company's guarantees instead of passing them on to Morris Motors. By the spring of 1928, the MG Car Company (Prop Morris Garages Limited) had been formed, and handbooks were produced for each of the cars.

Also, an MG had already won its first motor race. This was in 1927 when Alberto Sanchiz Cires, driving a 14/40 model in a one-hour event at the San Martin track outside Buenos Aires, averaged almost 62 mph.

Because the Company was now beginning to establish a separate identity, Kimber took the trouble to make it clear that this line must be pursued. His instruction to his sales staff made it clear that they should stress the MG aspect of the car and to divert attention away from the fact that they were still, basically, rebodied variations of Morris motor cars.

Even with much developing, the days of the 14/40 were numbered. Despite the fact that the car continued in the MG catalogue for the 1928 Motor Show with the words, '... this popular model still remains by far the best value in its class', sales were steadily declining and what Kimber needed was something to provide a fresh impetus to his uncanny knack of modifying a standard chassis into something very special.

What happened was that he started off modifying an engine and ended up with a completely new motor car, one which featured not only a six-cylinder overhead-camshaft engine but also a chassis frame of MG's own design. The engine was the work of one of Morris's subsidiary companies and had been fitted to a rather cumbersome, long-wheelbase Morris named the Light Six, which was a complete disaster as a piece of design; Kimber, however, bought one of the three surviving motor cars after the decision had been made to scrap those already produced. Kimber was after the engine and the first thing he did when the Light Six appeared at his factory was to dismantle the lot and throw nearly all of the chassis and its equipment away.

What emerged onto the Stand at the 1928 Motor Show was the MG Sports Six, a car which proved itself capable of out-accelerating both the 3-litre Lagonda Six and the Alvis Silver Eagle, and that from a power unit of only 2468 cc with an estimated output

of the prototype engines and had quickly realised the potential of both the power unit and the new Morris Minor chassis. By lowering the suspension, increasing the steering rake, making minor adjustments to the chassis and fitting an extremely light, boat-tailed, plywood body to the car, he ended up with the original MG Midget. As *Autocar* said on its introduction, 'The MG Midget will make sports-car history.'

Kimber, however, was to make history in more ways

of around 75 bhp. With a top speed in the region of 80 mph and with steering, roadholding and braking to match, the 18/80 was far in advance of anything Kimber had offered to the public before. But that was not the only surprise Kimber had on his stand.

William Morris had his own problems, some of them being created by the success of Herbert Austin and, in particular, by the success of Austin's immortal Seven. The decision had been made to produce a competitor to this motoring classic and Morris was very lucky in having available a Wolseley power unit of only 847 cc, but which produced sufficient power in its standard form for the word to go out to detune it before fitting it to what was to be the Morris Minor.

Kimber had been fortunate enough to procure one

than with one single concept. By 1929, MG had almost trebled the previous year's output. In two years, MG had outgrown its Edmund Road premises and so the Company moved to Abingdon, in Oxfordshire. Sales boomed but Kimber was still looking ahead. The Mark II version of the 18/80 featured a much stronger chassis than the original model. In fact, so many components were now being bought specially that it could be said that the Mark II was the first specific MG. It was also the catalyst for the next major step to be taken by MG—into factory-backed competition. Using the Mark II 18/80 as a basis, MG developed the engine by incorporating a new crankshaft and pistons, a crossflow cylinder head and twin spark plugs. By bringing the chassis equipment up to

Top: a superb example of a 1930 MG Midget. This model originally made its debut at the 1928 London Motor Show. It was powered by a four-cylinder, 847 cc Wolseley engine

Above: a 1936 MG PB. It used a 939 cc engine, developing 45 bhp at 5500 rpm

the competition standards of those days, MG produced the Mark III version of the 18/80, a fierce-looking piece of machinery, sometimes called the 'Tiger', which was to have its first outing at the Brooklands Double Twelve meeting of 1929.

Work was also progressing on a modified version of the tiny Midget. Attention had been paid to the brakes of the car with the net result that it could now stop very quickly as well as handle very well. The next step was to improve the power output. By altering the valve timing, power was increased from 20 to 27 bhp. Care and attention to detail were lavished on the engine and MG was encouraged to build five cars in all—each of which was to be raced at the forthcoming Brooklands race. Modified bodies were produced which featured cut-away doors and folding gauze windscreens.

In the event, the Mark III succumbed to mechanical failure after two hours of racing. The Midgets, though, ran almost faultlessly. At the end of the race, a Midget driven by Cecil Randall and F. M. Montgomery finished 14th overall, averaging 60.23 mph against a handicap target of 62 mph. Although two works Austin Sevens finished ahead of the five Midgets which reached the end of the race, such was the lowly position of a third Austin that MG won the Team

Prize. That was the beginning of the Midget's success in motor sport throughout the world. Rallies, trials, hill-climbs, circuit and track races, all of these types of events were to witness an invasion by enthusiastic amateur racing drivers, driving the small, neat, nimble products from Abingdon to success after success.

As can be expected, though, Kimber was not a man to rest on his laurels at all. He was already actively investigating the potential of a new model. Basic to the design principle of this new car was the fact that the chassis line passed below that of the rear axle, thus providing very low lines indeed.

So the EX120 was born as a prototype chassis with a wheelbase of 6 ft 9 in and was to have an important history and be of immense value to the Company. This was mainly because its conception and design were just what Captain George Eyston and Ernest Eldridge, two famous and successful record breakers, were looking for to attack the Class H (750 cc) One-Hour Record. Having discovered that work was being done on the Midget engine with this aim in mind, the two record breakers visited Abingdon and were shown the EX120 by Kimber. A decision was quickly arrived at, and a top security, experimental workshop was laid out in a part of the works; one man, full time, was placed at the disposal of Eldridge.

Modification followed modification and, by the time Eldridge had finished, the chassis and engine bore little resemblance to those of the still-current Midget. Proof of his ability was to be furnished within a short space of time. A faired-in body was fitted to the car and it was shipped off to the Montlhéry track, outside Paris, where the record attempt was to take place. On 30 December 1930, Eyston covered 100 kilometres at an average speed of 87.03 mph before a valve failure resulted in the car stopping short with 20 minutes of the hour still remaining. He had done enough to take several records but not enough to achieve his ambition.

On their return to England, a conference was held during which Malcolm Campbell's forthcoming attempt on the record with an Austin Seven was discussed. It was common knowledge that his target was

Below: the supercharged 1087 cc, 1934 MG K3, which was driven in the Mille Miglia by Lurani. It was fitted with the single-seater bodywork in 1937

Bottom: pictured in 1937, this is Goldie Gardner at the wheel of his MG Magnette K3 single-seater racing car

100 mph, and Kimber was determined that MG should be the first to win that honour.

Eldridge's advice was to use a supercharger. An extremely intensive development programme was instituted and, within four weeks, the Eldridge engine was converted for supercharging and was on its way back to France. At first, the record still proved to be elusive, even though the car's speed went up to 97.07 mph. Final modifications were made to the body and on 16 February 1931, Eyston broke four records at speeds up to 103.13 mph.

Despite amazing racing success, production at Abingdon, reflecting the current state of the market,

Top: the most famous MG of them all? This is the TC model of 1945. It was fitted with a four-cylinder engine of 1250 cc. This car proved very successful on the American market

Above: after the TC model came the TD, introduced in 1949. It, in turn, was replaced by this model, the TF, which first appeared in 1953. By this time the engine capacity had grown to 1446 cc

had fallen by 25 per cent. Towards the end of the year, MG had introduced the D-type and the F-Type, two relatively under-powered motor cars which caused no great stir in the market place. Overall, the MG range of motor cars was ageing and lacked the lustre one would have thought it should have possessed. Recognising this, Kimber set about designing a new Midget, one which would incorporate all the lessons learned from the C-types and from the EX120 and its successor the EX127, another record breaker which already held the 5-Kilometre record at a speed of 114.77 mph. A crossflow cylinder head was designed and the design was modified to cater for twin carburettors. These changes brought about an immediate increase in power from the 847 cc unit and the modifications were given some strenuous testing simply by fitting the new cylinder head to competition C-Types.

Once the decision had been made to go ahead with the new model, Kimber did not even wait until the 1932 Motor Show: he simply unveiled his car at the beginning of August—thus creating a double sensation at the time. The J2 Midget, which Kimber announced was recognised as a motoring classic from the very first day of its introduction. There was a 'rightness' about the design and the styling which

made the car immediately desirable. The low, rakish lines embodied in the design of the J2 were to be carried on in MG sports cars until the middle of the 1950s and the basic principles of simple, though proven, engineering design were to lay the foundation of a continuing success story of the MG sports car.

Not content with setting a motoring standard, Kimber also announced the J1 variant—which was an open four-seater—and the Salonette variations. He also announced J3 and J4 variations as well just to confuse the issue. He further strained the ability of the man in the street to differentiate between various MG models by introducing the Magnette range of cars powered by six-cylinder engines. As an indication of the confusion which could arise when considering the purchase of a new MG, one range of variations, the K Magnette Series, featured no less than three different chassis, four engines, three gearboxes and five body styles.

Despite this confusion on the Showroon floor, production for 1932 was up by 75 per cent and, although the year brought few notable successes on the track, the Company continued to involve itself in its now almost traditional record-breaking period at Montlhéry, taking some more class records, although nothing of real note.

1933 was to see a new impetus brought to the Company as Kimber introduced the K3 Magnette prototype. Powered by an 1100 cc supercharged engine, this new sports MG featured a 7 ft 6 in wheelbase. It certainly got off on the right foot, as three cars were entered for the 1933 Mille Miglia, two of them coming first and second in their class and, because of the rate of attrition of the event, winning the Team prize as no other complete team finished.

Success of this magnitude encouraged the great Tazio Nuvolari to agree to drive a K3 in the 1933 Ulster Tourist Trophy. Those lucky enough to be there that day witnessed a superb feat of driving skill as the diminutive Italian from Mantua broke the lap record no fewer than seven times, leaving it finally at 78.65 mph, a speed that was not bettered until 1951. The importance of maintaining the Company's record at Brooklands was also recognised and, accordingly, the Brooklands 500-mile race was won by a special, single-seater version of the K3, driven by Eddie Hall, at a speed of 106.53 mph.

All this success was beginning to place a burden on the fortunes of MG, however. The public are quick to applaud the entry of a new gladiator into the arena and even quicker to take him to their hearts if he begins to win against what appears to be superior odds. But when he confirms his early promise by consistently winning, then the fickle taste of the public is apt to desert him as it looks for new heroes. So it was that 1933 saw the public slightly blasé about MG successes which was reflected in slightly lower sales figures and pressure from William Morris to rationalise production and use more components from the 'parts bins' of the Morris Motor Company.

Kimber's answer was to rationalise, slightly, the model range for the 1933 Motor Show, dropping the 18/80 range completely and all the four-seater variants of the Midget range. He also introduced the KD engine for the K Magnette range and introduced a Continental Coupé type of body on the L-type Magna chassis.

In itself, this was not enough to bring about a resurgence of interest, so in the January of 1934, Kimber took the decision to drop the J2, stop production of the L-Magna and to reduce the number of variations on the K Magnette. Of course, he had a replacement for the J2 and in March 1934, unveiled the P-Type, a car which followed on the original concept of the J2. However, by giving it a wheelbase of 7 ft 3$\frac{5}{16}$ in and a track of 3 ft 6 in, together with a new three-bearing engine of 847 cc and 12 in diameter cable brakes, he produced a small, light sports car which was more in line with the gradually sophisticating taste of the public. He also introduced the N-Type Magnette which had an engine of 1271 cc, an 8 ft wheelbase, a 3 ft 9 in track and which featured a body mounted on a rubber-insulated sub-frame.

On the sporting side, Easter Monday 1934 saw Ronnie Horton take his single-seater Magnette around the Outer Circle of Brooklands at 117.74 mph, then use his Midget later in the day to set a speed of 116.64 mph over the same ground. Just to rub in his car's superiority, he came back with the Magnette for the Whit Monday meeting and set a speed of 123.58 mph for the outer circuit. Despite success of that nature, Kimber continued to instruct his staff to develop the Midget still further, and 1934 saw the introduction of the Q-Type prototype. Using a P-Type engine fitted with a Zoller supercharger, the Q-Type initially featured a power output of 100 bhp, but this was eventually raised by development to a fantastic 145 plus bhp. The Q-Type featured special brakes and a pre-selector mechanism for the gearbox. The wheelbase of the car was 7 ft 10$\frac{3}{16}$ in and the track was 3 ft 9 in.

It was around this time that Kimber was investigating the possibilities of independent suspension. Development work consisted simply of, initially, chopping off the rear end of a J2 and fitting it up with something that looked right. Pleased with the result, Kimber's men turned their attention to the front end and engaged on a similar empirical approach, with equally pleasing results. From these ideas it was relatively simple for the design staff to progress to building a stiff, true, Y-shaped frame on which to hang the new components. Fitted with a modified Q-Type supercharged engine of 746 cc developing 110 bhp at 6500 rpm the new car was named the R-Type and introduced on 25 April 1935. It was offered to the public at a price of £750, perhaps the most remarkably cheap, genuine, single-seater racing car ever to be offered for general sale.

To publicise his new car, Kimber instructed the works to prepare no less than six of them for the forthcoming International Trophy Race at Brooklands on 6 May. As previously seen, miracles of engineering and devotion were performed, miracles which were rewarded when an R-Type driven by Hall came third overall; Campbell won the 750 cc class and MG took the Team prize.

The result of much administrative activity was seen at the 1935 Motor Show. The whole range was tidied up and rationalised. All of the competition MGs were withdrawn from the MG catalogue. The PB, featuring an engine of 939 cc, was introduced and the original P model became the PA, gradually being allowed to die. A different body for the N-Magnette was introduced, but the real indication of the Company's new direction came in the unveiling of the SA. This was a big, plush saloon car powered by the 2062 cc Wolseley engine which used push-rod-operated overhead valves. The chassis had a wheelbase of 10 ft 3 in, a track of 4 ft 5$\frac{3}{8}$ in, hydraulic brakes and a synchromesh gearbox. It will be appreciated that the SA was a complete departure from the then-current MG practice and caused quite a stir when it was introduced. Unfortunately, so did the 2$\frac{1}{2}$-litre Jaguar SS saloon also introduced at the same Show which cost only £10 more and which, because of smoother and more organised production techniques,

was available to buyers shortly afterwards. This was in marked contrast to the shambles which followed the SA's introduction, the car taking six months to get into production.

Despite this setback, there was enough impetus in the Company for Kimber to be able to introduce the TA Midget in the spring of 1935. Called by some motoring correspondents a 'more mature' version of the Midget theme, the TA with a 52 bhp, 1292 cc engine, hydraulic brakes and a 7 ft 10 in wheelbase, gave a more comfortable ride, better handling and more performance than its predecessors. It was also better equipped to withstand the vagaries of the British weather and was a turning point in the evolvement of the Midget.

The 1936 Motor Show saw the Magnette series replaced by the VA. This was a 1$\frac{1}{2}$-litre motor car, available in open, coupé and saloon form, which offered fair performance and a lot more comfort than its predecessors. This theme of comfort was brought to its conclusion before the war with the introduction, in the summer of 1938, of the WA. Based on the SA chassis but with bigger brakes and a wider rear track, the WA was powered by a 2.6-litre engine and was available in saloon, tourer and coupé variations.

Even though any competition aspirations held by the remainder of the staff were kept in tight check, Kimber was able to persuade Morris to grant permission for a record-breaking special to be built for Colonel Gardner. Working, as usual, on a tight budget, the decision was made to purchase the ex-

Below: a 1939 MG WA drophead coupé being put through its paces

Bottom: although the MG company is best known for its sports cars, it has also produced some interesting saloon cars. This is the MG Magnette ZA introduced in 1953. The car was powered by a four-cylinder 1466 cc engine, developing 60 bhp at 4600 rpm

Eyston EX135 record breaker from its current owner and then equip this with a body designed by Reid Railton. A Centric supercharger was fitted to the specially built 1087 cc engine and in November 1938 Gardner established a new class record for the flying Kilometre of 187.62 mph, then set a new speed of 203.05 mph the following year. Meanwhile, the TA had undergone a metamorphosis into the TB by having a slightly smaller engine fitted and closer ratios in its gearbox. By the time that war was declared, 22,500 MGs had been produced, not all of them great but among them cars which had stirred the imagination and admiration of enthusiasts throughout the world.

By 1945, the TB was the only MG in production but by October the TC had been introduced and put into production. The TC was a car featuring the barest minimum of changes from its predecessors, but one factor, increasing the cockpit width by 4 in, was to help the car create its greatest mystique and help to conquer its greatest market—the USA. With shortages holding back production, only 1500 TCs were built in 1946 but one-third of these went for export.

Even with the shortages that were making business very difficult, MG found that Colonel Gardner had still retained his enthusiasm for record breaking. Utilising a 741 cc engine fitted with a Shorrock supercharger, Gardner took his by now almost venerable car to Belgium in October 1946 and recorded a time of 159.15 mph for the flying mile. In 1947, he simply disconnected two cylinders and claimed a 500 cc record at 118.06 mph. By September of 1949, he had a new 497 cc MG engine and proceeded to set a shattering speed of 154.23 mph.

Progress was also being made with the production MGs. By 1947, the factory was able to announce the Y-Type 1¼-litre saloon which featured a 1250 cc

Below: the MGA series of sports cars was first introduced in the autumn of 1955. The car was then powered by a 1½-litre four-cylinder, 70 bhp engine. Later a more powerful 1600 cc engine was fitted. Pride of the MGAs, however, was the Twin-Cam model introduced in July 1958. The car, as the name indicates, was fitted with a twin overhead camshaft engine of 1588 cc, which developed 108 bhp at 6700 rpm. Pictured is the MGA 1500

engine, independent front suspension and a box-section chassis. This four-door saloon was to lay the foundation for the next great success in the MG story as it was a Y chassis—shortened by 5 in and fitted with a TC body—which was the basis for the MG TD.

It was an immediate success and, within one year, over 10,000 cars had been sold to the export markets. Colonel Gardner had already commissioned work on a modified TD engine which eventually produced 213 bhp at 7000 rpm, and which was to help him secure records at Bonneville, Utah, in both 1951 and 1952. Also in 1952, a team of TDs brought off a team prize victory in the Sebring 12-Hour Race, a victory which sent the prestige of the car soaring with American enthusiasts. It was also the year in which the Nuffield Group was amalgamated with the Austin Motor Company to form the British Motor Corpora-

tion, and Lord Nuffield handed over policy control to Sir Leonard Lord.

The effect of an ageing car being offered in a fiercely competitive world in 1953 resulted in a 40 per cent slump in production. An attempt to face-lift the TD for the 1953 Motor Show resulted in the TF, a model which was roundly condemned—albeit a little unfairly—on both sides of the Atlantic as being indicative of a company which had lost its impetus and ability. The fact that the Triumph TR2 was also introduced at the same time did not help matters.

Even the introduction of the ZA Magnette, nothing more than a badge-engineered Wolseley, did little to help the Company as, despite its very good looks and outstanding performance, the security of the future of the Company rested on the sports-car scene rather than on the comfortable saloon market.

It was in the autumn of 1955 that the general public were introduced to a new MG—the MGA. The sleek, smooth body of the MGA was in complete contrast to those open MGs which had gone before. The car was a properly equipped, simply designed yet extremely effective synthesis of all that was good in current sports-car design. With its steel body and four-cylinder engine which developed around 70 bhp at 5500 rpm, the MGA restored the Company to the forefront of public taste and acceptability. A very well executed promotions programme was embarked upon and a selection of MGAs were sent to Montlhéry, culminating in John Gott covering 112.36 miles in one hour in the Le Mans car.

When road-tested it was found that the production car had a top speed in the high 90s, that it would accelerate from 0–60 mph in 15 seconds, and that fuel consumption usually averaged around 30 mpg. The MGA had good brakes, good roadholding, good handling and good steering. It had just about everything that the average enthusiast wanted and could afford. In 1956, 13,000 were built and in the same year, MG announced the MGA Coupé—another step in the right direction as MG showed how in harmony it was with the market's requirements.

Almost as a side effort, another record breaker was built, the EX181, and Stirling Moss recorded an almost incredible speed of 245.64 mph in the single-seater car, which featured an experimental twin-overhead-camshaft engine of 1½ litres capacity, in August 1957.

By July 1958, MG had announced the MGA Twin Cam with its 1588 cc engine developing 108 bhp at 6700 rpm, and disc brakes all round. They were needed as well, as the car could accelerate from 0–60 mph in 9.1 seconds and had a top speed of 111 mph—not a car for fools to play around with. This in itself was the car's undoing. It was too good, too near being a circuit racing car. Post-war cars had been fun, sporty, docile and reliable. Anybody could enjoy themselves without getting into trouble. The MGA Twin Cam needed people who were sensitive, skilled and knowledgeable. There simply were not enough of those to go around and only 2111 cars were built as warranty claims flooded back to Abingdon from all over the world.

Even so, things were still bubbling at Abingdon. The re-opening of the design office there and the decision to move Austin-Healey production to Abingdon had brought about cross-fertilisation of ideas with the net result that the design team had been working on the design of a new, small light-weight sports car using as many off-the-shelf components as they could squirrel from the 'parts bins' of BMC. The result was the Austin-Healey Sprite which, when introduced in

1958, was an immediate success. In 1959, with the factory concentrating purely on the production of sports models, 52,785 cars were produced, over 47,000 of them for export.

That year also saw the introduction of the MGA 1600 and the return of the EX181 to the Bonneville Salt Flats. The result of that particular exercise was the fastest speed ever recorded by an MG when, powered by a 1506 cc engine and driven by American Grand Prix racing driver Phil Hill, EX181 achieved a speed of 254.91 mph.

Despite the thriving sales of the Austin-Healey Sprite, market research discovered that there was still an unsatisfied demand for a really small Midget MG and so in 1961 not only did the A-H Sprite receive a facelift, but BMC also did some minor revision to styling and trim and introduced the new MG Midget. Even such a transparent piece of badge engineering from a concern famous for its almost cynical use of famous marque names failed to deter or undermine the residue of affection that the British motorist still held for the concept of the Midget. So, another success story was born. It is indicative of the depth of feeling that, despite the fact that the Sprite and the Midget were mechanically identical and despite the fact that the MG cost more, the MG Midget always sold consistently well.

By the beginning of the 1960s, it was obvious that the MGA was about to come to the end of the road as a concept, even if 1962 did see the 100,000th car roll off the Abingdon MGA production lines. Luckily, the first people to realise this were the design staff at the factory and by the Motor Show of 1962 they were able to unveil their next contender for sports-car sales honours. This was the MGB, a car which was still selling well way into the 1970s.

Visually, the MGB looked a bigger, heavier and more solid car than the MGA. In fact, in almost every physical dimension it was smaller than the A, albeit 2 in wider. Fitted with the ubiquitous BMC B-Type engine of 1798 cc, the MGB produced 95 bhp at 5400 rpm. The motoring press was delighted. With a top speed of 105 mph and a 0–60 time of 12.2 seconds, MG assured themselves of sales throughout the world for many years to come. By 1964, the car was selling abroad, at the rate of 30,000 a year. Back in 1962, BMC also took the opportunity to refurbish its basic front-wheel-drive 1100 cc car and put an MG badge on the front to offer the MG 1100. They also fitted both the Sprite and the Midget with the same 1098 cc power unit to replace the earlier 948 cc one. Perhaps a much more significant variation on the MGB theme came when in October 1965 BMC showed the motoring press the MGB GT. This closed Coupé, with a very small seat behind the two front seats, offered the keen motorist all the performance of the MGB but without the sometimes inconvenient problem of whether to have the hood up or down. Although it was around 2 cwt heavier than the open MGB, the GT, with its better aerodynamics, was almost as quick.

Encouraged with the success that they were enjoying, the design office at Abingdon proceeded to make a fairly major mistake when someone's enthusiasm got the better of their judgement and the MGB was transmogrified into the MGC—a 'new generation' Healey 3000. This beast, displayed at the 1967 Motor Show, featured a 3-litre BMC engine with no less than seven bearings supporting the crankshaft. Despite the fact that the unit produced 145 bhp at 5250 rpm, the general concensus of opinion was that the low-speed torque was insufficient to make the car truly attractive to those used to the general smoothness of the B and

the fact that the handling was markedly inferior also ensured the eventual doom of the car which petered out of production in 1969. By then, the BMC-Leyland Motors coming together to form BLMC had happened and the new masters were busy cutting things out of production in an attempt to rationalise production facilities. Perhaps their efforts were beneficial for the name of MG, because certainly the loss of the Magnette Mark IV (a restyled Austin Cambridge) and the demise of the MG 1300 (a larger engined version of the 1100) could not have caused much pain in Abingdon, while the production of the 250,000th MGB in 1971 must have reassured BLMC that the production of sports cars should be the main aim of the works.

An indication, though, of what might happen was inherent in the production of the MGB V8, an extremely quick vehicle indeed, which utilised the aluminium-block V8 which Rover initially developed from the basis of an American Buick unit. Although competent in itself, the car did display a seeming lack of interest in allowing or encouraging the people down at Abingdon to come up with something dramatic, something trend setting, something with sensational performance, something in keeping with the magic of those two simple initials—MG.

MG has come a very long way since its humble beginnings. Surprisingly, it has recovered from many setbacks, both administratively and financially. It has survived both good and bad management, keen interest and total lack of interest, it has survived the bad times and enjoyed the good times. Probably because everywhere in the world there is a sufficient number of people who will always think that 'sports car' is synonymous with MG.   TN

Top: the MGB, successor to the MGA, made its first appearance at the London Motor Show in 1962. The car was fitted with the BMC B-series engine of 1798 cc, which developed 95 bhp at 5400 rpm and gave the car a top speed of 105 mph. The model was then available as only an open two-seater, but in 1965 a GT was announced

Above: in 1961, MG revived a famous name from the 1930s. This was the 'new' Midget, which used the small BMC A-series engine. Pictured is the Mk III version of the Midget, which was powered by a four-cylinder 1275 cc motor

BGT V8

The MGB has long been one of the major supports of the British sports-car industry. Over the years it has been slightly revised in looks to keep it from showing its not-inconsiderable age.

Unfortunately, very little has been done to the 'B' to increase the performance which by the 1970s could easily be matched by many so-called 'sports-saloons'. However, mid 1973 saw the arrival of a V8 MGB; although only available in fast-back GT form, it more than compensated for the performance lag that the years had brought. So, although in 1975 the MG company still produced the 1798 cc car, they also had the V8, which utilised the Rover/Buick light-alloy 3½-litre unit, with enough power to put the car into the high-performance league. The figures show a top speed, in the order of a 124 mph, and a 0–60 mph acceleration time of 7.7 seconds.

The GT V8 chassis is identical to that of the smaller four-cylinder model, which is of the independent-front and non-independent-rear type. Braking is taken care of by front discs and rear drums, while the steering is of the rack-and-pinion type, with 2.93 turns from lock to lock. A four-speed gearbox with overdrive on top gear is standard.

The V8 uses the same neat body of the ordinary MGB GT, albeit with minor cosmetic changes, apart from those imposing V8 badges. The main external differences are the cast aluminium-alloy wheels, with chrome steel rims and 175 section tyres, tinted windows, twin exterior mirrors and head restraints.

ENGINE Front-mounted, water-cooled 90 degree V8. 88.9 mm (3.50 in) bore × 71. mm (2.80 in) stroke = 3258 cc (215.3 cu in). Maximum power 137 bhp at 5000 rpm; maximum torque 193 lb ft at 2900 rpm. Light-alloy cylinder block and heads. Compression ratio 8.25:1. 5 main bearings. 2 valves per cylinder operated, via push-rods and rockers, by a single camshaft at the centre of the V. 2 SU H1F6 sidedraught car-burettors.

TRANSMISSION Single-dry-plate clutch and four-speed gearbox with overdrive. Ratios 1st 3.180, 2nd 1.974, 3rd 1.259, 4th 1, overdrive 0.820, rev 2.813:1. Hypoid-bevel final drive. Ratio 3.07:1.

CHASSIS Integral.

SUSPENSION Front—independent by wishbones, coil springs, an anti-roll bar and lever dampers acting as upper arms. Rear—non-independent by a rigid axle, semi-elliptic leaf springs and lever dampers.

STEERING Rack and pinion. Turns from lock to lock 2.93.

BRAKES Servo-assisted discs front and drums rear. Total swept area 338.4 sq. in.

WHEELS 5 in cast-aluminium with chromed-steel rims.

TYRES 175HR–14 radial.

DIMENSIONS AND WEIGHT Wheelbase 91.12 in; track—front 48.82 in, rear—49.21 in; length 154.75 in; width 59.86 in; height 49.96 in; ground clearance 4.25 in; dry weight 2345 lb; turning circle between walls 34 ft; fuel tank capacity 12 gals.

BODY Coupé 2-door plus hatch-back. 2 seats with occasional rear bench seat.

PERFORMANCE Maximum speed 124 mph. Acceleration 0–60 mph 7.7 secs. Fuel consumption 22 mpg.

A TRIUMPH IN DESIGN

Giovanni Michelotti is one of Italy's greatest automobile stylists. Apart from his superb 'one-off' designs he has done much work for the British Triumph company

Above: a 'one-off' styling exercise by Michelotti; this two-door coupé was based on Jaguar mechanical parts

Below left: Vignale built this Michelotti-designed, egg-shaped Fiat Abarth 750 in 1957. It was photographed outside the Vignale showrooms, where it created a sensation in its bright red and black trim

Below right: Giovanni Michelotti, one of the world's greatest stylists

LATE IN THE YEAR 1959, and shortly after the announcement of the BMC Mini and the Triumph Herald, a Conservative MP stood up in the House of Commons and asked whether there was really no stylist in the British Isles sufficiently competent to render it unnecessary for BMC and Triumph to have to call upon a coachbuilder from '. . . the land of spaghetti' for their models.

The MP was referring to the work done by Pininfarina on the BMC 1500 cc range of cars and to a stylist whose name has drifted in and out of popularity for the past twenty years. The latter is a man of whom very little is known, yet his influence in European car design has been such that nearly every manufacturer at some time or another has experimented with some of his styling ideas; his name is Giovanni Michelotti.

Michelotti was born in Turin in the late 1920s, the son of a coachbuilder who was later to work for Pininfarina. Unlike the other big names in styling, Michelotti himself has never been a coachbuilder, considering that his work is more that of a stylist than of one who physically builds cars, although in recent years he has developed his own prototype workshop in Turin.

Michelotti was still very active in 1975 and did not seem to have lost any of his touch, but his heyday was the 1950s, when he peppered the styling scene and the glossy magazines with a whole array of cars, some of them on the most unlikely chassis, aided by the fact that he was consultant designer to Vignale and did many of Vignale's show cars during the period.

The styling of cars is an area where ideas can pass from designer to designer until one scarcely remembers the originator, but going back to Michelotti's early days in 1950 one can see some original work coming from him. This was long before he became known in Britain as the man who took the bulbous and ugly Standard Vanguard II and, with some subtle

modifications to the grille, the wheel discs and the front and rear screens, made perhaps not a silk purse out of a sow's ear but at least a much superior sow's ear.

The first signs of Michelotti influence can be seen in a Turin Show car, built in 1954 by Vignale for the Turin show and based on the Siata Fiat V8; it is interesting to note that with this car the stylist used a grille similar to that of the sports-racing Aston Martin DB3 of the period. Although Michelotti got no official credit for the car, there were indications in the design that he had certainly worked on it.

In 1955, although he still did not get individual credit, Vignale produced a styling exercise on the Lancia Aurelia GT, called the Azure Ray, which had predominant tail fins and an interesting plexiglass roof and double windscreen. The windows slid upwards to folding into the humps on the roof. The reason why this design obviously came from Michelotti was explained some years later, in an interview, when he enthused about the possibilities offered by the use of synthetic transparent resin tops. That same year he used plexiglass for another futuristic coupé, on a Fiat V8 chassis, called the Red Devil. The roof line overhung the back window and again there were those tail fins. It was in that same year, 1955, that he got his first

public credit for a one-off styling exercise, commissioned by Ghia-Suisse in Aigle near Montreux. The chassis he was given was that of a Daimler Regency with a 3½-litre engine, and the car was shown for the first time at the 1955 Geneva Show. Only the radiator grille identified it as a Daimler, but the coupé design was not far away from the original Jaguar-based Daimler body which came along much later.

Michelotti was by now getting better known and had moved from anonymity to notability, getting his name on his designs, and 1957 saw some of his most prolific yet diverse styling ideas. Like the frustrated artist looking for a medium of expression, Michelotti appeared to be given a free hand, and skill was in demand. He designed the Lancia Appia Coupé and designed two cars for Ghia Suisse, one based on the Chevrolet Corvette, but with an aluminium body, rather than the glassfibre of the production car, and rubber crash pads on the dashboard. The other car was a very special GT car based on one of Colin Chapman's sports racing Lotus XI's. The machine was owned by a Swiss enthusiast and he asked Ghia-Suisse to commission Michelotti to design a road car out of the lightweight space-frame racer. A year later, in 1958, the author saw the actual car competing in the

Above: Michelotti's interpretation on Triumph's TR5 theme; this car was built in 1968

Below left: much of Michelotti's work has been for the Standard-Triumph organisation. This is perhaps Michelotti's best-known design, the Triumph Herald

Below right: the Michelotti-designed Triumph Italia was based on the Triumph TR3 and shown in this form at the Geneva Show in 1958

GT class at the Ollon-Villars hill-climb and Michelotti had transformed it. In place of a very stark and functional racing car he had produced a stylish coupé using his favourite medium, plexiglass, for the roof and thin screen pillars. In complete contrast, he designed an egg-shaped styling car for Vignale, using the Fiat Abarth 859 chassis. Here one could see Michelotti's attention to every styling detail; this was one of the first cars produced with only a seat frame and slotted back rest. The front end was completely egg-shaped and the visibility was superb.

By now Vignale had been in consultation with Standard Triumph about the restyling of their cars and so Michelotti became involved firstly with his modifications to the Vanguard III, but more importantly with the Triumph Herald. While working on that design, he still had time to revamp the Triumph TR3, producing a sharply angled car, with tail fins and scalloped headlight surrounds, for the Geneva Show. Many of the exterior-styling ideas in this car were to be seen in modified form in the Triumph Herald. However, by the Turin Show he had produced a completely different Triumph Italia, this time with smoothed-off headlights, like a Lotus Elan, and much cleaner lines. Vignale were interested in building a number of these

cars for series production and the final version was produced a year later, yet another Triumph Italia.

Still in 1959, Michelotti anticipated the rage for Targa tops, detachable centre roof sections, in a Vignale styling exercise on the Fiat 1200 called the Wonderful, and Michelotti worked on the production design of the original Vignale-bodied Maserati 3500 GT, which went into production that year.

In the following year, Michelotti had his first of a number of Japanese assignments. This was to design a production coupé and convertible for Fuji to sell on the Japanese market, with coachwork to be built by Allemano. Three years later, he did work with Hino producing the Contessa Coupé.

His first use of the Targa top on a production car was the Triumph TR4, introduced in 1961, and by now he was on a long-term contract to Triumph, which in

Left: one of Michelotti's most attractive designs is this Spyder body on a Ferrari 4.4-litre chassis. It was displayed at the 1974 Turin Show

turn led to his other designs, the Triumph 2000 and the later 2000 PI, the Vitesse and the Spitfire. All of these tended to keep him out of the public eye in the 1960s and his name only rarely appeared on the odd one-off design, such as a sports coupé, designed in 1962 using a Conrero-tuned Alfa Romeo engine, and a really superb styling car for Triumph, which was shown at the 1964 Geneva Show based on the Triumph Vitesse. This was a coupé, but Michelotti still persisted in his glass roof panels which were again a feature of this car.

In the 1970s, Giovanni Michelotti was still in demand and, although he had spent nearly sixteen years working with Triumph on cars which were aimed for series production, he had lost none of his style. In the three years up to 1975 he had produced a number of show cars. His 1972 effort on a Fiat 128 Rally chassis, the Pulsar was a much better and much more stylish car than the ungainly Matra exercise of the previous

year, but alas Fiat produced their own coupé on this chassis and so it stayed a show car.

Michelotti had a stand at the 1974 Turin Show and produced three contrasting designs in the shape of a four-door gull-wing version of the Lancia Beta, with pop-up headlights, a Fiat 126 Egg model and his own Ferrari, based on the 4.4-litre V12 and featuring, yet again, his Targa-style roof.

Throughout his career, Giovanni Michelotti has never sought publicity like Giugiaro or the ultimate prestige of Pininfarina, but has, in his own words, always sought to equate the best possible styling with the most economic methods of mass production. In this he has been successful with many of his Triumph models and has been able to let his imagination wander throughout his career on the many show cars he has designed. In this way he has managed to survive twenty years in the styling business and still be in demand which in itself is an achievement.   GG

Top left: Michelotti's electric-powered city car, the Lem

Top right: first seen at the 1974 Turin Show, this is the Lancia Beta-inspired Beta Mizer. It featured four gull-wing doors and pop-up headlights

Above left: Michelotti's Fiat 128-engined Pulsar coupé

Above right: the sleek gull-wing Matra Laser of 1971

WARFARE ON WHEELS

Production of military vehicles has become highly specialised. Almost every modern fighting force in the world possesses a vehicle for every occasion

FOR CENTURIES, ARMIES HAVE DIVIDED their strength into infantry and mobile forces and these, in their turn, as the styles of warfare have evolved, have become either light or heavy units. Lightly equipped fleet groups of fighting men, either as infantry or cavalry, have always had the advantage of speed and manoeuvrability and have been employed to attack the heavier van of the enemy.

Even now, with the sophistication which has been introduced into modern conventional warfare, it is possible to trace the ancient equivalent from which they have evolved. Every army marches on its stomach and so must have supply; the baggage columns and supply trains carried the needs of the armies of yesteryear, and of course the trucks, fuel tankers, water carriers and mechanical repair vehicles are the direct mechanical descendants.

High-mobility troops, invariably mounted, have always been used as light cavalry, auxiliary or irregular formations and armed either with bows or, with the introduction of firearms, light weapons like the carbine. These forms of mounted troops have been used to attack supply columns, to parry the enemy in the rear and to engage similar hostile elements. Armoured cars, developed in 1913, took over from the horse in this respect and moved into a necessary mode of their own as mobile warfare increased.

Special tasks are required in many operations, and because of today's style of war they abound, mainly

Above left: an all-terrain, lightweight, personnel carrier as used by the Italian army

Left: the American Bantam company produced this pilot model of the Jeep during the early 1940s. Only seventy were made, of which eight had four-wheel steering for test purposes

Bottom: the Volkswagen-engined Schwimmwagen.

concerned with supply and handling problems. Bridge building, the demolishing of strongpoints and general sapping concerned the old armies as much as they do ours, but now the machine has eased the way.

Prior to the age of steam, all tractive effort was provided by the horse. It was, therefore, a traction engine which became the first vehicle to be used for mechanical military purposes. Traction engines, with their ability to produce harnessed power, were ideal for hauling the huge siege guns which were the vogue in the latter half of the nineteenth century. As early as 1857, a traction engine, designed by Charles Burrell, which was fitted with shoes on the wheels to give a lower ground pressure, had been constructed. These shoes were the idea of a man by the name of James Boydell. Attached to all four wheels, the shoes laid themselves in an endless belt as the wheels revolved. This was the earliest idea of the development which was to lead to the endless-belt track, first used on tractors and eventually on the tank. Although the Burrell-Boydell engine successfully towed a siege gun over a route chosen by the military, it was not selected for army service, due to the fact that the shoes broke up after a short time.

The siege of Paris in 1870 during the Franco-Prussian war gave eight Fowler traction engines the opportunity to prove the real value of mechanisation by hauling guns, coal and ammunition wagons. The

Above: the American Sims War Machine, built around the turn of this century. It was never put into mass production, although it had potential—if it didn't kill the enemy they would surely have died laughing anyway. The machine came fully equipped with weapons, ammunition boxes and a simple engine, plus pedals for unexpected emergencies. Bowler hats and bicycle clips were optional extras

manufacturers of the Fowler engine, John Fowler & Co of Leeds, built an Artillery Siege Train Traction Engine exclusively for military use. The Siege Engine weighed 12 tons and put out 8 hp from its single-cylinder engine, but this was powerful enough to haul a 38-ton gun and its limber up a beach and over a low sea wall. This Fowler engine also showed it could de-ditch itself and a four-ton field piece from marshy ground with the aid of its own capstan winch. Although advanced, the Fowler was never used by the military, as its arrival was during a peaceful part of the nineteenth century.

In 1899, the British had to contend with the Boer War, and by this time had had practical experience of traction engines on active service; Fowler traction engines were employed, and a number of these were used as armoured road trains. These armoured Fowler engines hauled several wagons which could carry either troops or 4.7 howitzers. The machines have the distinction of being among the first of the world's armoured vehicles.

Another noted traction engine used in the South African campaign was the powerful 70 hp McLaren engine. Commercial use of this vehicle in Africa evolved it into a useful machine which was of interest to the military. It had wide wheels for use on soft ground, a large fire box for wood burning and large water tanks for an extended range. The McLaren also had the useful advantage of being fitted with a seven-ton dismountable crane.

The practical use of mechanised transport had now been displayed and, in 1901, the British Government offered monetary prizes for the best-designed 'self-propelled lorries for military purposes'. The vehicles submitted for trial were from Thornycroft, Straker, Foden and Milnes-Daimler; all of them, except for the Milnes-Daimler, had steam power and they all sported heavy-duty springs and wheels. The success of the Thorneycroft and the Foden won their makers the prize and they became the first mechanical load carriers in the British Army.

The advantages of mechanised transport were not only being recognised by Europeans for, in 1899, an American, Major R. P. Davidson, armed a 6 hp Duryea tricar with another recent invention: the machine gun. Davidson's idea of flying patrols with tricars carrying four men, the gun and its ammunition was received with some acclaim, although his proposal for thus equipping certain units came to nothing. Davidson continued to experiment with his armed cars: next came a steam car built and manned by his pupils at the North-West Military Academy, then he fitted a pair of Colt machine guns to two Cadillac touring cars. Davidson's involvement in the early part of the century with these projects, later led him to play a major part in the development of American armoured cars.

Motor vehicles had now shown that they had the advantage of hauling cargo with reasonable reliability, and had the power and stamina to carry heavy weapons further and faster than any horse teams. The next avenue of experimentation to those with an eye to the future was the use of the motor vehicle as a troop transporter. One of the earliest examples of a lorry used for trooping was a 1908 Armstrong-Whitworth, which could carry either troops or cargo and, in the former role, it could carry 25 men on bench seats. This vehicle had a 40 hp four-cylinder engine and was built on a Maudslay chassis. The War Department did not accept the Armstrong-Whitworth but accepted the Maudslays which they tested.

In both Britain and Germany, where major advances were being made in transport, it was customary when the military went on exercise to hire extra trucks from commercial concerns to swell the numbers of the then-limited vehicles in service use. In the summer of 1908, the Germans had made good use of some Adler light-lorries hired for an exercise. A detachment of four lorries travelled 100 miles daily carrying supplies for the duration of the exercise. The British in the same year organised a manoeuvre to prove the practicability of carrying troops by hired vehicles. This was done in twenty-four buses hired from the London General Omnibus Co. The type of vehicles involved were De Dions, Vanguard Milnes-Daimlers and Straker-Squires. Some of the buses took ambulance roles, and the troopers carried a Maxim machine gun on their upper deck. Much was learned from this exercise and the knowledge was put to good use, when six years later buses were sent to the front in World War I.

Hired transport was of course non-standardised, so both the British and the Germans introduced a subsidy system whereby commercial transport types were sponsored providing they could be taken into the services. The Germans approved designs of a standard type from Büssing, Ehrhardt, Daimler and NAG. These lorries were built to a four-ton load capacity, and the specification included a minimum power output of 35 hp. The NAG lorry was the most powerful in the class, boasting a governed 60 hp engine

with forced lubrication and Bosch ignition.

The mainstay of the British transport force from 1913 onwards comprised the standardised trucks from Wolseley, Dennis and Thorneycroft, all in the three-ton class. These trucks were in the Class A of a similar subsidy plan which the Germans ran. Here, too, the basic specification was drawn up: a four-cylinder engine, water-proofed ignition, standard tyre and wheel sizes, weather equipment and a live axle with conventional drive were all compulsory for the Class A vehicles. The most popular was the Dennis, of which 7000 were built. The Thorneycrofts were often equipped as specialist vehicles with workshop bodies and equipment, one being a mobile field-gun version with a thirteen-pound gun. Over 5000 of the J-type Thorneycrofts were built, which had top speeds, from their 40 hp four-cylinder engines, of 14 mph.

At the beginning of World War I, the great powers still relied on horse transport for the bulk of their military mobility. It was the Navy, however, and not the Army who first made use of motorisation in a modern war.

The British Expeditionary Force involved against the Germans in the August 1914 Battle of Mons was backed by elements of the Royal Marines and the Royal Naval Air Service, both of whose task it was to defend the Channel Ports. With the shortage of vehicles—the army had only 2000—and remembering

Top: a Model T Ford truck, as used by the Royal Air Force during World War I

Above: used by the British forces during World War 1; this is the Lanchester armoured car. Lanchester are perhaps better known for their road-going peacetime creations

the success of the bus manoeuvres in 1908, the London General Omnibus Co were asked to provide buses for France; this they did, together with volunteer crews. Seventy-five Daimlers from the Tramways (MET) Omnibus Co were shipped over the Channel in early October. Here, the buses and their Royal Marine crews did patrol work and, when Antwerp was threatened, they rushed troops to the town's defence. When the town fell, many of the Daimlers were captured. Such was the haste to get the buses to France that, in the early days, they were to be seen in their MET livery complete with advertising and destination boards.

Daimlers were not the only buses to be used in the Great War; over 1300 AEC 'B' types were used. Many had their bodies removed for storage and were fitted with general-service cargo bodies. The 'B' type did useful work, a number being converted for staff vehicles and ambulances. The lesson learned from the bus fleet at war was that standardisation was all

Right and below: the Fowler traction engine was used to carry guns, ammunition, medical supplies and coal during the Franco-Prussian war of 1870. The engine was also fitted to this vehicle, the Artillery Siege Train Traction Engine, which was designed for military use but apparently never saw action, due to its arrival during a rather peaceful period of the 19th century

Far right: Lanchester and Austin armoured cars on parade in Victoria Square, London, on a 'Save for Victory' campaign during 1917

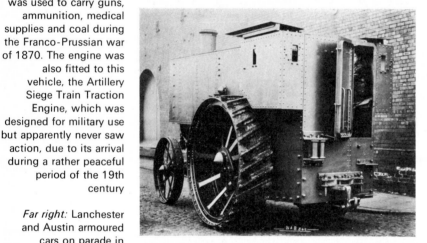

important. Many of the serving buses returned home after the war and were back on the streets after a thorough overhaul.

The Royal Naval Air Service was stationed in Northern France to prevent airships crossing the coast and going on to bomb London. Defending the RNAS airfields were motor-car patrols. It was quickly found that a motor car fitted with a heavy machine gun was an ideal combination for attacking German cavalry.

However, the armouring of the attacking vehicle was a decided advantage. The leader of the RNAS detachment, Commander Samson, gained permission to armour his cars with boiler plate. This was carried out to both a 45/50 hp Mercedes and a Rolls-Royce 40/50; protection was added at the rear to shield the gunner and shields for the driver and the radiator, were also attached. Boiler plate however, was a poor substitute for proper armour plate.

On the orders of Winston Churchill, based on the reports of Commander Samson, the Royal Navy designed proper armoured cars. These first Admiralty-pattern cars had full side and engine armour and were fitted to 40/50 hp Rolls-Royce models and some six-cylinder Wolseleys. Modification of the first Admiralty-pattern cars was carried out on some Clément-Talbot 25/50 hp chassis; higher radiator shields and better protection of the front wheels were interesting features and armament consisted of either one or two Maxim machine guns.

Commander Samson's use of Rolls-Royces as armoured cars was the beginning of the recognised shape of a turreted armoured vehicle. His cars were the standardised 1908 models, with straight-six 7428 cc engines developing 80 bhp and this, coupled with the

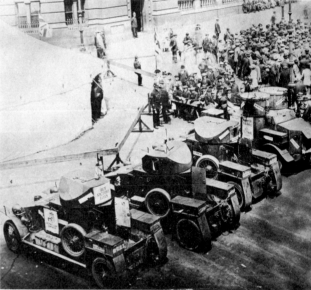

renowned reliability, made the marque famous as armoured cars. The Admiralty-pattern cars had their suspension strengthened, and the back axle was redesigned for the extra weight of the armour. Action was seen by Rolls-Royce equipped units in France, South-west and East Africa and some limited engagements at Gallipoli. Of the two RR armoured cars attached to a force operating in Russia until the Revolution in 1917, one is claimed to have covered more than 53,000 miles over virtually non-existent roads. The crew of the car was usually two, due to the lack of room, with the driver feeding the machine gun with one hand and driving with the other. In hot climates, the top turret plates were usually removed and sometimes even the turret itself. The guns carried were either Maxim or Vickers water-cooled machine guns. 1914-pattern Rolls-Royce armoured cars remained in service for many years, in both India and with the RAF companies patrolling the Suez Canal Zone between the wars. The 1920-pattern RR cars were very similar to the earlier models; both saw action early in World War II.

The second type of armoured car built in quantity for the Admiralty was the Lanchester, in some ways more suited to conversion than the Rolls-Royce. The armoured Lanchester used the 38 hp standard chassis which sported a six-cylinder, 4.8-litre engine producing about 65 bhp. Fully fitted out, it could achieve about 50 mph, which was fairly acceptable for a five-ton vehicle in 1915! Twin rear wheels and a doubled-up springing system kept tyre wear to a minimum. Crewed by three or four men, the Lanchester was armed with a Vickers or a Maxim machine gun; a Lewis machine gun was also carried. Lanchesters were used in the Russian campaign and probably hold the record for mileage in the Great War.

Due to the successful action of the RNAS units, the Germans, who had been on the receiving end, had taken notice of the armoured-car actions and had begun to design some versions of their own. Armoured prototypes from the main German motor manufacturers, Daimler, Büssing and Ehrhardt were con-

Top left: an armoured car built during 1904 by the Austro Daimler company. This was one of the earliest of the armoured cars; it used an in-line, four-cylinder, 4.4-litre engine, which developed 45 bhp

Centre left: a Rolls-Royce-powered armoured car, as used by the British forces during World War I. It was based on the Rolls-Royce Silver Ghost chassis and used a six-cylinder, 50 bhp, 7.04-litre engine

Bottom left: the first series Lancia IZ armoured car, as used by the Italians in 1915

sidered and all were large vehicles compared to the British equivalents. Daimler's offering had four-wheel drive, an 80 hp engine and a gearbox giving four forward and reverse gears. The car had flanges fitted to the outside of the wheels to prevent it sinking into the mud and carried no less than three Maxim guns. However, only two Daimlers were produced, as the firm was committed to other war work.

Ehrhardt's car was similar in both design and construction to the Daimler, and was powered by a four-cylinder 85 bhp engine. The third of the manufacturers was Büssing, who built a massive thirty-foot-long, four-wheel-drive heavy armoured car, powered by a 90 hp six-cylinder engine, with five forward and reverse gears. Three machine guns armed this huge machine, with alternative mounting points in the hull and the turret for the pieces. A mixed unit of all the three types of vehicle built did useful work in the Transylvanian Alps against the Romanians.

Lancia in Italy had produced a conventional but effective car called the IZ which was based on the IZ25/35 hp truck chassis. The Lancia had twin rear wheels and a small revolving turret which had the provision for a machine gun. The main armament of two machine guns was housed in the main turret beneath. As with other Italian armoured cars of the World War I period, the IZ featured wire cutters stretched over the hull to cut through any barbed-wire

Below: another of the armoured cars produced by Lanchester; this is their six-cylinder, 40 hp model, built during the period 1924–1931

Bottom: pictured is the chassis of the 40 hp Lanchester armoured car of 1926, seen here with a test load of cast iron

entanglements that may have been encountered.

Major R. P. Davidson, who built the Duryea tricar and Cadillac Balloon Destroyer, built in 1915 an armoured car with the Cadillac Co. It was fairly basic compared to the vehicles being turned out in Europe at that period: it had an open hull behind the driver, although a lower centre of gravity by mounting the engine deep in the chassis gave the Cadillac good cross-country performance for a two-wheel drive machine. Although it was the first armoured car to be built in America, its reception was luke warm and it failed to get into production.

An American armoured car that was to see action was the Jeffery-Quad. Built on one of the four-wheel-drive truck chassis which the Americans developed, it had a rectangular hull with a revolving turret. A number of Quads were supplied to the British and used in Ireland and India. Although still in use in India in 1924, they were renowned for being highly unreliable.

In 1917, the famous Model T Ford was provided with light armoured plate; the armoured Ford was to provide support for the heavy armoured-car units of the RNAS operations in Russia. Model Ts had already gained acclaim by their success in the Light-Car Patrols used in the African deserts against the Senussi tribesmen. Ts and the later model As and Bs were the cars for desert travel before World War II when the Long-Range Desert Group learnt so much about desert journeying.

The last of the Great War armoured cars was the 1918 Austin. Austins had been producing armoured vehicles for the Russians throughout the war, but supplies were curtailed when the Revolution of 1917 took place. Russian-bound Austins were diverted to Persia and used in Mesopotamia, and the Tank Corps also used them to good effect in France. The Austin had a vertical turret projecting out of each side of the hull with a spare wheel fitted beneath. The engine was an Austin unit that produced 50 bhp and gave a top speed of 35 mph. These vehicles were armed with Vickers guns or, in the case of the Tank Corps vehicle, the standardised Hotchkiss automatic guns.

The Americans had three years before they entered the war, and in this time they observed and decided that all their transport would be mechanical; they had already been building trucks for the British Government in huge numbers. The main type accepted by the British was the FWD model B, built by the Four-Wheel-Drive Co. Their three-ton truck had a four-cylinder petrol engine, with a three-speed gearbox and a two-speed transfer case. Because of the advantage of this transmission, the FWD was used as a gun tractor and a baulk carrier. Other American-built 4wd vehicles were the Knox, the Jeffery Quad and the Nash. When the Americans did arrive in Europe, most of their transport comprised these types with four-wheel drive, many of which were fitted with special bodies for the repair of artillery and other specialised uses.

Huge US mass production led to the proposed standardisation and to plans for both a truck and an aero engine named the Liberty. However, the war ended before either of these projects could be properly launched. This was perhaps fortunate, for the manner in which the various manufacturers interpreted the Liberty standards differed from company to company. As a stopgap, commercial trucks from Packard, Pierce-Arrow and Riker, as well as the 4wd makers, were used to swell the numbers supplied. Eventually, Liberty trucks of 3½ and 5 tons were built and these remained the core of the transport used by the US Army until just before World War II.

LANCHESTER ARMOURED CAR

In the 1930s, a now familiar class of vehicle was supplied to the British Army—this was the 15 cwt. Of the many designs, the Bedford is the most famous. Early models of the Bedford had an open cab, the crew being protected from the elements by aero screens and a canvas cape. At a later date, this was improved with a full hood. Morris-Commercial also produced a series of 15 cwt general-service trucks. The first of this new generation of service truck were the Guy Ant and the Commer Beetle. In 1937, Guy produced a 4wd version of the Ant which had ammunition storage and a steel body; it was used to tow an eighteen-pounder field gun (later replaced by a 25-pounder). The Guy was used throughout World War II, and was the first of similar gun tugs to be built by both British and Canadian manufacturers.

Since the early 1930s, the Germans had been amassing transport, the majority of which fell into no particular tonnage category; in fact, there were over 100 assorted types in service. To rationalise the transport system, the Snell Programme was introduced and the 100 designs were reduced to 30. Perhaps the best known of these was the Opel Blitz, a three-ton truck which was built in huge numbers. In standard form, the Blitz was a 4 × 2, with a six-cylinder 3.6-litre engine, giving 75 bhp, which drove through a five-speed gearbox. It had a steel cab and was the basis of many special body conversions; workshop, ambulance and

Below: the production of military vehicles had become very sophisticated by the 1970s. Vehicles have been built to cater for almost every conceivable condition experienced in warfare. Pictured are three types of vehicle in use with the Italian army. *Below left* is a small truck, perhaps a little larger than the Land Rover produced in Britain, which is used for carrying supplies etc; *Below right* is a truck not dissimilar to the British Bedford 3-tonners; pictured *bottom* is a heavy-duty truck which combines the duties of personnel carrying and supplies delivery

map-caravan bodies were among those fitted. In 1943, the Blitz was built by Mercedes-Benz, although they had their own competitive design in that class. The Blitz continued to be built in the post-war period and helped the German industry to get back on its feet. This period too, was when the Volkswagen Kubelwagen type 82 emerged: the wartime cousin of the famous 'people's car' which Hitler had promised to the German people. By using the floor pan and the running gear of the proposed 'people's car', the Kubelwagen with its light open body weighed only half a ton. Until 1943, it was powered by an 985 cc engine, replaced after that date with a 1131 cc unit. Used by all the German forces, the VW thrived in the deserts and on the steppe and by the end of the war, 52,000 had been built.

A close and perhaps more-glamorous relation to the Type 82 was the Type 166, the amphibious Schwimmwagen, which could negotiate waterways; a chain-driven propeller taken off the crankshaft gave the necessary propulsion. A total of 14,265 of these interesting Porsche-designed machines were built.

After the British Army had been forced to leave behind a large part of its transport in France, it was the American and Canadian auto industries who for the most part resupplied. Described as CMP (Canadian Military Pattern) and produced by Ford and Chevrolet, these trucks were built in the same class range as those

Left: the giant six-wheeled Mercedes-Benz as used by Adolf Hitler during World War II. It was powered by an in-line eight-cylinder motor of 5019 cc, which developed 100 bhp at 3400 rpm

in Britain: eight, fifteen and thirty cwt and three ton, as well as artillery tractors. The power units for these vehicles were either Ford V8s or Chevrolet in-line sixes. A combination of 4×2 and 4×4 trucks throughout the class range was fitted with general-service and special-task bodies. A total of 815,000 CMP trucks had been produced by 1945.

One of the old faithfuls of the war years was the 4×4 AEC Matador Medium-Artillery tractor. Produced in 1939, it was used to haul 4.5 to 6-inch howitzers. Powered by a six-cylinder $7\frac{1}{2}$-litre AEC 95 bhp engine, the Matador could haul $6\frac{1}{2}$ tons. 8,600 vehicles were built, some of which were used by the RAF, while a small number had caravan bodies fitted to provide accommodation.

The forerunner of the $2\frac{1}{2}$-ton range was based on a forward-control, 6×4 commercial model, later converted to 6×6. Production of this, and the more familiar bonneted 'Deuce and a half', was by the Yellow Truck and Coach Manufacturing Co, a sub company of General Motors. Yellow Truck was quite small, so Studebaker, who built a similar truck with a different engine, was used to swell the numbers, most of which were sent to Russia. The GMC pattern $2\frac{1}{2}$ was also produced by the truck-building firms of Reo and

International Harvester. Both the 6×6 and the 6×4 for non-off-road operation were fitted with all-steel cabs and cargo bodies; water and fuel tankers and a dump-truck version were also based on this chassis. Late production models lost the steel cab and gained canvas weather equipment instead. All versions were powered by a six-cylinder GMC petrol engine developing 104 bhp. Five forward gears, the first being ultra low for maximum tractive effort, gave the 'Jimmie' excellent cross-country performance aided by the two-speed transfer cases. Its successor, the M series $2\frac{1}{2}$ ton, began to replace the wartime version in the early fifties. Bearing a direct resemblance to its forerunner, the M series had a 147 bhp engine and, in 1975, was still in service with the US forces.

Another wartime truck with an ascending family tree was the Dodge. Produced first in half-ton form then uprated to $\frac{3}{4}$-ton capacity, the Dodge truck chassis was usefully used in weapons-carrier, ambulance and command-car form, the latter looking like a big Jeep, which could have given it its nickname of 'Beep'. The offshoot of the wartime model became the civilian Power Wagon, militarised for some countries and called the M601. Both the original, and Power Wagon and the post-war M37 Dodges were powered by six-

Bottom: Daimler-Benz of Germany recently developed this eight-wheeled amphibious armoured car. It is powered by a ten-cylinder multi-fuel engine. All wheels are driven and steered

cylinder 92 bhp engines. All had four-wheel drive, and the M37 had a low-ratio auxiliary gearbox and water-fording gear.

From 1967 onwards, the ¾-ton rating was superseded by the 1½-ton M715 Jeep truck, derived from the 'Gladiator Jeep'. 22,000 of these were produced as an interim model until quantity production of the 1½-ton-6×6, articulated 'Gama Goat' series of battlefield truck began in 1969.

Perhaps the most famous and familiar military vehicle of all time is the Jeep. Originally started as a project to replace the motor-cycle combination, and to provide transport for heavy weapons, the Jeep's reputation exploded with every impossible task it managed to perform. The MB model was used during the war, and, in 1975, some of the 632,000 of them were still being used along with the post-war civilian Jeeps.

Bedford's MW, or 15 cwt, was eventually used by most arms of the British forces, a large proportion of

Above: after World War II, practically every country with a motor industry produced field cars for military use. This is Red China's Peking BJ212, a four-door model introduced during the 1960s. Here Chairman Mao greets his followers

Left: developed in the late 1930s and used extensively by Hitler's Wehrmacht during World War II, this is the Volkswagen-powered KdF type 82, commonly known as the *Kubel-wagen.* Total production was about 52,000, in several versions

the 250,000 Bedford trucks built being of the 15 cwt class. The MW chassis carried a water tank, although some with GS bodies were converted to carry two-pounder anti-tank guns. Vauxhall, who produced the Bedfords, built three versions of the three-ton type, which was the largest practical size for mass production. Sharing both the chassis and the sturdy 72 bhp six-cylinder Bedford engine with the ML was the famous OY model. This retained the civilian cab, but was fitted with the squared-off military bonnet of the smaller MW. Besides the ordinary 4×2 truck, the OY chassis carried the usual service bodies of water tank, workshop and bowser.

With the exception of the Quad trucks of the 1920s and 1930s, the Bedford QL was the first four-wheel-drive truck that the British possessed. It was designed, built and tested in under four months, after the Government decided that the advantages of all-wheel drive were too good to miss. Vauxhall produced some 52,000 QLs, again with a great range of bodies: Bofors AA tractors, troop carriers and command and wireless trucks, several of which were still with the British Army in the early 1970s. The replacement of the QL started in 1952 with the three-ton (to be uprated to four ton in 1962), Bedford RL. Its six-cylinder engine of 4.9 litres was later improved to give 130 bhp from

the original 110 bhp. Bedford, in the mid 1970s, continued to supply the Army with a new series of vehicles, this time known as the MK, derived from the civilian RK.

Jeeps continued to be the standard British army ¼-ton 4×4 unit until the advent of the Austin Champ, which had independent suspension. Unfortunately, it proved to be rather complicated to run, the Land Rover taking over as the sole vehicle in this class. Military Land Rovers have 24-volt electrics and the latest lightweight air-portable models have been uprated to ½-ton. Modifications to carry firefighting equipment, anti-tank weapons and ambulance bodies give them scope for a range of many duties.

Scammell vehicles, beside having the longest-serving name in the British military vehicle inventory, are also among the largest. The R100 made its introduction in the late 1920s and went into active service just before World War II. For Artillery towing, the Scammell, or 'Coffee Pot'—so named after the protuberance on the top of the radiator—had a steel roof over the cargo area and a shell handling jib for supplying the 7.2 in gun it towed. Scammell recovery tractors with three-position jibs and eight-ton winches were the standard recovery vehicles for many years. Such a powerful vehicle made an ideal tug for a thirty-ton tank-

Top: the other side of war—apart from war machines a number of manufacturers have produced vehicles intended to save lives. This is the ¾-ton, 4 × 4 Dodge T214-WC54 ambulance built by the Chrysler Corporation. It was fitted with a six-cylinder engine developing 92 bhp. Some of these vehicles were also used as vans

Above: a ¾-ton, 4 × 4 Dodge T214 Command Reconnaissance vehicle. These were used by the US forces during World War II. The wheelbase of the T214 measured 98 inches and the overall weight was 5375 lb, or 5675 lb when fitted with a winch

recovery trailer, the whole outfit weighing just under twenty tons. The Scammells of this period all had 8.3-litre six-cylinder Gardner diesel engines which churned out 102 bhp at 1700 rpm. A six-speed transmission drove through the rear wheels only rather than providing power to all the wheels.

The range of post-war Scammell 'heavies', all of which derived from the civilian-produced chassis, were joined by the Thorneycroft 'Antar' tractors, originally designed for desert pipeline work. The later Scammell Constructors were Rolls-Royce-diesel powered, as were the more-powerful turbocharged Super Constructors; all had six-wheel drive. Antars were in use in 1975 with UK forces and with overseas armies. It is worth noting that examples of another famous 'heavy', the Diamond T, were still in service twenty years after the war's end.

From the onset of World War II, the British embarked on an armoured-car programme. When Operation Sealion, the proposed invasion of England, threatened, makeshift armoured vehicles called Armadillos were hurriedly constructed. Usually built on Bedford 30 cwt and three-ton trucks, a rudimentary 'armour' of two layers of timber with the cavity between filled with pebbles, provided the protection. Fortunately, the effect of these vehicles, with their light weaponry of a Boyes anti-tank rifle or a Bren gun each, never had to be proved.

Of the heavy armoured cars that were produced, the Daimler Mk 11, which weighed 7½ tons and carried a two-pounder gun, was the most widely used. It shared its H-drive pre-selector-style transmission with the lighter, faster Dingo scout car. This had five forward and reverse gears, which gave the little vehicle rapid speed for retreating after observation had

been completed; a swivel seat for the driver provided a dual-control position. The six-cylinder, 55 bhp engine of the Dingo gave way to 130 bhp worth of Rolls-Royce power for the post-war Ferret cars. The earlier variants were turretless like the earlier Dingo, although the vehicles in service in 1975 had a small revolving turret for a machine gun. Daimler sired the latest in the line of wheeled armoured cars. Called the Fox, it is protected with aluminium armour and propelled by a powerful militarised version of the 4.2-litre Jaguar XK engine; the Fox has power steering and disc brakes and is armed with an automatic cannon.

Heavier vehicles in use in 1975 were based on 6 × 6 Alvis chassis. The Saladin is a turreted armoured car, with a quick-firing 76 mm gun, and the Saracen is a twelve-man personnel carrier. Both have semi-automatic five-speed gearboxes and Rolls-Royce B80 8-cylinder engines.

By the time war in Europe had started, the Americans had developed a different style of armoured car, not in the true style, being more of an armoured truck. The White 4 × 4 scout car, although used in some numbers, was the forerunner of the 41,000 half-tracked vehicles which the Americans favoured. The adaptability of the latter proved almost unparalleled and, for years, many armies, including that of Israel, found them an irreplaceable form of transport.

Both the British and American forces used the six-wheeled M8 Ford-built car, which mounted a 37 mm gun and .30 machine gun. The M20 was a turretless version for use as a high mobility command car or cargo carrier. These vehicles were named Greyhounds by the British, who also labelled the Chevrolet-built M6 as the Staghound. American Staghounds mounted either a 37 mm gun or a pair of .50 machine guns, while those in British service were armed with a 3 in howitzer or a 75 mm tank gun. Power was provided by a pair of GMC 270 six-cylinder engines via dual hydromatic transmissions.

The only post-war American armoured wheeled vehicle of any significance was the Cadillac Gage. Designed around the Chrysler 361 V8 and the axles of the M series 2½-ton truck, its speed was 65 mph. Also, its amphibious capability made it useful for action in South Vietnam. Experiments were undertaken by the Lockheed Corporation on a novel 8 × 8 machine, dubbed the Twister, which featured an interesting suspension system and was powered by a pair of large Chrysler V8s. The Twister's acceleration was fierce for an armoured fighting vehicle, due to extensive use of aluminium armour.

An 8 × 8 drive layout was also favoured by the Germans for their wartime Büssing NAG Sd Kfz 232, a large vehicle in the vein of the World War I type of cars. A family of light armoured vehicles was also produced from the early thirties, based on a light 4 × 4 car chassis produced by Horch.

Because of the huge number of vehicles which have been produced for military use, it has only been possible to mention the better-known types. Many of the smaller countries have been equipped with American, British or Soviet equipment of either World War II vintage or of later production types and, until recently, the Soviet Union built vehicles patterned on US types. When great strides were made in vehicle design during World War II, a certain pattern was formed, and many of the current vehicles in production are modifications of those early types. In some ways, the simplicity of those basic types is more appealing than the complicated engineering that constitutes the modern military vehicle. **RP**

MILLE MIGLIA

One of the greatest motor-race series ever known was the Mille Miglia, which produced some of the most dramatic incidents in the history of motor sport

OVER THE YEARS the Mille Miglia has developed a reputation as one of the most difficult, tortuous, yet romantic races ever devised. It spanned a period of only 31 years, from 1927 to 1957, yet each race often packed in more drama and courage than a whole season of Grand Prix races. It is still spoken of with awe by those who were fortunate enough to participate or merely watch from the sidelines. Possibly only in Italy could such a long road race have persisted into the late 1950s, for most other countries had long before abandoned road racing and even placed severe restrictions on rallying. It was only an accident in the 1957 race, costing the lives of nine spectators, that forced the Italian Government to stop the event.

The idea for the Mille Miglia (1000 miles) came from four Italian enthusiasts who desperately wanted to emulate the Le Mans 24-hour race which had started in 1923. The four men, famous journalist

Above: the start of the first Mille Miglia on 26 March 1927 at Brescia; the winning car on this event was the OM of Minoia and Morandi, at an average speed of 47.99 mph

Giovanni Canestrini, Count Aymo Maggi, Franco Mazzotti and Renzo Castagneto decided that Italy's answer to Le Mans must be a road race. Since Castagneto was the secretary of the Brescia Automobile Club, the town of Brescia naturally had to be the starting point. The route mapped out was a figure-of-eight course round Italy, with the crossing point of the eight at Bologna, the start and finish being in Brescia. A great number of difficulties had to be overcome. The Government had to approve the scheme, various automobile clubs had to arrange checkpoints and organise refuelling depots and the police had to block off all access points and keep spectators off the road—a difficult job to organise over a few miles, but for 1000 miles of ordinary main road it was a Herculean task.

The first race, in 1927, was run in an anti-clockwise direction round Italy, the route running from Brescia down to Piacenza, then inland to Parma, Modena and

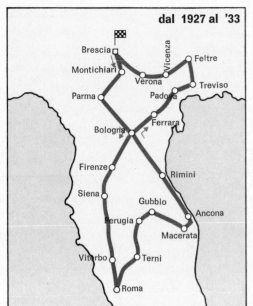

dal 1927 al '33

1940

1948

Bologna. The really hard work started after Bologna for the drivers had to cross the Appenine mountains to Florence before tackling the hills of Umbria down to Rome. From Rome the course turned east across the Abruzzi mountains to Ancona on the Adriatic coast, where the route turned northwards up the flat coastal strip, via Pesaro and Rimini, before turning inland once more back to Bologna then circling north via Padua, Vicenza and Verona and returning to Brescia. The actual distance was 1004 miles.

It was obviously inadvisable to have a massed start at Brescia so the cars were set off at intervals, with the smallest and slowest cars starting first. This gave faster drivers a great number of problems since they had to pass many slower cars on the poorly surfaced and narrow roads in the mountains, but the race was an immediate hit with both drivers and spectators alike even though the roads were theoretically still open to normal traffic. Winner of the first race was the OM of Minoia and Morandi, at an average speed of 47.99 mph, ahead of two other OMs. The relatively low speed illustrates the difficulties of the course; it took the winners nearly 21 hours of virtually non-stop driving to finish the race.

Although the era of the riding mechanics in Grand Prix races had come to an end they were still used in sports-car races, and in the Mille Miglia many cars had two drivers, for most men found they were unable to race for virtually a whole day without respite. Some drivers took a mechanic who could also give route instructions and take a spell at driving on the straight coast roads of the Adriatic, leaving the difficult mountain sections to the number one driver.

The Italian manufacturers quickly realised the publicity value of the Mille Miglia and a number of works entries were made in 1928. The race attracted many millions of spectators who turned the day into a great festive occasion, so manufacturers had a large captive audience of potential buyers. Alfa Romeo entered the 1928 event in some force, victory going to the car of Giuseppe Campari and Giulio Ramponi at an average speed of 52.27 mph, followed home by an OM and a Lancia.

The corpulent Campari won the 1929 race, once again accompanied by Ramponi, their average speed rising to 55.69 mph. An OM was second and another Alfa Romeo third.

Minor changes in the route were made each year, to

Top: three of the famous Mille Miglia routes. *Far left* is the most famous of all: the figure of eight that centred on Bologna. *Centre,* the 1940 1486 km route and, *right,* the 1826 km circuit used in 1947 and 1948

Above: the winning OM of 1927 seen at the pass of Raticosa. This car beat the favourite Alfa Romeo of Gastone Brilli

cope with road works and deviations asked for by local authorities, but the distance rarely changed by many miles, although it gradually increased. In 1930 the distance had crept up to 1018 miles and the event provided Tazio Nuvolari with one of his first great successes. He had been invited to join the Alfa Romeo team for the 1930 season and one of his first events for them was the Mille Miglia, which was traditionally held in early April. Accompanied by Guidotti, who later became team manager for Alfa Romeo, Nuvolari intended to drive his 1750 cc 6C Alfa Romeo single handed, relying on Guidotti only for signals to show dangerous parts of the route and for passing his food and drink. Nuvolari was up against some formidable opposition, notably his team mates Campari and Varzi, but there was also Caracciola in a Mercedes-Benz and Arcangeli in a 2-litre Maserati. The Alfa drivers practised the route assiduously, none more so than Nuvolari who was unfamiliar with the car. On the fast stretch down to Bologna Arcangeli led, but in the misty mountains of the Appennines Nuvolari showed a sixth sense for the road direction as he flung the car over gravel strewn roads. Guidotti confessed afterwards that Nuvolari's speed in virtually zero visibility terrified him. Although the little Alfa sports car could

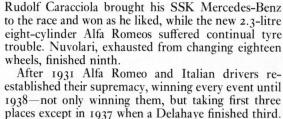

Rudolf Caracciola brought his SSK Mercedes-Benz to the race and won as he liked, while the new 2.3-litre eight-cylinder Alfa Romeos suffered continual tyre trouble. Nuvolari, exhausted from changing eighteen wheels, finished ninth.

After 1931 Alfa Romeo and Italian drivers re-established their supremacy, winning every event until 1938—not only winning them, but taking first three places except in 1937 when a Delahaye finished third.

The 1932 race gave victory to Borzacchini and Bignami in a 2.3-litre Alfa, after some of the leading names had dropped out. Nuvolari was fighting for the lead

barely exceed 100mph, it cornered like a dream and Nuvolari took the lead through the mountains. His only refreshment came from a flask of sweet tea, which had been fitted up with rubber drinking tubes, and the occasional piece of orange or barley sugar that Guidotti passed him. On the stretch to Rome Varzi regained the lead, a position he held until the Adriatic coast was reached. With the relatively straight and well surfaced coast road to come Varzi felt confident of holding his two-minute lead, but Nuvolari began driving like a madman, taking every bend as fast as was humanly possible, using his famous over-steering, tail-sliding technique to the full. The two minutes were gradually eaten away and, as Varzi had started a minute before Nuvolari, the 'Flying Mantuan' had only to hold station to win; but he ignored Guidotti's pleas to ease off and as darkness fell he pushed even harder. At the town of Peschiera Nuvolari caught Varzi's car, but Varzi was unaware of Nuvolari's presence as they rushed through the lighted streets of Peschiera on the shores of Lake Garda. To Guidotti's horror, Nuvolari switched off his headlights when they emerged into the darkness outside the town and he followed Varzi by means of his tiny red rear lamps. Still blissfully unaware of how close his rival was Varzi ate up the last few miles to Brescia, but with only three kilometres left, Nuvolari switched on his headlights and streaked past Varzi to reach the finish first. It was one of the first signs of the bravura which became a Nuvolari trademark in years to come. Nuvolari had averaged 62.51 mph and had sat at the wheel for over 16 hours without relief.

A legend had quickly grown up around the Mille Miglia that no foreign driver or car would ever win the race because of the high degree of local knowledge required, but the myth was shattered in 1931 when

Top: the year 1931 sees a car just about to traverse the bridge spanning the river Panaro at Modena

Above left: the victorious Alfa Romeo 8C 2300 of Borzacchini and Bignami in 1932

Above right: the Lancia of one of the women drivers on the 1929 event, Mimy Ayhner

with Caracciola and Varzi, but as he went through Florence, Nuvolari saw a wrecked car on a bend; he quickly snatched a glance at it to see if it was a team mate's car and in that split second he lost control and crashed his own car, only a few yards past the other wreck! In this race young Taruffi snatched the lead briefly in his Scuderia Ferrari Alfa Romeo, but his car lost its oil pressure and he retired.

For 1933 Nuvolari was accompanied in the Mille Miglia by his friend and mechanic Decimo Compagnoni. They drove a Scuderia Ferrari Alfa Romeo, now that the factory had withdrawn from racing, and their 2.6-litre Monza Alfa Romeo proved good enough to win. Despite losing the complete silencer system, Nuvolari kept the car in the lead for the whole race, winning by no less than 27 minutes at an average speed of 67.46 mph, despite a good deal of rain in the mountains. Second was the Alfa of Castelbarco/Cortese with Taruffi/Pellegrini third in another Alfa. A team of MGs was entered for the 1933 race, a class victory being gained by Captain George Eyston and Count 'Johnny' Lurani.

The weather in Italy in April tends to be capricious. Sometimes warm sunshine prevails, but more often drivers are faced with every type of weather from driving rain in the north and fog in the mountain passes to hot sunshine around Rome and on the Adriatic. In 1934 it chose to rain throughout most of the race, a feature which worked to the advantage of Nuvolari, who was driving a privately owned 2.3 Alfa Romeo against the works 2.6-litre cars. He was able to keep among the leaders for much of the race by using his superior skill on the wet roads, but he eventually had to give best to his old rival Varzi in a 2.6 and be content with second place. The MGs again took part in this event but they had to give best to Taruffi's 1100 cc

Right: the shortened event of 1940 was won by a streamlined BMW 328 coupé driven by Baron von Hanstein and Bäumer. This is the sister car of Cortese and Lurani

Below: fifth overall, and winner of the 1100 cc class, in 1934 was this Maserati of Taruffi and Bertocchi

Right: the joy of victory in the Ferrari camp after the 1949 event. No prizes for spotting the winner and co-driver, Biondetti and Salani, with their blackened faces

Maserati in the 1100 cc class, the little Maserati finishing fifth overall as well.

With the accent turning to the monumental Grand Prix successes of the German Auto Union and Mercedes teams, sports-car racing lost some of its appeal in the mid 1930s, but the Mille Miglia continued successfully, even if lacking in foreign opposition. The 1935 event went to Pintacuda/della Stufa, the 1936 race was taken by Brivio/Ongarao, while Pintacuda/Mabelli won the 1937 race, all of them driving Alfa Romeos. Brivio's win shot the race average up to 75.57 mph, but he was using the 2900A which was little more than a thinly disguised Grand Prix car. The 1937 winning car was a 6C 2300 with a special duralumin body.

For the 1938 race some changes were made to the route. This was as before down as far as Florence, but then the cars were taken westward to the coast which they followed all the way to Rome.

The 1938 race was a tragic one which nearly caused the abandonment of the event. A car plunged into the tightly packed crowd near Bologna, killing ten spectators and injuring a further thirty. The race was won by Biondetti/Stefani in a production version of the 2900A Alfa Romeo called the 8C 2900B, at an average speed of 84.13 mph.

Italy's dictator, Mussolini, bowed to public opinion after the tragedy and banned the race for 1939.

Despite the onset of World War II, Renzo Castagneto, who still organised and acted as starter of the race, decided to run the Mille Miglia in 1940, expressly against Mussolini's wishes. He was restricted to a 193-mile triangular course, running from Brescia to Cremona to Mantua and back to Brescia, and the event was named the Grand Prix of Brescia, although it was also listed in the programme as the 13th Mille Miglia. Despite the ersatz nature of the race and the wartime conditions it attracted a team of 2-litre BMWs from Germany and the very first Ferraris, the type 815s, which were little more than rebodied Fiat 1100s. Significantly, one of the 815s was handled by 20-year-old Alberto Ascari, then setting out on his illustrious career. The works Alfas and the Ferraris all ran into trouble and it was the works BMW of Huschke von Hanstein and Baumer that won the race at an average speed of 103.60 mph.

The war put paid to the Mille Miglia for six years, but Castagneto was determined to get the race going again. This proved to be a difficult task, for Italy had been ravaged by the war. In fact, when Castagneto attempted to drive round the route he was met by fallen bridges, great holes in the roads and complete devastation. But he persisted and finally announced that the race would be run in June 1947. Over 100 entries were received for the 14th Mille Miglia, included among them being the new 1½-litre Ferrari, Villoresi with a 2-litre Maserati and a host of the tiny new Cisitalias, one of which was to be driven by Nuvolari himself, at the age of 55, despite suffering from a serious chest complaint.

The route had been modified considerably, the main change being to reverse the direction of the race so that it now ran clockwise round Italy, leading from Brescia down the Adriatic coast, then across to Rome, returning northwards across the Futa and Raticosa passes to Bologna and then deviating through Asti, Turin and Milan before rushing back to Brescia along the autostrada. This increased the race distance to its longest ever figure of 1133 miles.

Nuvolari was given little chance in his tiny cycle-winged 1100 cc Fiat-engined Cisitalia, but even though the circuit now went the 'wrong' way and the ailing Nuvolari had had little chance to survey the route he once again began to throw his car around, to the great terror of his mechanic, Carena. By the time they reached Rome Nuvolari had built up a lead of no less than seven minutes over the 2.9-litre Alfa Romeo of Biondetti. Over the fogbound Futa and Rarticosa passes, which Nuvolari could drive over with his eyes closed, he extended his lead and although Biondetti closed up on the level ground towards Florence, Nuvolari still had a nine minute lead when they reached Bologna. Nearing Asti the Cisitalia rushed through a deep puddle and suddenly the engine stopped; Carana and Nuvolari desperately dried out the ignition, but they had lost fifteen minutes by the time the engine was running again. The exhausted Nuvolari once again began driving like a maniac although the rain had by now turned to hail and the open cockpit of the Cisitalia had been turned into a mobile swimming pool. But with the fast straight roads of northern Italy to come there was little that even Nuvolari could do about the big Alfa and the Cisitalia rolled into Brescia 16 minutes behind Biondetti. However, it was enough to convince Italian enthusiasts that the 'Flying Mantuan' was back at the top.

Nuvolari was to make one more glorious attempt at the Mille Miglia; he was offered a 2-litre Ferrari by Enzo Ferrari for the 1949 race, an offer which he gladly accepted. He started off more gently than usual, but he got into the lead as soon as the cars reached the Appennines and began to pull away from everyone else. His great rival, Biondetti, who was also in a factory Ferrari, conserved his car in the mountains, but Nuvolari pushed as hard as he could and at Rome he was 12 seconds in front of Alberto Ascari. Then Ascari retired and, over the Futa and Raticosa passes, Nuvolari pulled out an enormous lead of nearly half an hour. But the Ferrari was falling to bits around him; first the bonnet flew off and disappeared over his head down the mountainside; then his seat began to break up and after enduring the sliding sensation on every bend he threw the wrecked seat away and sat on a couple of bags of lemons and oranges. His pace hardly abated even though he was far in the lead and when he hit a pothole at over 100 mph, the car broke a spring shackle completely. He arrived at Bologna with a 35-minute lead over the canny Biondetti, but the body-work was falling apart and the chassis itself was beginning to break up. The mechanics took one look and told him to retire, but he gave them a rude sign and drove back into the race. But the car couldn't last much longer and when the rear brakes stopped working, nearly causing several accidents, Nuvolari was finally forced to retire at Villa Ospizio, once again completely exhausted by his efforts and the results of his illness,

which was finally to kill him four years later.

Biondetti won the race as expected and went on to take his fourth victory the following year when the circuit was again run anti-clockwise. The Bologna section was cut out, the cars being routed down the Mediterranean coast with the result that the race distance was reduced to 990 miles.

It was in 1949 that the unique system of race numbering was instituted; the cars were numbered according to their starting time so that a car starting at at 5.30 am was numbered 530 and so on. This enabled spectators to check on the progress of various cars.

Italy was becoming fully conscious of the motor car in the early 1950s and, although many still had to rely on the ubiquitous Lambretta scooter, a large number of people could afford a Fiat 500 or other small car and it soon became a point of honour among enthusiasts to enter the Mille Miglia. In 1950 the official entry list contained 743 starters, including many foreign entries, but it was not unheard of for keen drivers, who did not have the price of the entry fee, to slap some numbers on their road car, join the race at some deserted spot, dice happily down the route for an hour or two, then slip off at another deserted spot and motor contentedly home. Virtually everything on four wheels could be entered for the early post-war Mille Miglias and many drivers could be seen bowling along for hour after hour in tiny Isetta bubble cars and other tiny contrivances. They natur-

Above: Piero Taruffi's Ferrari overtaking a Delahaye in streaming rain in front of the crowd at Vicenza. Despite the weather, there were still masses of people lining the route

ally caused a great deal of trouble to the faster cars which had to overtake literally hundreds of slower cars and many collisions were caused by slower cars. However, the faster drivers accepted the problems, simply because it was the Mille Miglia, but several of the Grand Prix aces refused to have anything to do with the race and even the great Juan Manuel Fangio was none too keen on the race.

In 1950 the race reverted to a clockwise direction

Left: the route used for the last Mille Miglia events of 1954–1957

and it remained this way with minor alterations until the final event of 1957. The race came under attack from foreign teams once more, principally Mercedes-Benz and Jaguar; the firmly-sprung Jaguars seldom lasted long, but Karl Fling finished second with a Mercedes 300SL in 1952 behind Bracco's Ferrari. Stirling Moss got his Jaguar up to third place in 1952 before crashing and in 1953 Reg Parnell finished a fine fifth in a factory DB3 Aston Martin. A feature film called *Checkpoint* was eventually made, using the Aston Martin cars and the race as its background.

In 1953 the Mille Miglia became a qualifying round in the newly instituted World Sports Car Championship. This forced the organisers to weed out some of the slower cars, but in turn it also obliged racing-car manufacturers to enter the event if they wished to gain points in the Championship. The Ferrari stranglehold on the race, which had held since 1948 came to an end in 1954 when Alberto Ascari won in his 2.3-litre Lancia ahead of Marzotto's Ferrari. Both works Astons crashed in the race and Jaguar decided not to compete.

For the 1955 event Mercedes were determined to win with their 300SLR; they spent a great deal of money in preparing cars and giving their crews extensive opportunities for practising on the route. Stirling Moss was paired with British journalist Denis Jenkinson, who prepared a comprehensive set of pace notes so that he could signal the severity of bends to Moss. The system worked perfectly and Moss won the race at an average speed of 97.89 mph, nearly 10 mph faster than the previous race average. To maintain almost 100 mph over the undulating terrain of Italy seemed an impossible task before the race, but the 170 mph Mercedes never faltered once and Moss was able to push hard for ten hours. Castellotti in a 4.4-litre Ferrari drove single-handed and bravely against

the Mercedes, but he wore out his tyres too quickly and eventually blew up, while Piero Taruffi, who led briefly in a 4.9 Ferrari also retired. Fangio showed his quality by finishing second to Moss.

In a way the very speed of the Mercedes victory led to the demise of the Mille Miglia, for it suddenly became very apparent to disinterested parties in Italy that hundreds of cars were rushing about Italy at speeds of up to 170 mph, passing through throngs of completely unprotected citizens. Agitation for the abolition of the race began to grow.

The 1956 race took place as planned in early April and Castelotti gained his revenge, winning a very wet race at 85.40 mph, while Britain's Peter Collins finished second in another 3.5-litre Ferrari. The best Mercedes could do this time was sixth.

The 1957 event proved to be the last. Peter Collins led the race for a spell, in a Ferrari, but rear axle trouble put him out, while the Moss/Jenkinson partnership lasted only a few miles before the brake pedal snapped off in their Maserati. With Collins's retirement, Piero Taruffi got into the lead and, despite a grumbling transmission, the car held together to give Taruffi his long-awaited victory. Unfortunately, soon after Taruffi finished came the news that Count Alphonso 'Fon' de Portago had crashed his Ferrari only thirty miles from the finish. A tyre had burst and the Ferrari had scythed into the crowd at maximum speed killing Portago, his navigator and nine spectators.

The rising tide of public opinion soon forced the Government to prevent the race being held again. This time Renzo Castagneto was obliged to give in, although a couple of regularity rallies were held in 1958 and 1959 with the title of Mille Miglia. Naturally these attracted little interest and the Mille Miglia was no more.   MT

Above: the finish of the 1957 Mille Miglia. Again in rain, Piero Taruffi, with a Ferrari, crosses the line at viale Rebuffone, after passing the little 1500 cc OSCA of Cabianca. This was the last race to be held, leaving the Targa Florio as the only major road race

THE ARCH AMERICAN RACER

Harry Miller was one of the world's great automotive designers and perhaps the most important single figure in the history of American motor racing

IN ANY LIST OF THE GREAT MEN who have earned distinction in the design or manufacture of cars, Harry Armenius Miller must stand out as unique. Others might be described as artists, craftsmen, scientists, or even as simply inspired, but Miller alone admitted to an inexplicable occult inspiration as the source of his ideas, which simply came to him without any real working out. It seems certain that he possessed some kind of clairvoyant facility, notably in the ability to forecast the precise time when people would die, but as far as his role in the evolution of the car is concerned —and especially of the racing car, which was his prime concern during his heyday—it is apparent that he was not a practical engineer, nor in any way a theoretical one. He was a fund of inspired ideas, often years or decades ahead of their time, and he was fortunate enough to have working with him men of consummate ability in transmuting those ideas into substance. Because of the important part these men played in establishing the Miller legend, it is not always clear just how much was originated by Harry himself, but it seems likely that his was the inspiration for the design of a front-wheel-drive layout for a racing car with a conventionally oriented engine, and for the related adoption of the de Dion suspension that had been generally forgotten since the 1890s and that, after extensive use on American race tracks and in some Cord touring cars, was finally taken up to very good purpose by Mercedes-Benz in 1937, since when it has always been in use somewhere. In one other thing Miller was an undoubted first, although it had nothing to do with engineering ability, and probably nothing to do with clairvoyance either: he was the first man in the world to make a thoroughly successful business out of merchandising racing cars.

Miller's father, a cultivated German who had trained for the priesthood before coming to the USA where he worked as a schoolteacher in Wisconsin, spelt his name Mueller. His mother was Canadian and Harry, one of five children in Menomonie, not only spelt his surname the English way, but also rejected the education planned for him, so as to take a job in a machine shop at the age of 13. To Harry's credit, he worked hard, so that before long he had his own business, and was increasing his knowledge and experience in various branches of the automotive industry, notably in the design of carburettors, but also in the manufacture of pistons. By the time America entered World War I, he had established his own piston factory, probably the first in the USA to make pistons of aluminium, and by this time he was a well established specialist in carburettors, the first commodity with which he was to make really substantial money. It was in about 1909 that he built the first carburettor of his own invention, calling it the Master.

In those days, when the average carburettor was hopelessly incapable of providing proper mixtures of fuel and air in correct proportions over a wide range

of operating speeds and flow rates, the Master Automatic was a good deal better than average. It incorporated a barrel-type throttle with helical opening, which progressively uncovered a series of individually replaceable jets set in a bar across the carburettor bore, upstream of the throttle. Between the idle setting, at which only one jet was uncovered, and wide-open throttle, when they were all cleared, the Miller carburettor was not very good, but for engines that had to do a lot of full-throttle work and do it particularly well, it was eminently satisfactory, being taken up with enthusiasm for racing cars, police cars, fire engines and even aircraft. In particular, the racing-car applications brought Miller into contact with the lively American racing fraternity, much of it gathered along the West Coast where Miller had his factory in Los Angeles. However, he was to sell the Master rights in 1914 to the son of Charles Fairbanks (then Vice President of the USA) who set up a large factory in Indianapolis to build carburettors in quantities large

Below: the Miller of Count Zborowski leads the Alfa Romeo of Antonio Ascari, during the Grand Prix of France in 1924

Bottom: from 1926 to 1929 American racing was governed by the 1½-litre, 91 inch, formula. This is the front-wheel-drive, '91 inch', Miller-engined Packard Cable Special of Leon Duray

enough to satisfy a nationwide demand—whereas Miller's output had previously been a mere 60,000 or so per annum. When the deal was done, and Miller and Beasley (who had financed the original 1909 operation) had been bought out, Miller promptly set up the Miller Carburettor Co, to make a crude simplified form of the Master that, being suitable only for racing, was not in competition with the original Automatic. With the blossoming of the age of speedway racing on board and other oval tracks in the USA, the success of the venture was complete and lasted until well into the 1920s, when a superior carburettor produced by Ed Winfield (a former employee of Miller) supplanted it. Years later, Winfield paid his compliment to Miller with an evaluation of the man's place in the scheme of things: 'He was the originator in the automotive field of doing an artistic job on his machinery. He was more of an artist than an engineer. The one thing he insisted on—and that was pure Miller influence—was having everything well proportioned and well finished, regardless of structural quality. Others around him, like Fred and Leo, could worry about that.'

Fred and Leo certainly did, but they had the ability to do what Miller demanded, the gifts that he lacked, and the devotion to contribute more in sum to the lasting good reputation of Miller than did Harry himself or anybody else. Fred was of German parentage, too, his name being Offenhauser, and he was born in Los Angeles in 1888. By 1913, he was a first-class toolmaker and machinist working for the Pacific Electric Railway, but he went to Miller for a job that would allow him to make progress on his own terms and his own abilities. So well did he justify his claim that he was soon in complete charge of production in Miller's factory, giving it the reputation of being the cleanest and best run in the vicinity.

The other helpmeet was Leo William Goossen, the Michigan-born son of Dutch parents and the one and only man who could be considered truly responsible for the design of all effective American racing engines from 1920 until 1965. Having no choice but to go to

Above: in 1923 a new 2-litre formula was introduced into the American racing regulations. For this formula Miller produced the '122 inch' model, which was powered by a straight-eight, twin-cam, dry-sump, barrel-crankcase engine. It was a truly magnificent machine and no effort was spared in its preparation. For the next two years the Millers dominated American racing. Pictured is the 1925 Miller 122 racer. Although, by this time, the car was fitted with a supercharger, it was quite regularly beaten by the Duesenberg racing cars

work when only halfway through high school, he continued to study hard while working in the blueprint room at the Buick factory, and rapidly acquired a command of mathematics and engineering talents to match his exquisite and eloquent draughtsmanship. He was doing very well at Buick when illness forced him to leave for a kinder climate, and he left with a strong letter of recommendation in his pocket signed by the firm's General Manager, no less a man than the great Walter P. Chrysler. This was in 1919, and after convalescence he offered his services to Miller, who hired him on the spot. The age of really elegant Miller racers, the Golden Age of the American Racing Car (the expression is the title of a very fine work by the historian Griffith Borgeson) was about to begin.

Miller had built cars and engines before then. In fact, he had built his first car, a ramshackle device with a dog clutch and no gearbox, for his own use as early as 1905. It was late in 1914, though, that his first real task based on racing-car manufacture (as opposed to the repair work that had kept the shop busy for some time) tickled his fancy. This was to re-create the GP Peugeot that had been blown up early in the season by the racing driver Bob Burman. Miller undertook to do the work in four months and, with Offenhauser's aid, took the opportunity to improve upon the Peugeot design in many details. It was natural that he should employ his own light-alloy single-ring pistons, reasonable that he should replace the feeble Peugeot connecting rods by his own tubular forged pattern which was to remain a characteristic of the Miller engine for many years, and hardly surprising that valve and port sizes should be amplified. More interesting was his substitution of a single overhead camshaft, after the style of the 1914 GP Mercédès, for the twin shafts standard in the Peugeot that Henry had designed. Fortunately for Miller, the Burman car as reconstituted proved fast and competitive during 1915, although a tyre failure was to cause it to crash and kill its owner early in the following year. By that time, Miller was busy building an aero engine for the barnstorming pilot Lincoln Beachey, a six-cylinder unit generically similar in section to the GP Mercédès; it ran very well but, eventually, Beachey killed himself in a test flight to prove some new controls, and the whole project foundered. Nevertheless, it brought Miller's name to the attention of the aviation business, and in 1916 came a commission for a lightweight high-performance aero engine, which Miller neatly tied in with another for a complete racing car. He was thus able to build half a dozen engines, two for flight, and four (with much longer stroke) for the cars. He settled on a barrel-type crankcase with integral block and detachable head, in which the combustion chamber and valve layout were much as in Henry's engines, except for the single overhead camshaft.

When racing driver Barney Oldfield saw it, he decided he wanted something similar but even better, and, after conferring with Miller, had a new engine devised in which the head became integral with a separate block, and with desmodromic valve operation from two camshafts. This engine was designed to run up to 4000 rpm, a very high figure for the times, but it attracted less attention than the car in which it was mounted. This, which was christened the *Golden Submarine*, was (with the exception of its naked wheels, axles and dumb irons), a completely and quite beautifully streamlined affair, and it scored some notable racing successes. The fame it brought Miller was to stand him in good stead after the war, during which he was heavily engaged in the development of the King and Duesenberg versions of the Bugatti aero engine, and also created a very large V12 aero engine for yet another glamour man of American aviation, 'Dutch' Thompson.

At the end of the war, the Miller factory returned to normal work on carburettors and the like, only to be disturbed by a commission from a brewer to produce a radical racing car that might evolve into a volume-production sports car. The project eventually fell through, but it was work on this that gave Leo Goossen the chance to prove his abilities to Miller and, when the racing driver Tommy Milton ordered a new car, they were ready for him. In fact, Miller must have seen him coming, for this important customer was fobbed-off with an engine like Oldfield's; irate, Milton came back and insisted on something better, the specification of which he worked out with Goossen. The car was a three-litre twin-cam straight-eight that in most respects was a copy of the successful Henry-designed Ballot, but its exceptional performance was due to a clever new cam contour that Milton admitted pirating from Hall-Scott. Any part of the engine that was not otherwise inspired by the Ballot was derived from the straight-eight Duesenberg that Milton brought to the Miller factory to be copied or improved. It was ironic that this engine should win the 1922 Indianapolis race in a Duesenberg chassis driven by Miller's great rival, Jimmy Murphy. Half a dozen complete racing cars similarly powered were then ordered by Cliff Durant, and they were successful enough in the remainder of the season for Durant to order a team of new designs for the new 2-litre formula that took effect in 1923.

For Miller, this was like a dream come true. Instead of scratching from one project to the next, he could now go into business making racing cars on a regular production basis. Anybody else would have taken the chance to rationalise his production and make economies, but the last thing Miller ever could be was a businessman, and he reacted by devoting the new source of funds to making his cars more perfect in appearance and finish, more jewel-like in detail and more delicate in their fine balance of lightness and

durability, than ever before. Fine materials were bought from the small specialist firms that made high-grade alloys of steel and aluminium; brilliant artificers were set to machining engine and transmission components to the barest possible tolerances; even the side rails of the chassis were hand-beaten in the shop from mild-sheet steel over cast-iron formers, with such artistry that there was no trace of a tool mark on them when they were finished. Everything in the new 2-litre cars was beautiful—and most beautiful of all was the engine that Goossen drew up to the broad dictates of Harry Miller. It was a twin-cam dry-sump barrel-crankcased straight-eight, ostensibly similar to the earlier three-litre engine, but Miller had accepted the recommendation of Colonel Hall (of Hall-Scott) that

Top: Hollywood actress Paulette Goddard poses in an unnamed sports car, alongside the 2-litre, straight-eight Miller Special of Ralph DePalma

Above: Leon Duray's Miller-engined Packard Cable Special pictured at Indianapolis in 1929

Right: these pictures, taken at Monza in 1932, show the Miller of Leon Duray (in the black overalls) prior to the start of the Italian Grand Prix of that year. Duray was forced to retire from the race

Bottom: Harry Miller poses alongside the world's first four-wheel-drive racing car, which he built in 1932. Two of these machines, using V8 engines, were used at Indianapolis, but unfortunately they proved unsuccessful. The cars cost $15,000 and had a top speed of about 150 mph

the four-valve pentroof cylinder head should make way for two valves in a hemispherical combustion chamber, after the style pioneered by Fiat in 1921 and convincingly demonstrated by the Italian firm in the Grands Prix of 1922. Miller had his own contribution to make, however, and he did this in the light of his experience as a carburation expert: the straight-eight had a separate inlet tract for each cylinder, passing through one of the paired barrels of four Miller updraught carburettors. He went further in pioneering the use of ram pipes to achieve resonant tuning of the inlet tract, an artifice that he developed—in the absence of a dynamometer—by running trials at a

convenient oval track with a selection of ram pipes of various lengths and a stopwatch. It was to be a decade before this feature was emulated by F. W. Dixon on his Rileys and, in view of the tremendous success of Miller's cars in 1923 and 1924, it was surprising that this particular feature was not more widely adopted. The reason is probably that the entire racing world on both sides of the Atlantic was captivated by super-charging, introduced to sports cars by Mercédès, to Grand Prix racers by Fiat, and then to the American oval tracks by Duesenberg.

Still, throughout 1923 and 1924, the 2-litre (alias '122-inch') Millers dominated their scene. They developed about 120 bhp, and since they were all as fast as each other and were made in considerable numbers, they created some very close racing. They were more numerous than entry lists might lead one to suppose, for they were given all sorts of names. The Durant Special, the Studebaker Special, the HCS or Stutz, these and others were all Millers, and they were fast, maintaining average speeds as high as the 126.9 mph achieved over 250 miles around the $1\frac{1}{4}$-mile track at Culver City. Alas, none of them could quite hold the

new supercharged Duesenberg at Indianapolis in 1924, when the winner's average speed was 8% higher than that of the victorious Miller in the preceding year.

For 1925, the last year of the two-litre formula, everybody had superchargers, Miller included. Thanks to the gifted Goossen, Miller's centrifugal supercharging was effective and reliable, but Miller had something else that no other competitor had, something that was not Goossen's idea, nor Miller's, but which came from that inventive practical engineer Riley Brett, who worked for Jimmy Murphy: front-wheel drive. Murphy had been so taken with the idea that he set Miller to find a way of incorporating it in a racing car, only to be killed before Miller could deliver it. There had of course been front-drive racing cars before in America, Barney Oldfield having been very successful with a V4 Christy in the first decade of the century. Miller's first thought was to emulate the Christy layout, which featured transverse installation of the engine. With an in-line eight-cylinder machine, this was hardly feasible, and an alternative arrangement was eventually devised in which the engine was located more or less conventionally, that is to say longitudinally, in the chassis, behind the front axle line, but set back-to-front to drive a combined gearbox and right-angle transmission flanked by brake drums, from which jointed half-shafts led to the wheels, mounted at the extremities of a dead-beam axle. It was in effect a steerable de Dion layout, and its effect on the driver's technique was quite revolutionary. By keeping the throttles open, drivers found

Above: Harry Miller was one of the greatest designers America has ever produced. In fact, Miller has often been described as the most important single figure in American motor-racing history. His cars enjoyed great success on the circuits of America and helped establish his reputation as an ingenious and inventive designer. Here, a Miller Special competes during an early American oval-track race

that they could take the corners at Indianapolis much faster than ever before, although, if they lifted off, the cars became very difficult to control. The feature was judged valuable enough to have a substantial premium put on it, and Miller in his typically unbusinesslike way chose arbitrary round figures for his wares: 5000 dollars for a supercharged engine, 10,000 dollars for a rear-drive car and 15,000 dollars for a front-drive car. He did not go short of customers.

In 1925, he went a bit short of competition victories, however, for in that year it was the odd Duesenberg that played the hero while the Millers acted the crowd parts. It was the year in which Goossen set himself to design the engine that would have to take over in 1926 and remain in contention until the end of 1929, these being the years of the new 1½-litre, or 91 inch, formula. Superficially, he produced a short-stroke version of the existing engine, but it was refined in every minute detail. In fact, the front-drive '91 inch' Miller, which campaigned under a multitude of titles including Duray-Miller, Packard Cable Special and others, was the high point of Miller's achievement. It won everything in sight. It set a world's closed-course record of 148.17 mph that stood for 24 years. It took the International-class flying-mile record at 164 mph, driven by young Frank Lockhart, for whom the Miller was a basis for further development—a measure of which was the extra 98 bhp that Lockhart found beyond the 154 (at 7000 rpm) of the standard Miller engine, partly by adding an intercooler between the supercharger and the engine. Miller would not allow

Above: a Miller Special, as used for board track racing during the 1930s

Left: Tony Willman and Jack Petty pose in their four-wheel-drive Miller Special prior to the 1937 Indianapolis 500. Note that the car has been fitted with tyres of differing size. This is because of the anti-clockwise, oval-shaped nature of the Indianapolis circuit, which imposes greater stress on tyres fitted to the right-hand side of the car

the 'rookie' Lockhart to alter his engines. Lockhart responded by buying one outright and becoming a freelance driver. He had tremendous ability, and might have succeeded in his aim to capture the World land-speed record in his so-called Stutz Black Hawk. This was a finely streamlined little single-seater powered by two modified Miller 91 eights paired in parallel, ice-cooled, intercooled, highly supercharged and superbly prepared. A tyre burst during a warming-up run, and Lockhart (having already survived one such mis-adventure) was killed.

In 1930, a new stock-block or 'junk' formula replaced the old order and, although Miller 91 cars continued to do well, Harry gave up the motor racing business in disgust. Joining financier Schofield, he set out to carve a new career in aviation, but the slump hit the firm hard, and by 1932 it was bankrupt. Miller, whose name had been part of the deal, reversed his name and initials to found the Rellimah corporation, in which he was joined by Goossen and Offenhauser.

They tried a variety of things, as Miller was to continue to do until he died in 1943. Just one of those things was important: Goossen designed a twin-cam three-litre, four-cylinder, 16-valve engine (actually based on a marine engine he created in 1926) that remained in motor racing well into the 1970s. When Rellimah broke down, Offenhauser set up his own firm

to keep this engine in production. When he had gone, former associates Louie Meyer and Dale Drake took over, and the famous Offenhauser engine became the Meyer-Drake. When that firm finally ended its days, the Offenhauser name was revived—and still that incredible engine endured. In the unsupercharged days, it grew to $4\frac{1}{2}$ litres, and completely dominated American track racing. When the rules allowed it, the displacement was curtailed to 2.8 litres and a super-charger was added. And when finally turbocharging became the fashion, the exhaust-turbocharged 2.8-litre 'Offy' was the most formidable thing ever seen at Indianapolis, capable of rendering over 800 bhp for qualifying runs, or of running 500 miles competitively at a slightly lower rating.

It has always been, and still is, a superb engine, and the name it bears is a credit to Fred Offenhauser. Yet it is probably not fair to think of it as an Offy, nor (for all its characteristic features, culled from the Miller practice of the 1920s) as a Miller. If anything, it is a Goossen. Perhaps Harry, whose decline would make less inspiring reading than his rise, could see what was coming and knew himself a has-been. His name at least will not be forgotten, and his engineering style has lasted longer than anyone else's. With this much to its credit, his memory can afford due deference to the real designer who created his memorial in metal. LJKS

Outstanding despite handicap

TOMMY MILTON WAS, along with drivers like Ralph de Palma, Barney Oldfield and Peter de Paulo, one of the outstanding drivers in the early days of American track racing. Born in 1893, Thomas W. Milton had no sight in his left eye, but this handicap did not deter him from an

Below: Tommy Milton poses with Harry Stutz, following his 1923 Indy 500 win
Bottom: Milton and the double-engined Duesenberg, prior to his 156.03 mph run at Daytona in 1920

early ambition to become a racing driver, because he simply memorised the standardised eyesight test cards of the day! He had earlier shown promise as an automobile engineer and worked as a builder and tuner of racing cars. At the age of 17, he joined a barnstorming exhibition team driving a Mercer, but the ambitious Milton soon tired of the fixed results of the races in which he took part and was eventually sacked for disobeying team orders. He then joined the Duesenberg team which was enjoying considerable success at that time in the hands of drivers like Eddie Rickenbacker, Jimmy Murphy and Wilbur D'Alene. He was to have driven in the 1916 Indianapolis 500-mile race, but his car was not ready in time. However, he soon began to show that he was a driver of some skill by picking up many good placings on the board tracks, which were becoming popular in the USA at that time. Although he did not manage to win a race, he was placed 7th in the American Championship in 1916.

America's intervention in World War I kept him out of action until 1919 but he was made captain of the Duesenberg team for that season. He soon scored his first major victory by winning the 300-mile road race at Elgin, Illinois, at 73.9 mph; he had previously retired from the Indianapolis race after only 50 laps. Soon after his Elgin victory, he was badly burned in a crash

on a board track which put him out of racing until early 1920, but, during his convalescence, he designed and helped to build a twin-Duesenberg-engined car using a pair of the 5-litre, single-overhead-camshaft, straight-eight engines which were redundant because the Indianapolis rules were changed for 1920, reducing the limit to 3 litres. The engines were simply mounted side-by-side and drove by separate propeller shafts to a rigid rear axle fitted with two differentials. The 'Double Duesy' was tested at 151 mph by Milton's teammate Jimmy Murphy, and then Milton took it out on Daytona Beach and clocked up 156.03 mph over the measured mile. Milton claimed that this was the average of a two-way run, making it eligible for the land-speed record, which stood at that time to Horsted's Benz at a very modest 124.10 mph. Unfortunately, the governing body of motor racing in Europe, the AIACR, refused to recognise the run as it had not been carried out under their jurisdiction, but it was certainly recognised in the USA. Milton's speed was not officially bettered in Europe until six years later.

The rest of Milton's 1920 season was very successful, for he won three major long-distance races, finished third at Indianapolis and won the American National Championship.

For 1921, Tommy switched to a Frontenac for Indianapolis, although he also attempted to qualify a Durant-Duesenberg without success. The Frontenac went perfectly, to give Milton his first Indianapolis victory at 89.62 mph. Although his other successes were not so frequent as in 1920, he picked up enough good places to win his second American National Championship.

In 1922, Milton's Leach Special only lasted 44 laps at Indianapolis, but he picked up several victories and many places at the board tracks. He switched to Millers and Miller-powered cars after that and, in 1923, he won his second Indianapolis 500 in his HCS Miller Special at an average speed of 90.95 mph, to become the first man to win two Indianapolis 500 races.

Milton gradually began to wind down his own participation in races, but he still won a number of races in Miller-powered specials. His 1924 Indianapolis race lasted 110 laps, but in 1925 he finished fifth. On this note, he decided to retire from driving at the age of 32, but he kept his association with racing by designing and building a front-wheel-drive Miller-powered special for Cliff Durant to drive in the 1927 Indianapolis race. However, Durant was taken ill and was unable to drive, so Milton took over the car, qualified it and finished eighth in the race, despite severe overheating problems which obliged him to use a relief driver.

Like his former Duesenberg teammate, Jimmy Murphy, Milton took in one major European race during his career. He drove a Duesenberg in the 1925 Italian Grand Prix at Monza, leading the race at one stage, but eventually dropping back to fourth place after suffering a broken oil pipe.

Milton retired for good after the 1927 Indianapolis race, taking a job with Packard before forming his own company. He also remained active in racing as chief steward at Indianapolis and as a member of the American Automobile Association Contest Board. He died in 1962 at the age of 69.　　　　MT

GODDESS OF AUTOMOBILES

Belgium's Minerva company specialised in making high-speed luxury vehicles in the Daimler and Rolls-Royce mould

EVERY CAR-MANUFACTURING COUNTRY of any note has produced a top marque at some time or other. Rolls-Royce established a peak in this context for Britain, France had the Hispano-Suiza, Italy produced the Isotta-Fraschini in vintage times and Ferrari and other exotics since the war, Germany had top models from Mercedes, and America has contributed great and splendid automobiles such as the Duesenberg, Packard, Cadillac and Lincoln.

Belgium was never a major builder of cars, but if it did not make them in vast quantities, it had its *grande marque* in the celebrated Minerva, the Goddess of Automobiles.

It all began in 1897 when Sylvain de Jong commenced making bicycles and then branched out into supplying engines for the first motor cycles, a venture in which he was so well regarded that most of Europe's pioneer riders were propelled by little Minerva engines. Using his own expertise, de Jong had dabbled with a primitive motor car and a lorry before the close of the century and, by 1900, was sensibly making motor cycles of his own. Serious car manufacture was begun by the Antwerp factory in 1904 following experiments, a couple of years before this, with a four-cylinder 6 hp unit which was based on the Panhard system of a front-mounted engine driving the rear wheels.

These initial production Minervas were soundly constructed but by no means revolutionary machines. They used T-head engines and, by starting with a twin-cylinder unit and adding cylinders to it, a primarily 1.6-litre model could be made available as a 2½-litre with three cylinders, or as a bigger four-cylinder car of over 3 litres capacity. It might be thought that, at this early period of the automobile movement, de Jong would have been happy to have three sound models with which to entice customers. But, perhaps because Belgium was scarcely a wealthy country, the Minerva Company also ventured into the realms of cyclecar construction. They called this very simple device the Minervette. It used a single-cylinder engine, of a mere 636cc, at the front of a chassis and a simple transmission which consisted of a two-speed gearbox and final drive, driving to one of a pair of back wheels by a chain. They were able to offer this water-cooled contraption for the equivalent of just over £100. Fortunately for the reputation of Belgium and the future fortunes of the Minerva concern, this did not prevent proper cars of increasing horsepower emerging from the works of the Company, which was known as Minerva Motors SA of Antwerp. The Hon C. S. Rolls, of Rolls-Royce fame, began to sell Minerva cars in London, and it may have been his influence which brought more powerful models into the catalogues and showrooms. At all events, it was a 14 hp 3-litre Minerva that attracted the interest of Rolls, rather than the little twin-cylinder and four-cylinder models. This shaft-driven Minerva Fourteen

Two seats in front, four inside, of which two are folding, cloth or leather lined, with large headings, silk curtains, electric light, speaking tube, removable front glass, bevelled glass.

18 h.p. Four-Cylinder Minerva Landaulette

Chassis, with Tyres - £415   Limousine Landaulette - £595

Lamps and Horn extra

Above: our photograph shows an example of early Minerva advertising Depicted is the 18 hp four-cylinder Minerva Landauiette of 1908

Left: created for the Kaiserpreis race of 1907, this is the distinctive vee-radiatored Minerva racing car. These cars were fitted with 8-litre engines featuring overhead inlet valves and five-bearing crankshafts. Unfortunately, their attempt to win the Kaiserpreis was unsuccessful. At the Circuit des Ardennes, however, where this picture was taken, the cars scored a great triumph by taking first, second, third and sixth places

the Minerva followed Daimler in adopting the double-sleeve-valve engine of the American inventor, Charles Y. Knight. By 1910, after a brief period when L-head side-valve cars had been made alongside the new valveless ones, all Minervas, as all Daimlers, were to the new, silent, if smoky, pattern. It was from this sleeve-valve basis that the well remembered Minerva top models emanated.

Something historians debate is whether Daimler or Minerva were first with a Knight-engined car in their catalogues. However, be that as it may, both companies started this trend with a 38 hp model, powered by big four-cylinder engines of 124 × 130 mm. Dual ignition

was a modestly priced, well sprung car of decent performance. It had a pressed-steel frame instead of the wooden frames used by the original chain-driven Minervas and it was possible to buy one in London, with body, ready to use, for only £285. This was enough to put the name of this Belgian car firmly on the European map, and the Antwerp Directors enhanced the Minerva reputation still further by sanctioning motor racing.

They had brought out a fast Sixty in 1907 and led on from this to building a team of racing cars for the Kaiserpreis race that year. Unfortunately, they were unsuccessful, although fielding special cars with overhead inlet valves and five-bearing crankshafts. Two of the drivers were Moore-Brabazon (later Lord Brabazon of Tara) and Algy Lee Guinness; Brabazon later took his Minerva to the opening Brooklands meeting, only to have it catch fire. However, in the Circuit des Ardennes race, Brabazon finished first, and he was followed home by Koolhoven and Guinness with Warwick Wright taking sixth place, all in Minervas. This was a nice walk-over for de Jong and for a time, he continued to make conventional big-engined four-cylinder Minervas, such as the 5.9-litre; there was also a very good 102 × 115 mm 3.7-litre car capable of exceeding 50 mph which sold for £465.

After establishing itself as a sound poppet-valve car,

Above: Léon Molon drives his 3.3-litre Minerva to third place in the 1914 TT, held on the Isle of Man. These machines were fitted with sleeve-valve engines, developing 70 bhp at 2800 rpm

Right: pictured is an in-line, 6600 cc, 40 hp, eight-cylinder Minerva engine of 1929, while below it is a four-cylinder, 4-litre engine of 1930

Bottom: the magnificent Minerva 30 hp of 1921. It was fitted with an in-line, six-cylinder Knight engine of 5340 cc

and trough-and-dipper lubrication were common to both these makes that had come under the Knight engine spell.

Anyway, the formula worked. King Albert was a customer for a 37 hp Minerva in the year of its introduction and smaller models, like the 2.3-litre 16 hp and a 4¼-litre 26 hp Minerva, were immediately available for lesser mortals who wished to come under the sleeve-valve spell and smoke screen. These Knight Minervas now began to assume the luxury image that the post-war models are associated with. Magnificent closed bodies with every possible convenience were normal wear, and yet these were fast cars which began to demonstrate their reliability and pace in many of the more important trials and rallies, in places as far afield as Sweden, Russia, New Zealand and Spain. The big 'fours' carried on, acquiring improved cooling and lubrication as the years rolled on. The famous 38 hp Minerva was enlarged until it had a swept volume of 7.4 litres. It was an imposing car, with a wheelbase of 11 ft 4 in, but was less expensive than a contemporary Daimler just prior to the outbreak of war, and much less expensive than the Silver Ghost Rolls-Royce, that was still wedded to valves-and-tappets.

Minerva was now on the crest of a financial wave. Motor-cycle manufacture had ceased in 1910 and, before the Kaiser stopped play, the Belgian Company was offering the 75 × 120 mm Fourteen to its less-affluent supporters. This sold for £340 as a chassis from the newly opened and quite magnificent showrooms at Minerva House in Chenies Street, in the heart of London. Moreover, there was a brave attempt to prove the sleeve-valve system in racing, with a team of Minervas entered for the 1914 Tourist Trophy race in the Isle of Man. These were very special 3.3-litre cars, able to give 70 bhp at 2800 rpm, with a safe engine limit of 3300 rpm. They were driven in the contest by Riecken, Porporato and Molon, and went round blinding others with great smokescreens! They were not fast enough to vanquish the winning Sunbeam, however, but this TT appearance was a convincing demonstration of Minerva reliability, and of faith in the valve system that they had adopted four years earlier. They took second, third and fifth places.

The war years were occupied with making vehicles for the Army, including armoured cars, until the factory was overrun. With the Armistice, de Jong was ready to resume where he had left off, using machine tools imported from America and his own coach-building shop at Mortel. In the latter respect, Minerva again paralleled Daimler, and soon had a reputation for making rather dull, dateless carriages which were, nevertheless, extremely well built. They were comfortable and elegant, although a Minerva was usually a more ponderous beast than a Rolls-Royce, except in its more sporting manifestations, or when endowed with other people's bodywork. The first of the post-war models to foster this tradition was the 20 hp NN type, with neat monobloc cylinders and the expected cantilever rear springs of a heavy and sedate car. This was the 1919 offering. But, by 1921, a 5.3-litre six-cylinder model was ready. Not much development work was deemed necessary, although the cone clutch gave way to a single-plate type, and the former foot-operated transmission brake was changed for hand-operated rear-wheel retardation.

Minerva engines were farmed out to a few other manufacturers, and in 1922 a small brother to the big Minervas appeared, in the form of the Type TT. This had a sleeve-valve motor of under 2 litres capacity and, as with the small Rolls which was to appear in 1923, a central lever to change gear with.

Top: the four-door, six-cylinder Minerva 30 hp of 1925. This was typical of the large cars upon which the reputation of the Minerva company was established

Above: 'The Goddess of Automobiles' was the slogan by which the Minerva company was known. Its cars were large, luxurious and very well made. This is a Minerva coupé de ville model of the early 1930s

Mainly, however, the Minerva reputation lay with large cars, but these offered good value for money. The 30 hp six-cylinder followed natural processes of development, such as being provided with front-wheel brakes in 1923. There were various model permutations down the years, including a 2-litre 'small six' which was an 'Americanised' version of the larger cars, but retaining their seven-bearing crankshaft. In time, cast-iron sleeves gave way to steel ones, which gave the Type AK 32/34 hp model (which replaced the long-established 30 hp) quite a good performance, helped by its engine size of almost six litres. Oil radiators and dual-choke carburettors followed and the new-found sporting image was acknowledged when a team of AK Minervas was entered for the 24-hour race at Spa.

Even after the death of de Jong in 1928, Minerva flourished, and progressed along the lines of Daimler and Lanchester. That is to say that a long line of small and larger sixes was augmented in 1930 by a straight-eight, which used sleeve valves. It had a 90 × 130 mm engine, a wheelbase of 12 ft 9½ in, and was surely the only model—it was known as the Type AL—on which the outsize steering wheel favoured by Minerva did not look quite so enormous! You could buy a limousine in London for £1875, with servo brakes, the back springs now being half-elliptics.

It is remarkable how strong the similarity between Daimler and Minerva was. In London, Daimler Hire was well known and the London Minerva agents copied this with Minerva Hire. But, alas, the end was in sight: the English Company was bankrupt by 1932. On the Continent, the name of Minerva lingered on and will forever be associated with some of the world's finest town-carriages, especially in 32/34 and straight-eight form.   WB

A PROVING GROUND FOR DESIGN

The Motor Industry Research Association's proving ground in Warwickshire has been created to solve any problem that a motor-car designer may encounter in the course of his task

THE EARLIEST MOTOR CARS were tested by their manufacturers in the most haphazard fashion, according to the whims of the band of ex-bicycle makers and coachbuilders who created them. The most effective means of developing a car was to enter it in races and hope, with a little luck, to reach the finish successfully. Not only did these early and rather dangerous races ensure rapid developments in performance and reliability, but they also gave the winners a degree of invaluable publicity.

These days, no motor manufacturer would think of exposing a prototype family saloon to the public gaze, let alone test it in front of them in active competition on a race circuit before putting the model on the market. Yet it is a curious fact that it was not until well after World War II that the British motor industry got together and created its own private, and secret, complex of research laboratories and test tracks. Thus it was that an RAF wartime airfield of no particular distinction was redeveloped into the Motor Industry Research Association's establishment at Lindley, near Nuneaton, Warwickshire.

MIRA, as it is known, was partially opened in 1951, but additions continued to be made to the facilities on the Proving Ground's 650-acre site both before and after the official opening in 1954. The project was partially supported by the Government, the Department of Scientific and Industrial Research providing one third of the annual income while the rest was paid by the several hundred member companies who made use of the Proving Ground.

All that the public ever sees of MIRA is an anonymous block of brick 'quality architecture' set back from the A5 London to Holyhead road, and housing the administration and laboratory departments. People with business on the Proving Ground itself enter the

Below: a Reliant Scimitar GTE passes a Bond Bug on the 2.8-mile banked circuit. There is a minimum speed limit of 70 mph on the outer banked section which can be negotiated 'hands off' at 80 mph. There are also electronic timing lights fifty feet apart on one section that can measure speed, by checking time to one ten thousandth of a second

Inset: an aerial view of the MIRA complex at Lindley, near Nuneaton, Warwickshire. The linked horizontal straights are to the right

site here and show their Driving Permits to the security official at the gate. They drive straight past the labs and disappear out of sight over the top of a gently rising slope, pass some traffic lights, and dip down into a tunnel under one of the banked turns of the high-speed circuit. All users of the Proving Ground must go directly to the Control Tower—the original RAF building, in fact—and report to the Proving Ground Manager, or his staff.

The facilities at their disposal are highly varied. Possibly of the greatest interest to the ordinary motorist is the banked high-speed circuit where secret prototypes, sometimes conveyed to the Proving Ground in covered trailers, can be driven round in tests at well over the legal limit. This triangular 2.8-mile circuit is four lanes wide, the inside lane having been widened by four feet in 1974 to cope with the latest juggernaut lorries. The circuit is marked out with quarter-mile posts so that a best one-way top speed can be calculated. A dotted yellow line in the middle of the track reminds drivers that the two right-hand lanes, which are steeply banked in the three turns, are limited to traffic travelling at a minimum of 70 mph. The banking can be negotiated, theoretically, 'hands off' at speeds of up to 80 mph—faster than that and the driver has to start 'driving' the bends. Racing cars are not allowed to be taken to the Proving Ground but it is well known that an unofficial lap record was set by Jaguar test driver David Hobbs in the XJ13 at an average speed of over 150 mph. The forces imposed on the tyres with a car pinned up the banking at such high speeds are far beyond those reached on an uncambered road, of course, and the high-speed circuit is nowadays unsuitable for sustained high-speed testing of many high-performance saloon cars, let alone the exotic modern sports cars.

Within the triangle formed by the banked circuit

Below left: giving the suspension a tough time on the 1.5-mile pavé circuit; the surface is of granite setts laid in an irregular pattern. If there is any component on the car that is likely to drop off or shake loose, then a quick drive along the pavé will ensure that the problem will be brought to the fore

Below right: a Hillman with suspension fully extended on the long-wave pitching surface, which has waves of four-inch amplitude and pitches of forty feet

there are a further two circuits plus various special test facilities. The 'No. 2' circuit is a fast one-way 2.3 miles with three tight left-hand bends, and it is used primarily for brake testing. A water splash is situated close-by so cars can ford through and then check their brakes whilst thoroughly doused. Not far from the water-splash is the dust tunnel—200 feet long and capable of writing off a new car in seconds without putting a scratch on it. The fine china clay dust which is emitted is virtually impossible to remove as it gets into every part of the vehicle—useful research for export models but not very pleasant for the drivers!

A wide variety of horrors lie in wait for the unfortunate test cars, including 1½ miles of different types of continental pavé, half a mile of washboard surface, an 'Australian creek crossing', a long-wave pitching surface, corrugated sections, all sorts of bumps, an Australian 'spoon drain', deep and shallow wading troughs and a jet-powered cross-wind generator.

In the early 1960s, a special 1.38-mile ride and handling course was opened. This circuit was artificially constructed to simulate the worst possible combination of bad road conditions imaginable. In the mornings, traffic travels in a clockwise direction and at lunchtime the entrance and exit signs are reversed. Taking the morning direction, the circuit starts with a series of bends with extremely severe adverse cambers and leads into a straight with a waved surface of varying pitch. This is followed by a decreasing radius right-hand bend with a corrugated surface, a mock road crossing with high cambers, and a steeply rising left-hand bend near the start of which is sited a plateau with a very rough railway level crossing. At the top of the hill, the road falls away again sharply into a vicious dip followed by another hill which the road follows in a right-hand turn. Coming off the hill a driver can take a series of alarming ridges, improperly

Left: 'mud plugging' a Land-Rover on the 4.5-mile cross-country track. On this circuit, the vehicles come up against hazards like potholes, gullies, ruts and rocky passes

Below: there are four test hills at MIRA, ranging from 1 in 6 to the steepest 1 in 3. On the steeper gradients, cars with weak handbrakes find it difficult to remain stationary, and some low-powered cars even find it difficult to move in any direction other than down!

installed cat's eyes, drains, tramlines, gutters and a canted straight at very high speeds (if necessary). At the end of the course there is a highly crowned bend.

You might be forgiven for thinking that any car that can take on that sort of road and be pleasant to drive would be remarkable, yet a curious fact has been revealed by the road-test staff of a well-known weekly motoring magazine (three magazines have been permitted to take out membership of MIRA): a punishing and unrealistic ride and handling course such as this can develop the 'proving ground special', a car that seems excellent on the test track at which it was set up, but which is not so impressive under ordinary motoring conditions.

The remaining facilities within the perimeter of the high-speed circuit are the 250 ft diameter steering pad, the noise generating surfaces, and the wind tunnels in which aerodynamic studies can be carried out on actual cars and on scale models.

It could be argued that the most useful circuit of all at the Proving Ground is the 4½-mile cross-country track, which follows a punishing path around the outside of the high-speed circuit, for here much of the development work on the famous Land-Rover was carried out. This circuit is in almost constant use nowadays for endurance testing of the latest cross-country and dual-purpose vehicles. Also outside the high-speed circuit are the four test hills, going from 1-in-6 to 1-in-3, and the twin horizontal one-mile straights. The latter facility, completed in the mid-sixties, is linked at each end by banked turns which can, in emergency, be tackled at very high speeds. These dead-level straights are used for timing acceleration and are marked out in quarter miles and at the kilometre points by trackside posts.

Security at MIRA was tightened up even more in 1974 with the building of a second guarded gate

between the laboratory complex and the proving ground. This is the result of a MIRA Council decision to permit the Department of the Environment 'to conduct a completely separate enterprise' in a new building near the horizontal straights. This is claimed to be for the purposes of Government-sponsored research into the 'E-marking' system of standardisation in certain aspects of European car design. Rumours have been put forward of other interesting projects that will be carried out in these new premises, but MIRA, as ever, keeps its secrets.

What of MIRA's future? In 1970, the Society of Motor Manufacturers & Traders' (SMM&T) system of across the board subscriptions was stopped, and in 1973 the Government grant was phased out. Vauxhall built their own proving ground at Millbrook and used GM's European facilities. Chrysler have excellent testing facilities in France, as does the Ford Motor Company in Germany. Of the 'Big Four' car manufacturers in Britain, British Leyland remains the biggest user of MIRA's Proving Ground and they have made an attempt to buy it outright. This was turned down by the Council because of objections from other principal members and because it would have deprived the dozens of ancillary part manufacturers—makers of brake linings, tyres, etc—of an essential testing facility. These days, members pay a big annual subscription individually, and then pay by hour for the use of the test tracks.

MIRA's future, which, despite the link with the DoE, remains in the independent hands of the MIRA Council, depends on its ability to continue to operate as a profitable contract research association. Now that

Above: the twin one-mile horizontal straights that are linked, at either end, by large-radius banked turns; these can be negotiated at up to 55 mph, so that flying starts can be made from the beginning of the measured mile. The two twenty-foot carriageways have marker posts at regular intervals, so that accurate measurements can be made from the car or lorry that is being tested

some British-built Fords are designed in Germany (and *vice versa*), some French-designed Chryslers are made in England, and even all the British market 'German' VW Beetles are made in Belgium, there is no need for a single Proving Ground which all car makers can share in order to produce world-beating vehicles. The test tracks remain fairly busy with the activities outlined above, but MIRA's financial future lies firmly in the hands of the boffins in the labs.

They can conduct all manner of research projects into automotive and related subjects. In addition to aerodynamics, engine work, vehicle safety, impact tests, corrosion studies, and research into handling, ride, vehicle noise—it is a case of 'you name it, they do it'—they are free to carry out long and short-term research projects for industries not connected with vehicles at all, but which might make use of the special talents of MIRA's scientists. They possess comprehensive laboratory facilities including a general lab, electronics lab, a giant refrigerator plant which can contain a complete car and leave plenty of room to spare, a chemical lab, engine dynamometers, and an anechoic chamber (free field room): this chamber is a big room in which all echo is damped out, thus facilitating fine research into noise. To be inside the anechoic chamber is weird and oppressive and few newcomers can stand the painless torture for long! All this is obvious enough, of course, but the point is that the MIRA scientists possess an unrivalled fund of experience in their field. Now that they are free to take on work from firms outside Britain, and even in some cases outside EFTA and the EEC, they should be assured of a busy and profitable future. TD

AN ALL-ROUND VIEW FROM THE DRIVING POSITION

A mirror is a legal requirement on any motor car. Mirrors, correctly used and properly positioned, can play a vital part in road safety

A REAR-VIEW MIRROR is needed for two main reasons. Firstly, it is vital for safe driving on today's fast and crowded roads and, secondly, it is a legal requirement.

The law is quite specific: every car must be equipped with a rear-view mirror which can be fitted either inside or outside. There are at least two types of outside fitting mirror; the first is the common wing mirror and the second the door mirror, which is usually clipped rather than screwed on.

The door mirror is very useful in that it is close to the driver's eyes and so gives a wide field of view, something which goes a long way towards eliminating the blind spots which can be found with other types.

In a van it is essential that some form of exterior mirror be fitted, so that the driver can still see behind his vehicle when the load compartment is full and the rear window obscured. It is preferable to have two wing or door mirrors in this case, otherwise, the rearward view will be very limited.

Safety is quite important with a rear-view mirror, in more ways than simply providing vision to the rear. A plain-glass interior mirror can cause very serious cuts in the event of an accident in which the driver or passenger is thrown forward; the answer is to fit a protective surround to the glass—and this is usually done.

Most modern mirrors incorporate other safety features like shatterproof glass. The edge-protection function is achieved by means of a plastic casing which holds the glass in place even if it is broken by an impact. Some others have a mounting which is designed to collapse if a force is exerted upon it during an accident.

Methods of mounting the mirror vary. The most basic fitting is a single shaped arm screwed into the head framing of the roof and fitted with a friction-fit ball and socket at the mirror end to allow accurate adjustment. Others are attached directly to the windscreen glass by means of an adhesive pad, while a less permanent alternative to this is a simple rubber-sucker fixing. This is ideal for an extra mirror for the instructor occupying the passenger seat with a learner driver, or for a mirror with 'smoked' glass to reduce the glare from the reflected headlights of following cars.

The size, shape and type of mirror can vary considerably. The standard fitting is likely to be a simple flat glass type, plastic-edged and metal-backed. Alternatives are available and include convex glass instead of flat. These reflect a far wider area than the flat type but tend to distort as well as reduce the size of the reflected image. Getting used to them can take some time.

Other types have tinted glass to reduce reflected headlamp glare while there is a further type which incorporates a dual function—an ordinary mirror by day and an anti-dazzle capability at night.

One version of this has a hinged reflector mounted behind a piece of plain glass. With the reflector tilted

Above: a tinted overtaking mirror mounted on the driver's door for easy adjustment from the interior. Although the field of view is greater from a mirror in this position, one has to turn one's eyes further to see rearwards than one would from a unit mounted on the car's wing, for example

Right: a streamlined wing mirror that creates less drag than the conventional type

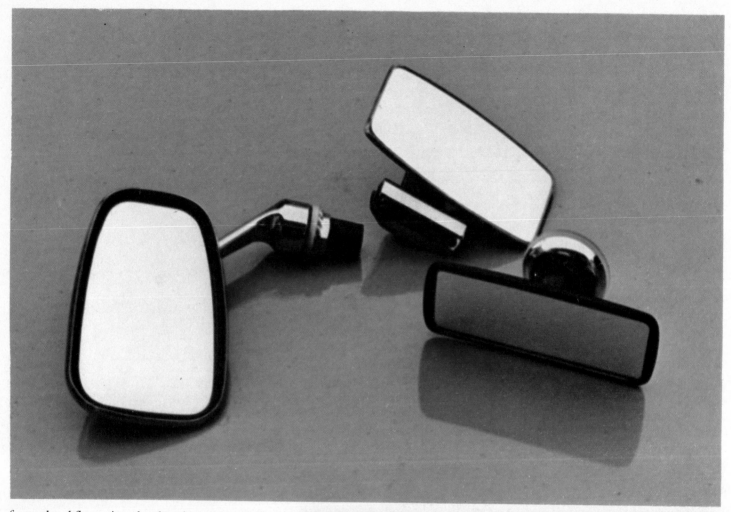

forward and flat against the glass, it acts as an ordinary mirror. Flicked back into its secondary position it gives reduced reflective power. The reflector is generally moved manually but there are modern versions available which are operated by a photo-electric cell, triggered by headlamp glare.

A choice between flat or convex glass is available with wing mirrors, too, and finding the correct mounting position and then aligning them correctly is a job for two people. One makes the adjustments to the mirror while the other sits in the driving seat and directs him. It must be positioned so that the driver can see it unobscured by windscreen pillars and should reflect the side of the car as well as the overtaking area behind it.

Even with a combination of wing mirror and interior mirror, it is sometimes impossible to eliminate the blind spot caused by the rear-window pillars. There is an interesting wing mirror available which has its glass located in two planes, designed to eliminate the blind-spot problem.

Wing mirrors tend to be in a vulnerable position and can be struck by passers-by when the car is parked. They can also suffer from the vigorous brush action in a car wash. For this reason, many are designed to pivot under pressure and spring back afterwards—a very useful facility.

Another modern tendency in mirror fitting is to mount it on the car door instead of on the wing. The advantages are convenience in looking into it, and the ability to clean rain off it if necessary from inside the car and to adjust it easily while travelling. They are ideal for vans and motor caravans, as well as being suitable for use on cars.

Other versions of rear-view mirrors which must be mentioned are the special adaptations used by vehicles towing a caravan or boat. The simplest conversion is an extension mirror attached to the existing wing mirror with an adjustable spring-loaded clamp.

For those who tow an extra large caravan, a long-armed mirror is available. The arm is a telescopic tubular unit, adjustable and fitted to the driver's door.

One more version of the rear view mirror for the caravan enthusiast is the periscope, which fits to the front of the car roof. The driver looks through the screen into the eyepiece end and, by means of mirrors, back along the top of the car through the front and rear windows of the caravan to get a view of the traffic behind. The device is adjustable and usually fits by means of suction pads and mounting brackets.   JJ

Top: a wing mirror, a clip-on overtaking mirror and a suction-sticking inside rear-view mirror

Above: when adjusting mirrors, always clasp the outer frame, so that finger prints are not put on the mirror surface, thus causing annoying distractions that can command the eyes' focus

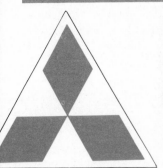

A SMALL PART OF AN EMPIRE

The Mitsubishi motor car is a recent development. The Mitsubishi organisation, however, can trace its history back to the nineteenth century when they built ships

IN COMMON WITH other Japanese motor-car builders, the Mitsubishi Motor Corporation, manufacturer of the Mitsubishi range of motor cars, is a relatively young company in terms of motor-manufacturing history. Of the firms in Japan producing motor cars, however, Mitsubishi is one of the few, if not the only one, which can trace its origins back before 1900. The direct origins of the company stem from a company which was called Tosa Kaisei-Shosha that was founded in 1870. This company was renamed Mitsubishi Shokai in 1873, and two years later the Mitsubishi Mail Steamship Company. Mitsubishi means 'three diamonds', which gives the company its red three-diamond trademark. A year later, the company was again renamed, becoming Mitsubishi-sha Ltd, and merged with the Government-owned Nagasaki Iron Works which themselves had their origins in a forge set up by Tokugawa Shogunate in 1857.

In 1917, the Mitsubishi Shipbuilding Co Ltd was formed and, in the same year, the Mitsubishi Model A, based on the Fiat, became one of the first commercially manufactured Japanese cars. Roughly twenty of these cars were built and sold, although experiments and development work continued until 1921 when the Mitsubishi Internal-Combustion Engine Co Ltd was formed from the previously named Mitsubishi Internal-Combustion-Engine Manufacturing Company Ltd.

The creation of the Mitsubishi Aircraft Company Ltd, in 1928, was followed by the founding of Mitsubishi Heavy Industries Ltd in 1934, and much of the intervening space of time was spent at the Kobe Works in the production of heavy trucks and buses.

During World War II, production was converted to the manufacture of tanks and it was not until 1946 that production of three-wheeled trucks and large-sized buses was resumed. Under the Enterprise Reorganisation and Readjustment Law, passed in 1950, which was aimed at putting war-ravaged Japan back on its industrial feet, the company was reorganised. This reorganisation, which was completed in 1952, resulted in Mitsubishi being divided into three divisional companies: the Mitsubishi Shipbuilding and Engineering Company Ltd; Shin Mitsubishi Heavy Industries Ltd; and Mitsubishi Nippon Heavy Industries Ltd. In 1953, Mitsubishi signed an agreement allowing them to manufacture Jeeps under licence.

It took eight years from the reorganisation before the first of the new generation of Mitsubishi passenger cars rolled off the production line—this was the Mitsubishi 500. Powered by a two-cylinder, four-stroke, overhead-valve, air-cooled, 20 hp engine, it was a small four-seater featuring synchromesh on second and third gears and a single-dry-plate clutch.

Since 1967, Japan has maintained its position as the second-largest motor-vehicle-producing country in the world, the USA, of course, being the first. The industry's annual production, including parts and

bodies, amounted to about 5800 billion Yen, and in 1973 automotive exports accounted for 16 per cent of the national total. Production of vehicles in 1973 was 7,082,757 units, an increase of 12.5 per cent over the previous year, with passenger cars accounting for 63.1 per cent of the total. Of the total production of passenger cars in 1973, 44.2 per cent were in the 1001 cc–1500 cc class; 39.2 per cent were in the 1501 cc–2000 cc group; 8.4 per cent in the 360 cc group; 5.9 per cent in the 361 cc–1000 cc class and 2.3 per cent in the over 2000 cc sector.

It is interesting to note in particular that the 360 cc class of vehicle, a phenomenon peculiar to Japan, experienced a remarkable change in fortune. Produced as a move towards mass motorisation in the formative days of the Japanese motor industry, and fed by Government concessions in taxation, registration and driving-licence requirements, it occupied a modest 16.8 per cent of the total Japanese car market in 1965. In 1970, the under-360 cc class took 30.4 per cent of the home market—but no sooner had the market been established than it began to decline, occupying only 8.4 per cent of the market in 1973.

Turning to the design front, it is interesting to note that, when the Japanese motor industry began to cater for the mass market in the mid 1950s, it found itself supplying a consumer educated to US standards and tastes. Before the war, both General Motors and Ford assembled cars in Japan, and, after the war, seven years of occupation by US forces helped particularly to shape Japanese attitudes towards passenger cars. Consequently, such tradition as there was, when production began in earnest in the sixties, stemmed largely from Detroit. As a result of this, when the cars appeared on the US market they had a styling which was familiar to the American consumer and were hence that much more acceptable.

In 1962, the first Mitsubishi Colt made its public début in Japan. Two years later, the present holding company was formed by a merger of the former three divisional companies, under the pre-war name of

Above: the first Mitsubishi, that saw the light of day back in 1917. Based on a Fiat, the Model A was one of the first commercially available cars in Japan, although the production span only ran to about twenty cars

Mitsubishi Heavy Industries Ltd. In the same year, Mitsubishi's top-of-the-range Debonair was shown.

1966 saw the launch of the Mitsubishi Minica 360 saloon, powered by a 356 cc air-cooled, two-stroke, two-cylinder engine. By this time, the Colt saloons (of which the smallest had fastback styling and was powered by a three-cylinder, two-stroke engine of the DKW type which developed 41 bhp) were being powered by 1000 and 1500 cc oversquare, push-rod, four-cylinder units and had front suspension by coils and wishbones in place of the transverse leaf springs of the smaller types. The Debonair was now a 105 bhp six with six-seater coachwork, four headlamps and the

same time, the Debonair received a new overhead-camshaft power unit. It was also in 1971 that a late version of a Mitsubishi single-seater, roughly conforming to Formula Two rules, won the 1971 Japanese Grand Prix for single-seaters.

1972 saw the introduction of the Colt Galant L Series and the Minica F4. The pushrod Colts now had bigger 1.4-litre engines, and the overhead-camshaft, four-cylinder Mitsubishis catered for everything from 1.4-litre saloons to the GTO-MR Series, which used a twin-cam, twin-carburettor 1597 cc engine developing 125 bhp, a five-speed all-synchromesh gearbox and servo-assisted front disc brakes.

Above: the Mitsubishi 500 of 1959, which was powered by a twin-cylinder four-stroke, overhead-valve, air-cooled engine; producing 20 bhp. The car had synchromesh on the upper two of its three gears

Above right: the two-stroke, two-cylinder Minica 360 of 1966

choice of all-synchromesh or automatic gearboxes.

In 1968, Mitsubishi Heavy Industries established a technical link with the Ford Motor Company and Mobil Oil Company in the United States for the development of an anti-pollution device. This was one of a number of technical agreements which the company signed with American companies for technical liaison on motor-vehicle components, such as steering columns, dynamo relays and electro-magnetic clutches.

In 1969, the motor-vehicle headquarters of Mitsubishi were relocated in a new building in Tamachi. A new Automobile Technical Centre was opened in Okazaki-shi the same year and the Colt Galant Series and new Minica were introduced. By this time, Mitsubishi were producing 128,000 cars a year, giving them just under five per cent of the Japanese market, and 209,000 commercial vehicles and buses.

A year later, the motor-vehicle headquarters of the company were separated from Mitsubishi Heavy Industries Ltd, and established as the Mitsubishi Motor Corporation. 1970 was also the year in which the Colt Galant hardtop and GTO were introduced.

In 1971, the Colt Galant Coupé FTO and Minica Skipper were introduced and small trucks and ultra-large dumper trucks were developed. The Skipper was powered by a single-overhead-camshaft in-line, two-cylinder, 360 cc power unit mounted conventionally and driving the rear wheels via a conventional transmission and drive train.

Although the Mitsubishi Corporation's connections with the Chrysler Corporation in the USA go back as far as 1925, the first phase of Chrysler's equity participation in the Japanese company was not officially announced until 1971, when, in June of that year, Chrysler took a 35 per cent interest in a new joint company with Mitsubishi.

As a result of this business and technical agreement, the overhead-camshaft Colt Galants appeared on the American market in 1971 and were sold through the Chrysler Corporation's Dodge dealer network. At the

In the same year, the company remodelled their medium and heavy-duty truck ranges. It was also the year that Mitsubishi announced their new anti-pollution clean-air system and as a result their Saturn engine passed the 1973 USA Emissions Standards. In the competition field, 1972 was the year which saw two Colt Galant 16 LGSs take first and third places overall in the Seventh Southern Cross International Rally.

1973 was the year in which Mitsubishi introduced four new passenger cars: the Colt Galant FTO Coupé, the Colt Galant GTO 2000, the Lancer 1200 cc and 1400 cc and the New Colt Galant 1600 cc and 1850 cc. In the Eighth Southern Cross International Rally that year, Colt Lancer 1600 GSs swept the board, taking first, second, third and fourth places. By the end of that year, the Mitsubishi range boasted four model series: the Minica, the Lancer, the Galant and the Debonair, with nearly 50 model derivatives. Smallest of the range was the three versions of the Minica saloon and the Skipper Coupé, which were all powered by a front-mounted, four-stroke, two-cylinder, in-line, 359 cc power unit which delivered 30 bhp (DIN) at 8000 rpm. The two-door, four-seater cars had full synchromesh, four-speed gearboxes and a top speed of 71 mph; their overall length was 117.91 in.

The Lancer range—a name 'on loan' from the Chrysler bank of model names—comprised 18 derivatives of two and four-door saloons and coupés, with the 1200 models powered by a four-stroke, three-crankshaft-bearing, four-cylinder, in-line, ohv, 1187 cc unit which delivered 70 bhp (DIN) at 6000 rpm; the 1400 model powered by a four-cylinder, five-crankshaft-bearing, 1439 cc unit which gave 92 hp (DIN) at 6300 rpm; the 1600 models powered by either a four-cylinder, five-bearing, ohv, 1597 cc unit producing 100 bhp (DIN) at 6300 rpm or a five-bearing, ohv, 1597 cc that produced 110 bhp (DIN) at 6700 rpm. With a conventional, full synchromesh, four-speed transmission, the five-seater cars had independent front suspension and rigid-axle rear suspension.

The Galant series offered the low emission, air injection, 1597 cc, 97 bhp (DIN) at 6300 rpm unit giving 99 mph in the 1600 saloons and hardtops, with the top of the 1600 range GL MCA 11 being powered by a four-cylinder, in-line, 1597 cc five-crankshaft-bearing, ohv, slanted, ohc unit. The Galant 1850 GL saloons and hardtop were powered by a 1855 cc unit which produced 105 bhp (DIN) at 6000 rpm with the SL-5 version having a five-speed gearbox.

The Galant 1850 GS-5 saloon and hardtop were both powered by a 1855 cc unit which gave 115 bhp at 6200 rpm while the Galant 2000 GL-11 saloon and hardtop were powered by a 1995 cc engine that produced 115 bhp at 6000 rpm. All four models had a five-speed, full synchromesh gearbox. The GS-11 saloon and hardtop versions of the Galant 2000 were powered by a 1995 cc unit which produced 125 hp (DIN) at 6200 rpm which gave the cars a maximum speed of 115 mph. The Galant FTO 1600 GSR Coupé was powered by a four-cylinder, ohc, in-line, five-bearing, 1597 cc unit which gave the car 110 bhp (DIN) at 6700 rpm. With a five-speed box, the two-door car had a maximum speed of 112 mph.

The Galant GTO series of coupés had as bottom of the range the 1700SL, which was powered by a four-stroke, four-cylinder, twin-overhead-camshaft 1686

Top left: the 1964 Mitsubishi Debonair saloon. This car was powered by a six-cylinder 105 bhp engine

Top right: the 1972 Colt Galant GTO GSR, which was powered by a 1995 cc 125 bhp engine

Centre: the 1975 Lancer 1400 two-door, introduced in Britain in late 1974

Bottom: a 1600 Galant four-door, which was powered by a 100 bhp engine

cc engine which gave 105 bhp (DIN) at 6300 rpm and a top speed of 109 mph. The 2000 GTO SL and 2000 GTO SL-5 models were both powered by a 1995 cc twin-ohc unit which gave 115 bhp (DIN) at 6000 rpm and the slightly faster top speed of 112 mph. The SL-5 version had a full synchromesh five-speed gearbox. The GTO 2000 GS-5 and GTO GSR were both powered by the same 1995 cc unit as the SL and SL-5 models, but with modifications that boosted the power to 125 bhp (DIN) at 6200 rpm.

The top of the Mitsubishi range, the Debonair Executive saloon, had a four-stroke, six-cylinder, 1994 cc, seven-crankshaft-bearing, ohv unit which as standard gave 130 bhp (DIN) at 6000 rpm and the option of another unit that produced 120 bhp (DIN) at 6000 rpm. The four-door, six-seater cars had independent front suspension and rigid-axle, semi-elliptical leaf-spring rear suspension. Transmission to the rear wheels was through a four-speed full-synchromesh gearbox and a single-dry-plate clutch.

By 1975, the Mitsubishi Motor Corporation had a capital of 35,177,000,000 Yen and employed about 22,000 people. It was part of one of the largest companies in the world, with the Mitsubishi empire taking in interests in the manufacture of heavy machinery, ships, rolling stock and aircraft.

In 1974, the Cooper Car Co Ltd was set up in conjunction with the Mitsubishi Corporation to import Mitsubishi cars into the UK for the first time, and were to be marketed under the brand name Colt. With headquarters in Cirencester, the joint company showed five models at the 1974 International Motor Show at London's Earls Court in October. A month later, the company were importing through Newport, the Lancer 1400 two-door, two-door de-luxe and four-door de-luxe and the Lancer 1600 two-door, (five-speed gearbox) de-luxe, the Galant 1600 four-door de-luxe and 1600 two-door coupé, the Galant 1600 four-door and estate and the Galant two-litre, four-door de-luxe and two-litre, two-door, coupé. BJ

The Grand Prix race ace from Algeria

IN THE EARLY 1930S, motor racing was becoming increasingly popular throughout Europe. Although Italy and France still dominated the majority of major events through Bugatti and Alfa Romeo, a number of young drivers were attracted into motor racing from countries which were not normally strongholds of the sport. Even Britain had seldom provided winners in International races but, with the arrival of the Bentley at Le Mans, British cars and drivers soon gained acceptance. For drivers from less well developed countries, however, it was more difficult to break into racing, because there was seldom any native motor industry and very often no surfaced roads at all to race or even practise on.

For Guy Moll, a young Algerian with a Spanish mother and French father, the way was smoothed to a certain extent by his friendship with Marcel Lehoux, who had already established a reputation in North Africa, where he had won such events as the Casablanca, Algerian and Tunisian Grands Prix. Moll began racing in Algeria with a Lorraine-Dietrich, taking part mostly in small local events. By 1932, his friend Lehoux was an experienced and successful driver in European events, and he invited the young Moll to race his Bugatti in the Marseilles Grand Prix at the featureless Miramas track. This was Moll's first race in Europe and he finished third behind the Alfa Romeos of Ray-

mond Sommer and Tazio Nuvolari, a performance which attracted much attention from other drivers and team managers.

For 1933, Moll began in Europe by driving a Bugatti in the Pau Grand Prix, which was run in appalling snowstorm conditions. Lehoux won the race, but Moll got through into second place in very unfamiliar conditions. Later in 1933, Moll bought a Monza Alfa Romeo. This was the Grand Prix version of the 8C 2300 sports car, although it was not as fast as the P3 Grand Prix car which some other drivers were able to use, especially those under contract to Scuderia Ferrari. Despite this handicap, Moll finished third in the Nimes GP, behind Nuvolari and 'Phi Phi' Etancelin. He then followed up with more third places at Nice, Comminges and Miramas, and a second place in the Monza GP.

Moll's skill was recognised by Enzo Ferrari in 1934, and he was asked to join Scuderia Ferrari to drive the 2.9-litre P3 single-seater Alfa Romeo which Ferrari was racing on behalf of the works, who had withdrawn from racing following nationalisation.

Moll immediately began to shine in the P3, even though the more powerful and larger Mercedes and Auto Unions were joining in the Grand Prix circus. His greatest victory was in winning the Monaco Grand Prix, but he also won the Avusrennen on the banked Berlin circuit in a

Top: Guy Moll, pictured after his win in the 1934 Monaco GP. To his right is a very youthful Enzo Ferrari
Above: Moll's last race—the remains of his Alfa Romeo, following his crash in the 1934 Coppa Acerbo at Pescara

streamlined 3.2-litre version of the P3 which developed 265 bhp. He also finished third in the French GP at Montlhéry behind teammate Chiron, and was second in the Targa Florio and second in the Coppa Ciano behind teammate Varzi's P3, beating Nuvolari's Maserati into third place.

The young Moll's career had been meteoric, for even when the powerful German cars were eclipsing the Italians he was still able to race on level terms with them.

However, his meteoric career came to a tragic end in 1934 during the Coppa Acerbo. Moll was dicing for the lead in his P3 with Luigi Fagioli's Mercedes when his car suddenly flew off the road at near maximum speed when both were lapping the Mercedes of Henne. Moll was killed immediately, the cause of the crash never being satisfactorily explained. Only two years later his mentor, Marcel Lehoux, was killed in an ERA.

In later years, Enzo Ferrari commented that, had Moll lived, he would have become one of the greatest drivers of all time.   MT

Road racing on the RIVIERA

MONACO
2 AVRIL 1934

6ème GRAND PRIX AUTOMOBILE

Right above: Achille Varzi's Bugatti T51 leads Tazio Nuvolari's Alfa Romeo Monza 8C during their epic dice in the 1933 event. Although after much changing of positions Nuvolari led into the last lap, the Alfa's engine blew up, leaving Varzi to win

Right below: after the 1933 event, poster painters were quick to publicise the race for 1934; this shows Nuvolari leading Varzi

Vittorio Brambilla's Beta March 741 amidst the scenery that makes the Monaco GP the most glamorous in the world. In this, the 1974 GP, Brambilla was involved in an accident on the first lap, which eliminated his car and six others

Inset top: 1964 World Champion John Surtees with Ferrari in 1964

Inset bottom: Clay Regazzoni in the 312 B3 Ferrari on his way to fourth place in 1974

THE MONACO GRAND PRIX is unique in the motor-racing calendar. The most prestigious, most glamorous and most picturesque Formula One race in the world, it is one of the few pre-war 'classics' to survive, albeit with several alterations to suit the mood of the day. Its round-the-houses character remains unaltered, and each year the race attracts spectators in their thousands. It is a tourist attraction and hotels both ultra-expensive and less-expensive for miles around are fully booked months in advance.

Yet the race came about almost by accident. In 1928, the Automobile Club de Monaco were anxious to be officially recognised by the *Association Internationale des Automobiles Clubs Reconnus*, the forerunner of the *Fédération Internationale de l'Automobile*, as a national authority instead of a regional French club. For some years they had organised the Monte Carlo Rally, but as it was held over the roads of Europe rather than those of the tiny Principality of Monaco itself, the AIACR did not react to the club's request too warmly. In retaliation, Antony Noghès, President of the AC de Monaco, said that the following year there would be 'an international race which will be held on the territory of the Principality and which will excite world-wide interest'. How could the AIACR refuse official recognition now?

Noghès then had the task of living up to his am-

bitious statement and scoured the roads of Monte Carlo in an effort to find something suitable. The result was the round-the-town-and-along-the-harbour-front circuit that was utilised in the same form from 1929 until 1972. Before 1952, the official distance was given as 1.976 miles, although since then, the figure was altered firstly to 1.954 miles and then, in 1973, in order to meet modern safety requirements and satisfy demands that the pit area should be changed, the length was increased to 2.037 miles. First reactions to the idea from the motor-racing world of the 1920s were ones of amazement and bewilderment. How could the Monégasques seriously expect to hold a motor race on the ledges of the face of a cliff and through main streets?

As is only too well known, the experiment was an immediate success. One hundred laps demanded immense skill and stamina from the drivers, and strength and staying power from the cars.

The race developed into a duel between expatriate British driver 'Williams' in his works Bugatti T35B and Rudi Caracciola's unwieldy 7.1-litre Mercedes-Benz SSK, a battle 'Williams' easily won when Caracciola squandered four-and-a-half minutes refuelling and changing wheels. The following year, Caracciola was refused permission to start as the big Mercedes was considered unsuitable for the track after practice, leaving the race open to the works and privately-entered Bugattis. Eventually, privateer René Dreyfus in his own 2.3-litre T35B beat the works 2-litre T35C of Louis Chiron, but only after Chiron had slowed in the closing stages owing to clutch, ignition and throttle maladies. Chiron, the Frenchman who resided in Monaco and the crowd's favourite, made amends the following year with an impeccable drive to victory in the new works Bugatti T51.

For 1932, there were changes: tramlines had been removed and parts of the track were resurfaced—and Bugatti were beaten. Chiron led the opening laps in his works Bugatti T51, but clipped Polishman Count Stanislas Czaykowski's spinning Bugatti at the chicane on the harbour-front and rolled three times. Fortunately, Chiron was only slightly hurt, but it gave the race to Tazio Nuvolari's works Alfa Romeo Monza 8C. Nevertheless, it was a close shave for the Italian as his fuel tanks were all but dry at the end of the 100 laps, and second-man Rudi Caracciola in another Alfa had dutifully slowed to allow the team leader to win. In 1933, Caracciola crashed in practice, putting himself out of racing for a year, but even the absence of the German ace paled into insignificance thanks to a desperate duel between Italian rivals Achille Varzi and Tazio Nuvolari. Varzi, at the wheel of his works Bugatti T51 won after Nuvolari stopped while leading on the last lap.

Louis Chiron seemed destined for a comfortable victory in 1934, nursing his Alfa Romeo P3 round well in the lead. With less than two laps to go, he lost concentration and spun at the Station Hairpin and before he could remove the car from the sandbags, teammate Guy Moll stole through to win his first Grand Prix. The final three pre-war Grands Prix were dominated by the German Mercedes-Benz team. Italian Luigi Fagioli led from start to finish in his 4-litre Mercedes-Benz W25 in 1935, nursing the car in the closing laps as his teammates Manfred von Brauchitsch and Rudi Caracciola had both retired. In 1936, when the other German team, Auto Union, joined the fray, it poured with rain and made conditions treacherous. Added to this, Mario Tadini's Alfa Romeo trailed oil from a fractured pipe and the chicane section became almost impassable with cars

spinning and crashing. Chiron, a new member of the Mercedes équipe and his teammate von Brauchitsch were among those eliminated, while Fagioli crashed there later and another fancied runner, Bernd Rosemeyer (Auto Union C-type), was an early casualty, too. Nuvolari excelled in the conditions, urging his underpowered Alfa Romeo 8C ahead until his brakes weakened. Presently, eventual winner Caracciola forged ahead, to be followed by the Auto Unions of Achille Varzi and Hans Stuck. In 1937, von Brauchitsch beat Caracciola after a race of rivalry between the two top Mercedes drivers.

The race was cancelled in 1938, the top teams' demands for £500-per-car starting money proving too much for the AC de Monaco's budget. In 1939, the threat of war meant no Grand Prix so there was an 11-year gap before the event was run again in 1948. For the new Grand Prix formula—1½ litres supercharged, or 4½ litres unsupercharged—an odd collection of Italian, French and British machines appeared. Jean-Pierre Wimille's little 1430 cc Simca-Gordini led briefly, only to be overwhelmed by first Giuseppe Farina and then Luigi Villoresi in their Maserati 4CLs. Farina sped on to win.

No race was run in 1949, but in 1950 a race qualifying for the then-new World Championship series was organised. Juan Manuel Fangio's Alfa Romeo 158 took an early lead, but on the first lap his teammate, Giuseppe Farina, spun at the left-hand corner on the quayside known as Tabac. Luigi Villoresi (Ferrari 125) scraped through, but nine other cars were eliminated due to Farina's error; Fangio went on to win.

The rising cost of organising a full-scale Grand Prix meant no race in 1951, but a sports-car race was substituted for 1952. Yet another multiple pile-up spoilt the race, leaving it a Ferrari benefit. Sadly, Italian veteran Luigi Fagioli subsequently died of injuries received when the 1935 winner crashed in practice.

It was 1955 before Formula One racing returned to Monaco, the event being given the 'courtesy title' of Grand Prix d'Europe. From Italy came the Ferrari, Maserati and Lancia teams, Gordini represented France, Vanwall upheld Britain's honours and Germany's all-conquering Mercedes-Benz team completed the first-class field. Juan Manuel Fangio and Stirling Moss soon established the familiar Mercedes-Benz 1–2 formation until exactly half-distance when Fangio's car broke its transmission. Moss took over the lead, but after 80 laps his engine exploded and that was that. Alberto Ascari inherited the lead (he had been all but a lap behind Moss), but the crowd at the chicane apparently distracted him by waving furiously —and Ascari's Lancia plunged straight into the harbour. The Italian swam to safety practically unhurt (ironically he was to lose his life in a testing accident only a few days later). This handed the race to the Frenchman Maurice Trintignant with his supposedly uncompetitive Ferrari 625.

Stirling Moss (Maserati 250F) won a well-judged race in 1956, forcing the usually smooth Fangio (Lancia-Ferrari D50) into making several mistakes. Fangio had eventually to take over teammate Peter Collins's car, but could not close the gap to the smooth Moss. In 1957, it was Moss's turn to err. Driving a British Vanwall, he led until he entered the chicane too quickly on the fourth lap. Moss crashed and knocked poles acting as barriers onto the track. Peter Collins (Ferrari 801) crashed into the quayside in avoidance, but Fangio threaded his Maserati 250F through. Tony Brooks (Vanwall) crept by the wreckage, but he was hit by Mike Hawthorn's Ferrari 801 which, in turn, lost a wheel and crashed into Collins's machine. Fangio was left to win as he pleased from Brooks who had managed to continue. The hero of the

Above: Lorenzo Bandini driving a Ferrari in the 1967 event, his last race. Later in the race, Bandini clipped the chicane and his car overturned in flames. He was trapped underneath and died in hospital a few days later

Left: official practice for the 1972 event sees the Yardley McLaren M19s in convoy coming out of the tunnel; the drivers are Hulme and Redman

race, however, was Jack Brabham who worked his 2-litre Cooper T43-Climax into third place at one stage, only to break down on the 100th of this (for once) 105-lap race.

The writing was on the wall, however, as Brabham's tiny Cooper demonstrated that light weight and nimble handling was more important than sheer speed and, in 1958, a 2-litre Cooper-Climax, handled by 1955 winner Trintignant, won the race; the following year, Brabham won, his Cooper now 'grown-up' to the full 2½ litres and showing greater agility than the Ferrari Dino 256 of Tony Brooks which followed it home.

In 1960, Stirling Moss began a chapter in motor-racing history by notching up Lotus's first-ever Grand Prix win at Monaco. Driving Rob Walker's privately-entered Lotus 18-Climax, Moss clearly demonstrated just why he was at that time the world's best driver. He did it again, more so, in 1961. In the first year of the 1½-litre Grand Prix formula, only Ferrari were prepared with new engines, the tough V6s having a 30 bhp advantage over the 'vintage' four-cylinder Coventry Climax engines used by the British teams. Yet Moss outdrove the Ferraris of Americans Richie Ginther and Phil Hill plus Germany's Wolfgang von Trips to win by 3.6 seconds.

Moss' near-fatal accident at Goodwood prevented his participation in the 1962 Monaco Grand Prix, or any other for that matter. This was the era of new-emerging drivers such as Jim Clark of Lotus and Graham Hill of BRM. Both took turns to lead before their machinery failed, handing victory to Bruce McLaren (Cooper T60-Climax). A first-corner accident, in which three cars were eliminated and others delayed, resulted in the death of a trackside marshal, hit by a flying wheel from Richie Ginther's BRM P48.

For three years, Graham Hill and BRM dominated Monaco, the Briton excelling at this round-the-houses circuit. In 1963, Clark was once more the pacemaker, only to have his transmission lock solid on lap 79 when the gearbox selected both second and fourth gears simultaneously. Hill was able to lead his teammate Richie Ginther home to a 1–2 BRM victory, as he did in 1964 when once more Clark led, but first had the rear anti-roll bar come loose and later lost oil pressure. In 1965, another Hill victory seemed a boring certainty until lap 25 when he had to swerve to a halt in the escape road at the chicane to avoid a stranded car. Graham climbed out, pushed his car back on to the circuit and continued, now fifth. Hill then began an epic drive which took him back into the lead on the 65th of the 100 laps.

In 1966, the 3-litre Formula One now in force, Jackie Stewart, driving a 2-litre BRM P261, proved that a car developed from the old 1½-litre formula had more stamina than the 3-litre machinery. Only four cars were classified as finishers, BRMs taking a 1–3–4 result. In 1967, the race's outcome was pure tragedy. Chasing leader (and winner) Denny Hulme's Brabham BT20 Repco, Italian Lorenzo Bandini crashed his Ferrari 312/67 at the chicane. It overturned on the straw bales and caught alight. Bandini later died of severe burns and internal injuries. Repercussions led to a tough tightening up of safety measures at all Grand Prix circuits, Monaco in particular. No straw bales were to be seen in 1968, only lines of steel guard-rail which, ugly as they looked, were safer and more effective. The 1968 race went to Graham Hill, who notched up his fourth victory at Monte Carlo driving a Lotus 49B-Ford. Only five of the 16 starters finished, accidents or transmission failure decimating the field.

Uproar was caused in 1969 when, halfway through practice, the FIA put a ban on aerofoils on Formula One cars. Jackie Stewart's Matra MS80-Ford appeared well on the way to victory when a drive-shaft universal joint broke, allowing Hill to his fifth Monaco victory, Hill once more driving a Lotus 49B-Ford. In 1970, there was a startling conclusion: Jack Brabham (Brabham BT33-Ford) apparently had a secure lead as the race entered into its final stages, but Jochen Rindt's Lotus 49C-Ford was making up ground extremely quickly. On the final lap, Rindt had Brabham well within his sights, although victory did not seem possible. Into the last corner Brabham was slightly baulked by a backmarker and missed his braking point, ploughing instead into the barriers and allowing Rindt to snatch a last-ditch victory. 'Black Jack' extracted his car to salvage second place.

The 1971 race witnessed a start-to-finish victory by Jackie Stewart in his Tyrrell-Ford, and a similar pattern emerged in 1972, although this time the race

Above: rain is almost unknown at the Monaco GP, but 1972 was an exception. In this picture, a Brabham BT37 leads a pack, but the race that year was won by Jean-Pierre Beltoise who was uncatchable in the torrential conditions

was held in pouring rain and Jean-Pierre Beltoise drove the race of his life to lead throughout in his Marlboro-BRM P160B.

In 1972, a revised layout was incorporated into the circuit to satisfy safety demands. A pair of chicanes around the swimming pool were incorporated, several other parts being slightly altered, to allow a safe pit road uninterrupted by race traffic. Although the new section was narrow, the drivers approved and Stewart scored yet another runaway victory. In the closing stages he allowed Emerson Fittipaldi (Lotus 72-Ford) to close the gap slightly, but Stewart was in no mood to concede defeat and won by 1.3 seconds, (in fact, Stewart and Fittipaldi collided on the slowing-down lap, Stewart relaxing and not noticing Fittipaldi in his mirrors. In 1974, Ronnie Peterson's Lotus 72-Ford (an old car brought in to replace the new Type 76 at the last moment) conquered some tough opposition.

Although these days most teams wish the race was eliminated from the calendar on personal grounds—the circuit is just too tight for modern-day Grand Prix cars, which almost tear themselves apart in the battle—to the spectator, Monaco is *the* Grand Prix of the year. For sheer spectacle, noise and scenery, it has no rival.   MK

Above: Ronnie Peterson, with his John Player Special Lotus 72, lifts a wheel on his way to victory in 1974

THE HIGH-STREET GP CIRCUIT

had to watch their exit from this bend or the waiting kerb would be ready to knock a wheel out of line—or if the car managed to mount the kerb, a fire hydrant could inflict even more damage. A couple of sandbags placed in front of the hydrant were all that was deemed necessary in the cause of safety—and they were mainly to protect the hydrant! The road then curves gently to the right as the cars accelerate along the road past the Hotel Bristol, reaching about 130 mph as they enter the *St Dévote* right-hander. This fast, uphill right-hander is very tricky, especially so in the wet, and has caught out many a driver. The road climbs steeply uphill towards the Casino Square, the cars accelerating hard through a couple of slight kinks until hard braking is required for the very fast left-right flick through the bumpy Casino Square, past the doors of the Hotel de Paris, which is followed by a downhill plunge to the *Mirabeau* bend, named after a hotel long ago demolished. This sharp right-hander leads to a short downhill section including a right-left flick before hard braking is required for the Station Hairpin, named after the railway station which, again, is no longer there. This first-gear left hander is followed almost immediately by the right-handed *Mirabeau Inferior* corner which leads straight down to the sea front at the

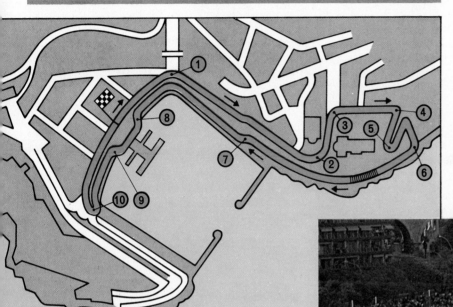

IT IS NOT SO MUCH the Monaco circuit which drivers like, as the sheer glamour which surrounds the actual race. Perched on the cliffs of the Cote D'Azur, Monaco clings tenuously to its tiny foothold on the shores of the Mediterranean, a sovereign country ruled by Prince Rainier and his fairy-tale Princess, Grace. With its towering apartment blocks, hotels and tax-haven offices, the famous Casino and the glittering harbour, jam packed with the yachts and motor boats of the rich visitors, Monte Carlo is attractive enough as it is, but at Grand Prix time the population trebles as crowds pour in from all over the world. For a driver to emerge from the cloistered calm of the Hotel de Paris and walk down the hill to the pits is the most ego-boosting trip of the year, for every window is packed with fans calling out drivers' names and the road is jammed with enthusiasts demanding autographs.

The actual Monaco circuit is something of an anachronism in today's motor-racing atmosphere where safety is all-important, because it does not have wide run-off areas, wire-mesh safety catch fences and all the other appurtenances of modern safety circuits like Paul Ricard, Nivelles and Dijon. Perhaps it is the very danger inherent in the circuit which awakens some of the latent desire to conquer the elements present in every driver.

The circuit was first used in 1929 and hardly changed at all until the early 1970s. In 1929, when the race was won by the mysterious 'Williams' in a Bugatti at the low average speed of 49.83 mph, the race started on the concrete-block harbour-front road, running on a slight left-hand curve until a sharp right-hand turn is reached. This is the first-gear *Virage des Gazometres*, so named because a gasometer used to dominate the skyline close to the corner, but it has long since been dismantled. Until guard rails were installed, drivers

Above: a Brabham BT42 chases a Surtees around the swimming-pool extension at the Monaco circuit

Above left: the Monaco corners—**1** Sainte Dévote; **2** Hotel de Paris; **3** Casino; **4** Mirabeau; **5** Station hairpin; **6** Portier; **7** Chicane; **8** Virage du Bureau de Tabac; **9** Swimming-pool diversion; **10** Gasometer hairpin

Portier right-hander. The cars accelerate away from this 40 mph corner on a slightly curving right-hander until they enter the famous tunnel which itself continues curving to the right. Cars enter the darkness of the tunnel at over 120 mph and burst back into the sunlight for the fast downhill stretch back onto the seafront and through the chicane; the position and severity of the chicane were altered after Bandini's fatal crash in 1967. The cars then rush along the quay, into the fast left-handed *Tabac* corner, named after a tobacconists kiosk nearby. The circuit used to run directly back along the quayside to the Gasometer turn, but in 1973 a chicane was formed by running the circuit round the swimming pool which is built into the harbour; this gives four extra bends and slows the cars considerably before they return to the Gasometer hairpin turn.

The circuit length was originally 1.9 miles which was covered 100 times in a Grand Prix, but the number of laps was reduced to 80 in 1968, the year after Bandini's death, because it was felt that tiredness had caused his crash. The extra distance round the swimming pool raised the lap distance to 2.037 miles, but the number of laps was reduced to 78, giving a race distance of 158.8 miles. MT

AN ANGLO-FRENCH ALLIANCE

The luxury Monica was designed in England, built in France and fitted with an American engine

Above: the pre-production Monica, which was powered by a 5.9-litre Chrysler engine. For economy reasons, a 5.6-litre unit was to be used in production cars

Top right: the neat pop-up headlights

Centre right: prototype number two with Deep Sanderson badges. A later model in the background shows how much more beautiful the Monica became

Centre bottom: the massive rocker wishbone arms acting on the coil springs in the engine compartment

APART FROM THE FACEL VEGA, France has built few luxury cars since the war, mainly because of a car-taxation policy which legislates heavily against any machine with an engine of 2.8 litres or more. So there was great interest when it was announced in 1972 that a French company would build a luxury four-seater GT saloon.

The car was the brainchild of Jean Tastevin, proprietor of a company called Compagnie Francaise des Produits Metallurgiques, which specialised in building railway rolling stock. In 1967, Tastevin foresaw that the demand for railway wagons would gradually ease off, so he began to look around for alternatives to occupy his factory at Balbigny, near Lyon. Being a motoring enthusiast, he decided to build a sports car and, by sheer coincidence, he read a report in a French motoring magazine about the British Racing Car Show in London which mentioned a highly tuned engine being produced by Chris Lawrence. Lawrence was, at that time, well known in British motor-racing circles for his very fast Morgan sports cars which were powered by tuned Triumph engines, and at the Racing Car Show he had exhibited a 2.6-litre version giving a claimed 150 bhp. This engine seemed ideal to Tastevin as it would be adequately powerful for a sports car, yet still be below the French 2.8-litre taxation limit.

Tastevin eventually established contact with Lawrence and asked him if he could supply 500 engines a year, but Lawrence knew that this was a very tall order for his small workshops. It was soon evident that Tastevin had no clear idea of the design of the car, so Lawrence persuaded the Frenchman to let him carry out the complete design of the car. The initial plan was for a two-seater sports car powered by the Triumph engine but, by 1968, Lawrence had convinced Tastevin that a better market lay in the luxury-saloon-car field, so the emphasis was switched from the sports car to a bigger four-door four-seater. The Triumph engine was not suitable for this car, so

Above: another view of the pre-production car

Left: the Monica's súmptuous interior

Lawrence decided to use the Martin V8, a 3-litre engine which had been used almost entirely in motor racing. However, there were many problems involved in persuading this engine to run reliably, something it had frequently failed to do in its racing days, and much time was lost in finding someone to make it work properly.

The chassis design was quite advanced, for it featured a semi-space-frame construction of square-section steel tubes, with built up sheet-steel structures to take the front and rear suspension and the scuttle area; the front sub frame was bolted on rather like that of the Jaguar E-type. Additional chassis stiffness was imparted by the sheet-steel side box members which contained the fuel tanks, but these had to be re-sited later because of European safety legislation. The front suspension utilised a pair of vertically mounted coil spring/damper units, operated by large rocking-arm upper wishbones, while conventional lower wishbones were fitted. One stipulation made by Tastevin was that the car should run very straight at speed on bumpy French roads, so a de Dion rear axle was specified for the rear suspension, location being by radius arms and a Panhard rod, with coil springs as the suspending medium. The differential was taken from the Rover 3500, using a crown wheel and pinion made by Hewland, but a novel refinement was the addition of a nosepiece giving the choice of two axle ratios, the idea being to use a low axle ratio around town and to change to the high-geared one for fast cruising; a lever arrangement in the cockpit allowed the axle ratio to be changed while on the move. The German ZF 5-speed gearbox was specified, rack-and-pinion steering was fitted and braking was by 12 in ventilated Girling discs at the front and 10 in non-ventilated discs at the rear of the car.

The body went through many changes of design, the prototype mostly being made in aluminium, but it was finally decided to build the body in steel with final assembly being undertaken at the Balbigny factory. Several years were lost in sorting out the body design and in attempting to obtain reliability from the Martin engine. Production was about to begin in 1972, but Tastevin decided that the Martin engine was not good enough and he rapidly switched to the American Chrysler V8 engine and three-speed automatic gearbox used by several other exotic-car builders. However, for the strong-armed type, the ZF five-speed box was still available. Lawrence engineered the new installation and tested the car quickly, a small pilot production line getting under way in 1973.

By 1974, the Monica (named after Tastevin's wife, Monique), was finally in full production at no more than one or two cars a week, priced in Britain at around £14,000, making it one of the more expensive cars available in Britain.   MT

MONICA

The CFPM Monica prototype was built by the British Deep Sanderson company and was originally intended to be powered by the British Martin two-cam V8. However, after troubles with what was essentially a temperamental detuned racing unit, the production cars were powered by big, lazy Chrysler 5.6-litre units. This engine was probably more in keeping with the character of the Monica which was designed to be a fast four-door, four-seater grand tourer.

The 5.6-litre engine, as fitted to the 1973 Chrysler, Dodge and Plymouth cars, produces 290 bhp at 5000 rpm and 330 lb ft of torque at 3800 rpm in the Monica. With this, the company claims a top speed of 150 mph for the car. There is a choice of two transmissions: the rugged German ZF five-speed unit, or the silky-smooth Torqueflite made by Chrysler. These are used in conjunction with an

ingenious two-speed final drive.

The car utilises a space-frame chassis of square tubing, along with sheet-steel structures, to take the suspension, and side box members for reinforcements. Independent suspension is used at the front, comprising wishbones, coil springs, an anti-roll bar and telescopic dampers, while the rear is semi-independent by way of a de Dion axle, torque arms, a transverse linkage bar, coil springs and telescopic dampers.

Servo-assisted disc brakes are used all round and power-assisted rack-and-pinion steering gear looks after directing the luxurious four-door, four-seater, £14,000 motor carriage.

ENGINE Front-mounted water-cooled 90° V8. 102.5 mm (4.04 in) bore × 84 mm (3.31 in) stroke = 5572 cc (340 cu in). Maximum power 290 bhp at 5000 rpm; maximum torque 330 lb ft at 3800 rpm. Cast-iron cyl-

inder block and heads. Compression ratio 8.5:1. 5 main bearings. 2 valves per cylinder operated, via pushrods and rockers, by a single camshaft at the centre of the V. 1 Carter downdraught four-barrel carburettor.

TRANSMISSION Single-dry-plate clutch and five-speed manual ZF gearbox. Ratios 1st 2.910, 2nd 1.780, 3rd 1.220, 4th 1.0, 5th 0.845:1. Optional torque converter and three-speed Chrysler Torqueflite automatic gearbox. Ratios 1st 2.450, 2nd 1.450, 3rd 1, rev 3.340. Hypoid-bevel two-speed final drive.

CHASSIS Space-frame with sheet-steel reinforcing super-structures.

SUSPENSION Front—independent by wishbones, coil springs, an anti-roll bar and telescopic dampers. Rear—semi-independent by a de Dion axle, torque arms, a transverse linkage bar, coil

springs and telescopic dampers.

STEERING Power-assisted rack and pinion. Turns from lock to lock 3.5.

BRAKES Power-assisted discs all round.

WHEELS 14 in diameter light-alloy.

TYRES 215/70VR × 14.

DIMENSIONS AND WEIGHT Wheelbase 109.05 in; track—front and rear 59.84 in; length 194.88 in; width 71.65 in; height 52.36 in; ground clearance 5.90 in; dry weight 3638 lb; turning circle between walls 29.4 ft; fuel tank capacity 24.2 gals in two separate tanks.

BODY Four-door, four-seater sports.

PERFORMANCE Maximum speed 150 mph.

THROUGH THE SNOW TO THE SUN

Formerly one of the most glamorous events on the rally calendar, the 'Monte' is now but a pale shadow of its once-glorious self

THE MONTE CARLO RALLY ranks with the Monaco Grand Prix as being one of the most glamorous events on the motor-sporting calendar, partly because the contestants end up in the Principality of Monaco at the end of the event and partly because the far flung starting points add a touch of adventure to the event. In truth, the rally has lost much of its glamour in recent years, largely because modern cars, shod with spiked tyres, find little difficulty in covering the long, boring mileages to Monaco before the short, tough meat of the rally is actually reached.

The Monte, as it is commonly known, is one of the oldest rallies in the world, having started in January 1911, and in '75 is the oldest event still being run. The idea of the first event was to give competitors a long, tough drive down to the Mediterranean from such diverse starting points as Vienna, Brussels, Paris and Berlin, each group covering a pre-determined mileage, according to the difficulty of their journey, before joining the common route to Monaco. There were no special tests incorporated since it was a difficult enough task to even get to Monte Carlo over the unpaved, snowbound roads of the Alps. Only 23 crews left the various starting points and a complete week was allowed for the rally, the average speed being set at 15 mph. The winner was Frenchman Henri Rougier driving a Turcat-Méry.

The event stirred the imagination of motorists on the Continent, with the result that the following year's event attracted no less than 87 starters. Additional starting points at Geneva, Turin, St Petersburg, Amsterdam, Le Havre and Boulogne were arranged and the winner this time was Beutler in a Berliet, who started from Berlin.

The onset of World War I brought the rally to a rapid halt and it was 1924 before it could again be run; but there was no doubting the enthusiasm of competitors who set off, this time in March, for the annual haul to Monte Carlo. Increasing interest in Britain persuaded the Automobile Club de Monaco to include a British start for the first time and from then on British participation increased virtually every year right through to the 1960s.

For 1925, the rally reverted to its traditional January date, for only in the depths of winter could the snow be virtually guaranteed on the Alps. Also in 1925 the rules were modified to include bonus points depending on the difficulty of the various starting points, and a fifty-mile mountain regularity test was included at the end of the rally to help determine any ties.

As road surfaces and the quality of the cars improved so it became more difficult for the organisers to determine the winner on the road section because by the early 1930s many cars were reaching Monte Carlo unpenalised. It was therefore left to the bonus system of points and the mountain test to determine the winner, but this often failed, so a short driving test event was staged on the quayside in Monaco. It very

Above: the winning Delahaye of Le Beque and Quinlin in 1937, seen on the post-rally trials at Monte Carlo

Right: weighing-in for a competitor in the 1936 event

often transpired that the winner was only found after this acceleration and braking or figure-of-eight test had been completed—a very unsatisfactory state of affairs. This is not to minimise the difficulties of the road sections from certain countries, because the roads were very often impassable. The Athens starters fared very badly because of deep snow which was invariably found in Salonika and it was not until 1931 that an Athens starter even got through to Monaco—Bignan in a Fiat—but even after that it was very seldom that a starter from Greece got through. Donald Healey won the 1931 event in an Invicta. The bonus points for Athens starters were high, say 500 points, against the 488 allowed for competitors from John o'Groats, Scotland, while some of the other far-flung points like Tallinn in Russia, Palermo in Sicily, Stavanger in

Above: a Porsche 911 forging through the sunshine on the 1968 Rally. In this event, Porsche were, in fact, victorious

Left: on the same rally, the Mini Coopers dominated the lower placings, finishing third, fourth and fifth

Above right: Sandro Munari and Mario Mannucci with their HF Lancia Fulvia on the 1972 event. The Italian pair won this event, and went on to win again in 1975, this time with a Lancia Stratos

Many ingenious devices were used to conquer the snowbound roads; some cars were fitted with twin rear wheels to give better traction and others could be fitted with skis on the steered wheels. Another way to beat the snow was to lighten the car to its barest essentials, some drivers even fitting a fabric body in place of the metal original. Virtually any type of vehicle could be entered, and it was quite common to see a bus complete with passengers bound for a pleasant winter break in Monte Carlo.

World War II put a stop to the rally until 1949 when interest again resumed at almost fever pitch, with no less than 208 starters, of which more than 40 started from Glasgow, which was now the British starting point. Britain had seldom provided any spectacular performances in the Monte, although the Hon Victor Bruce won the 1926 event in an AC and in 1949 the best placed British car was a Bristol driven by a French crew, although Leonard Potter's Allard and Ken Wharton's Ford were fourth and fifth. The rally was still little more than a glorified holiday trip to Monte Carlo, with the rally decided on a regularity run and driving test at the finish. Some of the trophies awarded, such as the Country Club Cup, the Late Public Schools MC Cup (for the best performance by a public-school driver) and the Noghes Trophy for the best performance by the oldest competitor, give some indication of the rather frivolous nature of the event. There was also a Comfort contest which was awarded to the best equipped and most luxurious car—invariably won by Mike Couper's immaculately prepared Bentley.

By 1951, the number of entries had risen to 337, a large proportion of them British, but the best Britain could do was third with a Mk V Jaguar driven by Cecil Vard, the rally being won by Jean Trevoux in a Delahaye for the third time. However, the Jowett

Norway and Bucharest were also given high bonus points. The snag with this system was that the bonus points were awarded to a start before the rally, so if this venue had good weather the starters from there had an advantage. However, quite a lot of the pre-rally interest centred on which starting-point to choose.

By the mid 1930s, British interest in the rally was high; of the 133 starters in the 1937 event, 17 started from John o'Groats and a number of other British drivers started from places like Amsterdam, Umea and Stavanger. That year the rally was decided on a tedious regularity run and an acceleration and braking test on the quayside.

Jupiter won the 1½-litre class.

By 1952, the entry list had swollen to 369, the importance of the event rising along with the entry list. Grim weather conditions everywhere caused many retirements and only 15 cars were unpenalised by the time the 163 survivors reached Monte Carlo. Of the finishers, 50 cars took part in the final regularity run over the Col du Braus, in which the cars had to average 45 kph, and it was the Allard driven by Sydney Allard which finally emerged the winner. This was the first win by a British car in 21 years and probably the only time the rally will ever be won by a car driven by the man who designed and built it. In second place came

Top right: an Alpine-Renault gets dangerously near a snow bank. These cars were victorious in 1971 and 1973

Above: cornering hard in a Fiat 124 Spider

Stirling Moss driving a Sunbeam Talbot 90 in his first ever rally! He beat the Mercedes-Benz team who were using Grand Prix drivers like Rudi Caracciola, Hermann Lang and Karl Kling.

The 1953 rally attracted a record entry list of 440 cars, of which no less than 253 got through to Monaco with no loss of marks. Since only 100 were to take the final mountain regularity test, the rest were eliminated in the acceleration and braking test. Competitors had to average 45 kph (29 mph) again on the regularity test and it was the Ford Zephyr of Dutchman Maurice Gatsonides which finally won the event from the Mk VII Jaguar of Ian Appleyard.

For the 1954 event, it was realised that the rally had to be tougher, so the final regularity run was lengthened to 165 miles and a race round the Monaco Grand Prix course was also instituted as a deciding test. These tests eliminated many cars and the winner was Louis Chiron's Lancia.

An even stiffer event in 1955 was won by the Sunbeam Talbot Mk III of Per Malling who started from Oslo. The number of entries had dropped to 319 and it was obvious that the more difficult event and the arrival of works entries had persuaded the more casual entrants to pull out.

The next British win came in 1956 when Ronnie Adams won a fairly easy event in his Mk VII Jaguar, but it was another eight years before a British car won again. The 1957 Rally was cancelled because of another fuel crisis—the Suez crisis which caused petrol rationing in several countries.

The system of determining the winner was gradually modified so that driving skill counted for a great deal, but in 1961 the organisers brought a ruling into play which caused a great deal of ill feeling. This was called the factor of comparison, an equation which took such factors as power and weight into consideration.

Left: a BMW 2002Tii getting tweaked up on a loose surface. Note that the car has a third windscreen wiper mounted on the roof

The end result was that the factor favoured big cars with small engines such as the French 850 cc Panhard which took the first three places on the 1961 event, despite being considerably slower than many other cars. In 1962, the formula gave a considerable advantage to the Saab of Erik Carlsson. This combination also won the following year.

In 1964 came the first of three wins for BMC whose Mini-Cooper was ideally suited both to the event and the factor of comparison. By now, the rally was being decided on special stages closed to the public, and the cars were becoming very specialised, as drivers

Above: despite being successful rally cars, the RS Escorts have had little luck on the Monte Carlo rally. The later RS Escorts had what were virtually Formula Two power units, but they could still not sought and highly valued victory

competed with each other to find the best combination of tyres. Paddy Hopkirk won the 1964 event; his teammate, Timo Makinen, won the 1965 rally in snowstorm conditions and the Minis would also have won the 1966 event but for a controversial and much debated decision by the organisers to disqualify the works Minis because they, and several other cars, were using quartz-iodine lights which contravened the regulations. Since British cars occupied the first four places, this elevated the Citroën of Toivonen to first place, a fact which brought accusations of a 'hometown' decision. The resultant publicity brought more attention to the Mini than if they had won, and Mini sales on the Continent received a tremendous boost that was gratefully accepted.

After this event, the factor of comparison was abandoned and the event was run on a scratch basis. Just to emphasise that the Mini was the best car for the event, Rauno Aaltonen won the 1967 rally in his Mini-Cooper after a close tussle with Ove Andersson's Lancia.

As rallying became more and more professional, so the private entrants were squeezed out and the entry list for the Monte dropped every year as more and more private owners gave up the struggle. British entries dropped away to virtually nothing and the Glasgow start had to be abandoned. By 1968, the Mini was no longer competitive and the initiative passed to the Porsche, Alpine-Renault and Lancia teams. Porsche won in 1968, 1969 and 1970, Alpine took the first three places in 1971, Lancia won in 1972 and Alpine took another 1, 2, 3 win in 1973. The rally fell into disrepute that year when a group of disgruntled competitors who had been forced out of the rally by a blocked special stage, blockaded the rally route to try and stop the remaining cars from finishing the whole of the rally.

The rally was not held in 1974 because of the fuel crisis and although it returned in 1975 only 98 competitors started, with victory going to Munari's Lancia Stratos. The rally came in for a great deal of criticism, because it still contained a high proportion of non-competitive road mileage at a time when fuel conservation was vital. The event had also lost its status in the European Rally Championship and it seemed that the rally's future was by no means assured.   MT

LUXURY MOTOR CARS WITH SWISS PRECISION

Swiss garage owner Peter Monteverdi first produced racing cars, before turning his attention to the manufacture of high-speed luxury touring cars

SWITZERLAND HAS PRODUCED few motor cars of her own and all cars now have to be imported. However, in 1967, a Basle garage owner and former racing driver, Peter Monteverdi, decided to build a fast two-seater GT car. Monteverdi had constructed his own racing cars, known as MBMs, but he retired after a serious crash and concentrated on his booming BMW sales outlet. He had often wanted to build his own car and, in 1967, he decided to take the plunge. To make the operation economical, he used a large number of bought-out components so that he needed little factory space; in fact, the cars were assembled in his BMW workshops by the mechanics, in between servicing the BMWs.

The basic design of the new car, known as the 375S, was drawn up by Monteverdi himself, but his only major job was to design the chassis on which to hang all the bought-out components. This chassis was a massive creation in square-section steel tubing with built up superstructures to take the front and rear suspension. This was built by an outside contractor in Basle, as were the double front wishbones which were manufactured from sheet steel. Coil spring/damper units were used at the front and at the rear, the rear suspension also utilising a de Dion axle located by a Watt linkage and parallel trailing arms. Steering was the German ZF power-assisted cam-and-peg layout

Above: the 375/4 Limousine with its sleek front and angular rear

Below: the 375L Monteverdi

and braking was by 12 in outboard front discs and 11.8 in inboard rear discs from Girling. The engine chosen for the 375S was the 7.2-litre Chrysler V8, mated to the Torqueflite three-speed automatic transmission, with the rest of the drive train coming from Britain's Hardy Spicer. In standard form, this engine gave 375 bhp, but a 400 bhp version was also available and the model fitted with this engine was known as 400SS. The attractive bodywork was

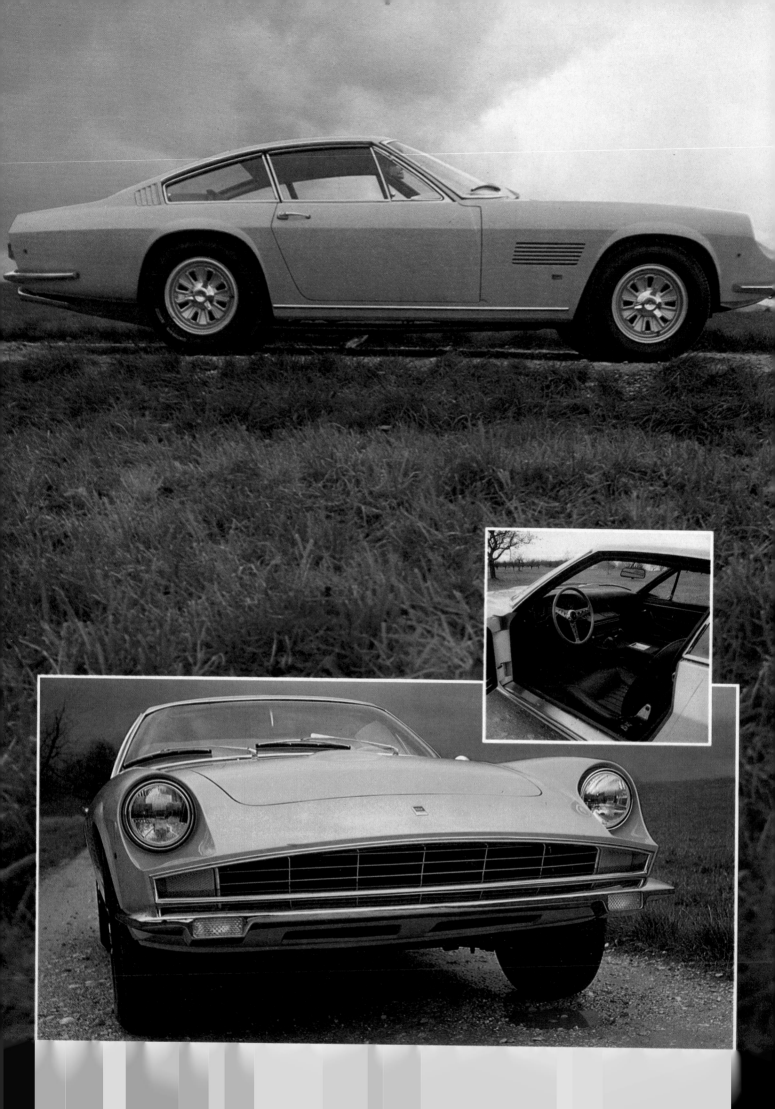

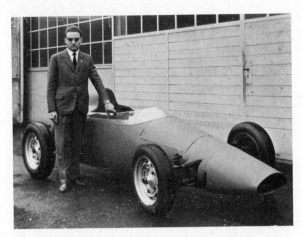

designed and built by Fissore of Turin, but put on to the chassis in Basle. The car was good for a top speed of over 140 mph and could accelerate to 100 mph from rest in a little more than 21 seconds.

The 375S and 400SS were in production for only about a year before they were joined by the 375L (for long). This was mechanically very similar to the two-seaters, but its wheelbase was increased to allow the fitment of two rear seats. Fissore modified the body to fit the new chassis without altering the lines too much, and the new car found quite a steady demand from wealthy drivers. A small export market was also undertaken and a number of cars were sent to Britain, marketed by the Hexagon Company.

Sales continued sufficiently well over the next couple of years to encourage Monteverdi to indulge in his ambition of building a mid-engined car to rival the Lamborghini Miura. The mid-engined Hai (or shark) 450SS was unveiled in 1971 at a price tag of close on £13,000, and it immediately attracted attention because of its brutal good looks. Mechanically, the car was very similar to the front-engined car, using a tubular-steel chassis with double-wishbone front suspension and the de Dion rear suspension modified so that the de Dion axle kinked over the transmission. The big Chrysler 'Hemi' engine was mounted in the

Opposite page: the Fissore-designed 375S manual-transmission coupé

Above left: Peter Monteverdi with his three-cylinder DKW-powered Formula Junior car of 1959

Below: looking like an early Ford Mustang coupé was this BMW 2002-engined prototype

centre of the car, protruding into the passenger compartment, and was mated to a ZF five-speed gearbox. Four-wheel disc brakes by Ate were fitted as standard and the manual version of the ZF worm-and-roller steering was standardised. The body, designed by Trevor Fiore and built by Fissore, featured pop-up headlights and a miniscule rear boot. Despite a top speed of around 160 mph and good handling, the lack of accommodation for both passengers and luggage and a poor gearchange restricted sales to just a few examples and production soon ceased.

In 1972, Monteverdi produced two more new models, the 375/4 and the Berlinetta. The 375/4 was a four-door, four-seater GT saloon intended to attack the luxury-saloon market owned almost exclusively by Rolls-Royce and Mercedes. Again, the car was mechanically similar to its forerunners apart from a much longer wheelbase of 10 ft 5 in. With a heavy new body from Fissore, the 375/4 scaled over two tons, but it was still capable of reaching 140 mph and accelerating from 0 to 60 mph in 8 seconds with the 7.2-litre Chrysler engine. However, this 17 ft-long machine did not attract much attention from wealthy potential buyers, and was soon dropped.

The Berlinetta was a high-performance version of the early 375S two seater. The chassis was again much the same as before, but it was fitted with the high-performance engine from the Hai which was claimed to give 450 bhp. The car was given new styling treatment, and a top speed of 180 mph was claimed for it, but the great weight and modest aerodynamics prevented the car from topping the 160 mph achieved by the Hai.

The mainstay of production continued to be the 2+2 375L but, as safety and pollution regulations began to bite and fuel prices began to soar, demand for Monteverdis slackened, reducing production to a trickle by late 1973.

In early 1975, the Monteverdi was still technically in production, but demand completely dried up and Peter Monteverdi concentrated on his BMW distributorship which still thrived in its Basle head-quarters.   MT

FOUR FAMOUS MOTOR RACE CIRCUITS IN ONE

Montlhéry, which comprises two banked and two road circuits,
was completed in 1924 and was the third and last banked track built in Europe

Right: this is a layout of the full Montlhéry circuit, which measures 7.8 miles in length. Depending upon which sections were used, the track could be divided into four separate circuits. The first full road circuit measured 4.7 miles per lap, the second 5.7 miles, while the banked section measured 1.58 miles. The entire project, completed in 1924, cost the equivalent of £500,000

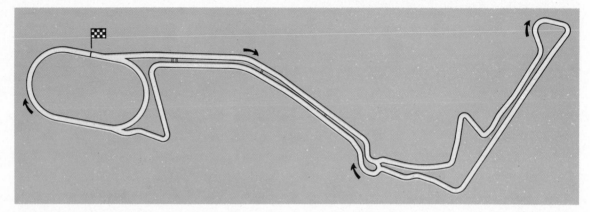

Below: the start of the GP de l'Ouverture, held at Montlhéry in 1924, showing the banked section of the track in the background. Note also the incomplete spectator grandstands

THE MONTLHÉRY AUTODROME, built about fifteen miles from Paris on the Paris-Orleans road, was the third major banked circuit to be completed in Europe. The Brooklands track in England was the first in the world in 1907, Italy's Monza track was completed in 1922 and the Montlhéry circuit was finished in 1924. It was the idea of a newspaper owner named Lamblin who felt that France, as the major motoring power, ought to have a banked high-speed track for use both by industry and for racing.

The track was designed to have two steep concrete bankings at each end, linked by short unbanked straights, to give a lap distance of 1.58 miles, considerably shorter than the 2.75-mile Brooklands circuit. However, right from the start, the track also had available a series of road circuits which could be used

in conjunction with the bankings or entirely separately if required. Four different circuits could be used; the full 7.8-mile circuit incorporated the bankings plus a long road section out to the Virage du Gendarme and back again along a parallel road, but there were also circuits measuring 5.7 and 4.7 miles. The building of the complete project, which was known officially as Linas-Montlhéry, cost £500,000.

The first event was held in October 1924 and it attracted a number of British drivers who were interested to see how the track matched up to Brooklands. Parry Thomas and Ernest Eldridge took their cars and were much impressed by the surface of the track. Montlhéry also had an advantage over Brooklands in that night racing could take place, while there were no noise restrictions such as at Brooklands.

The track boasted a number of garages situated under the bankings and, soon, motor manufacturers and racing teams were basing themselves there permanently so that they could develop new cars. Record breaking became a popular pastime at Montlhéry, because it could go on uninterrupted throughout the night if necessary.

The 1925 French Grand Prix was the first major race held on the track, using both the bankings and the road circuit. Run over 80 laps of the 7.8-mile course, Benoist and Divo won for France in their Delage, taking 8 hours 54 minutes 41.2 seconds to cover the 621.4 miles: an average speed of 69.7 mph. In the race, Antonio Ascari was killed when his Alfa Romeo hit the fencing on the road section and overturned. However, a relatively small crowd of 30,000 turned up for the event and most went away disappointed, for the tiny cars looked lost on the great concrete bowl of the banked circuit.

The main activity at Montlhéry was record breaking, for literally dozens of drivers could be on the track at any one time, all looking for a record of one sort or another. George Eyston, Freddie Dixon and Gwenda Hawkes were regulars at Montlhéry, because its newer surface was much smoother than that at Brooklands. Gwenda Hawkes established the record for the banked circuit in her Derby-Miller with a lap at 145.94 mph, this record remaining unbeaten for several years until Raymond Sommer pushed it up to 148.4 mph in his 3-litre Alfa Romeo.

The French GP returned to Montlhéry in 1927 where Robert Benoist won a much-shortened race, run over 373 miles. He won at an average of 77.24 mph in his Delage. Also run there in 1927 was the *Automobile Club de France's* 'Free for all' race won by Divo's Talbot, and the *Coupe de la Commission Sportive de l'Automobile Club de France* which was run to a fuel-consumption formula and won by Boillot's Peugeot. There was also a 24-Hour sports-car race called the Grand Prix de Paris which was won by the 4½-litre Bentley shared by Clement and Duller.

The French GP was next run at the track in 1931.

Above: the last Grand Prix held at Montlhéry was the French GP of 1935. Thereafter, the circuit was used mainly for sports-car racing and record breaking. The last race held at Montlhéry was in fact for single-seater Formula Three cars and took place in 1972. Our picture shows sports and GT cars lining up for a race during the late 1950s

This was a 10-hour race which attracted a good entry, and was won by the Bugatti of Chiron and Varzi. 1933's GP went to Campari of Maserati and in 1934 the powerful new German Auto Union and Mercedes-Benz cars attracted an 80,000 strong crowd. But the German cars all retired, leaving Chiron to win in an Alfa Romeo. However, they made no mistake the following year when Rudi Caracciola won for Mercedes-Benz.

In 1936, the French decided not to run a race to Grand Prix rules because they did not want to witness another German victory, so they ran a sports-car race instead. This was won by the Bugatti of Wimille and Sommer, a similar race the following year being won by Chiron's Alfa Romeo.

The 1935 French Grand Prix was the last Grand Prix event held on the Montlhéry track, for the surface was now beginning to break up badly and, as it was not a profitable concern, there was no money available to resurface the track. From then on, the track was used mostly for testing and record breaking, but the Bol d'Or races were held there in 1937, 1938 and 1939 and, after the war, in 1954 and 1955. From '47 onwards, the Coupe du Salon and the Paris Grand Prix became the main annual races at Montlhéry.

In 1948, the Paris Grand Prix was held at Montlhéry as was the *Coupe du Salon* meeting, invariably held at the time of the Paris Motor Show in October. A long-distance sports-car race, the Paris 1000 Kilometers was also established, run over 129 laps of the 4.7-mile circuit. In 1964, this became a qualifying even for the World Sports Car Championship, the race being won by the Ferrari of Graham Hill and Jo Bonnier. During the race, a Jaguar hit a stationary car in the pits, killing two drivers and three marshals. The race was not held the following year but was revived in 1966. However, the circuit gradually fell into disuse again because of the poor state of the surface and the last race of any importance run there was the *Coupe du Salon* in 1972 which was run for Formula Three cars. The lap record is held by the Matra of Beltoise and Pescarolo at 103.033 mph.   MT

HOME OF THE ITALIAN GRAND PRIX

Of the three banked circuits built in Europe, only Monza is still in use.
The banked section has now been discarded, however, for reasons of safety

Above: the first Italian Grand Prix was held at Brescia in 1921. The following year, however, saw the event being transferred to the newly completed Monza circuit. Shown is the start of the 1925 event

Right: these two photographs were taken during the Gran Premio Fiera di Milano, held at Monza in 1924. In those days, the track comprised a banked section plus a road course, the total distance of which was 6.214 miles. The banking was, however, abandoned for Grand Prix events after the tragic Italian GP of 1961, although sports-car races took place there until 1969

THERE HAVE BEEN THREE major European banked race tracks; Brooklands, Montlhéry and Monza. There have also been one or two short-lived tracks such as the Spanish Sitges circuit and the French Miramas track, but neither of these was a fully banked track.

Monza was the second major banked track in Europe, Brooklands being the first in 1907. The Monza Autodrome was constructed in 1922, reputedly in the amazingly short time of one hundred days, the track being laid out in the huge royal park close to the small town of Monza, which itself is about 10 miles north-east of Milan.

As originally laid out the track provided both a road course and a banked track which could be used separately or combined into one; the banked track was of 2.8 miles length and the road course measured 3.4 miles, the two of which could be combined to form a 6.214-mile circuit.

The Italian Grand Prix had been held for the first time in 1921 at Brescia but it was immediately switched to Monza for the 1922 event, which was held over the full 6.2-mile course. The race was run over a distance of 500 miles for the then current 2-litre formula and was won by Bordino's Fiat at a speed of 86.89 mph. Other major events held on the track were the Voiturette Italian Grand Prix for 1½-litre cars and the Monza Grand Prix which was usually for Formula Libre cars.

The Italian Grand Prix was run over the full 6.2-mile circuit until 1928, the average speed rising to 99.14 mph that year when Louis Chiron won in a Bugatti. The Grand Prix was not held in 1929 and 1930, being replaced by the shorter Monza Grand Prix. At the 1929 event Varzi won in an Alfa Romeo, putting the race average up to 116.83 mph.

The 1931 European Grand Prix was run over the 6.2-mile course and the Italian Grand Prix returned

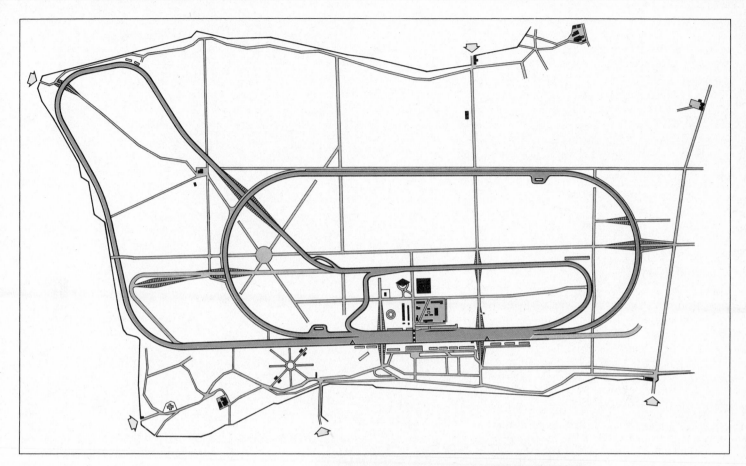

for 1932 and 1933 over the same circuit. The fast track suffered from some serious accidents, notably in 1928 when Ernesto Materassi's Talbot crashed into the crowd, killing both himself and twenty spectators. The crowds on the road circuit were protected only by wooden fences although the bulk of the crowd were placed in wooden grandstands along the main straight opposite the pits. The 1933 Monza Grand Prix was also a tragic event because three drivers, Borzacchini, Campari and Czaykowski, were all killed when they spun off the track on a patch of oil during a heat.

In 1934 the organisers decided to use a shortened 2.485-mile road circuit, known as the Florio circuit in order to try and slow down the new Mercedes-Benz and Auto Union monsters, but it made no difference for a Mercedes-Benz finished first and an Auto Union came second in the Italian Grand Prix.

For the 1935 and 1936 Italian Grands Prix the organisers lengthened the Florio circuit by adding two slow chicanes in order to nullify the power advantage of the German cars but Auto Union won both races. For 1937 the Grand Prix was switched to Leghorn but this time Mercedes-Benz won so the race came back to Monza again for 1938 over a slightly lengthened 4.35-mile Florio circuit. This made no difference either for an Auto Union won again, although it was piloted by Italy's hero, Tazio Nuvolari.

The banked track was demolished in 1939 and the Italian Grand Prix was not held that year. No more racing was held at Monza until 1948 when the road circuit was quickly refurbished and the Monza Grand Prix was held to Formula One rules, being won by Jean-Pierre Wimille's Alfa Romeo. The Italian Grand Prix was held that year at Valentino Park, Turin.

The new road circuit measured 3.915 miles and in 1949 the European Grand Prix was held there, being won by Alberto Ascari's Ferrari at 105.09 mph. The Grand Prix remained on this circuit until 1954 but in

early 1955 an entirely new banked circuit was constructed. This had part of the banking sunk below ground level and the upper portion raised on concrete pillars; the main straight was not banked so that cars could interchange from the banked circuit to the road course. The banking passed over the road course by means of a bridge and the distance of the combined road and track circuits was the same as the very first track at 6.214 miles. The 1955 Italian GP was held on the combined tracks, Juan Manuel Fangio winning in his Mercedes-Benz at an average speed of 128.5 mph, a considerable increase on any previous Italian Grand Prix speed. The track became immensely popular with spectators because those in the grandstands could see the cars emerging from the banking and racing past the pits in very close bunches. In 1955 the length of the road circuit was modified to 3.573 miles and the 1957 Italian GP was run on this track, the race speed then

Above: a layout of the Monza race circuit. Also shown in this picture is the oval banked section which has now been abandoned. Apart from the Grand Prix circuit, a short circuit, the Pista Junior, has also been created. In spite of the loss of the banked section, Monza is still one of the fastest race tracks in the world. To combat the problem of dangerous high-speed slipstreaming, two chicanes were incorporated into the road circuit in 1972

Left: Louis Chiron's Alfa Romeo competing in the 1933 Italian Grand Prix at Monza. During the race, three drivers, Borzacchini, Campari and Czaykowski, spun off the track on a patch of oil and were killed

Left: John Surtees's Ferrari leads the BRM of Jackie Stewart, the Lotus of Jim Clark and the BRM of Graham Hill during the 1965 Italian GP at Monza. Surtees eventually dropped out with clutch trouble and victory went to Stewart, who led team mate Hill home by only four seconds

dropping to just over 120 mph.

Unfortunately, the hasty construction of the track seemed to have affected the surface and the banking became very bumpy, causing some suspension failures and creating many complaints from drivers. However, in 1957 the track owners decided to invite a number of Indianapolis track cars and their drivers over to Italy for a race on the banked circuit only, omitting the road sections. The Indy cars proved as fragile as their European counterparts and the race, which was called the Race of Two Worlds, had to be split into heats so that repairs could be made between heats. The Americans put on a stupendous display of speed and bravery which was much admired by spectators and rival European drivers alike. The race was won by Jimmy Bryan at an average speed of 160.06 mph. The event was repeated in 1958, and despite stronger European opposition, the Americans triumphed again, Jim Rathmann winning at 166.72 mph.

Between 1957 and 1959 the Italian GP was held on the road circuit and in 1959 a short link road was added to the road circuit to provide a 1.48-mile short track for smaller events. The 1960 Grand Prix reverted to the combined banked and road circuits but virtually all drivers except the Italians boycotted the race because of the bumpy banking. However, the race was again used on the combined banked and road circuit in 1961 and most drivers agreed to race this time. Unfortunately, German driver Wolfgang von Trips was killed when his Ferrari left the track on the road circuit, killing several spectators as well.

The banking was abandoned for Grand Prix racing after 1961 and all subsequent races have been run on the road circuit. However, the Monza 1000 Kilometre sports-car race was instituted in 1965 and this event used the combined banking and road circuit until 1969.

The road-circuit lap times became faster and faster as the 3-litre Formula One cars improved, and in 1971 Peter Gethin won the Italian GP in a BRM at

150.76 mph. The racing was very close but drivers felt that the slipstreaming techniques necessary at Monza were very dangerous and two chicanes were incorporated into the track for 1972 in order to slow cars down and break up bunches of cars. The fastest race lap put up on the road course prior to the use of chicanes was made by Henri Pescarolo's BRM at 1 min. 23.8 secs during the 1971 race: 153.5 mph.

The future outlook for the Monza track was bleak in 1975 for the owners were reluctant to destroy a large number of trees which the racing community felt should be removed because of their closeness to the circuit. At that time it was planned to close the track completely and allow the Monza park to revert to a leisure area.   MT

Above: sports-car racing has proved very popular at Monza and the Monza 1000 km event is now one of the most important in the sports-car-racing calendar. Here a Chevrolet Corvette leads a Martini Porsche and a works Ferrari 312 during the 1971 event

'THE CAR OF COMFORT WITH A RESERVE OF SPEED'

The Moon Car Company was successful in its early days, but was held back when it combined with the New Era Group, which finally foundered

'THE CAR OF COMFORT with the Reserve of Speed,' that was the slogan of the Moon Motor Car Company of St Louis, and it certainly encapsulated their sales philosophy of offering the middle-class motorist a vehicle which tended to have ideas above its station, with better styling and performance than were normal in its price bracket.

The Moon company—headed by Joseph W. Moon, who had emigrated from Scotland—were builders of horse-drawn buggies before they turned to motor manufacture. Their first products, though, were a far cry from the buggies, for Moon engaged Louis P. Mooers as designer. Mooers had been designer with Peerless of Cleveland, Ohio, where he had produced some formidable racing cars, as well as refined touring cars; he was also a racing driver of some note.

His first car for Moon was the Model A, a 30/35 hp model using a proprietary Rutenber engine with four cylinders, and the pre-war models were large, well-built cars of distinctive appearance. Two four-cylinder cars, of 5.2 and 5.8 litres were available in 1912, joined by a six-cylinder model the following year.

By 1916, there were only sixes, with 3.6 and 5-litre Continental power units, the marque soon acquiring an imitation Rolls-Royce radiator to head them. Before long, Moons were available in Britain, where the agents were North Western Motors of Norton Street, Liverpool, who also handled the obscure Dixie Flyer

Below: a 1911 Moon; it used a 30/35 hp four-cylinder Rutenber engine. Like most Moons, it was well made and represented good value for money

from Louisville, Kentucky. At first, they imported the 3177 cc 6–42 23.6 hp six, which had overhead valves and Wagner electric lighting and starting, the five-seater tourer, painted Moon Blue (what else?) costing £575 complete with 'genuine tan Spanish upholstery'.

The design had retrogressed by 1922, for the engine now had side valves, although the Moon touring car was now £25 cheaper, while 12 months later the Moon stand at Olympia was graced by the Stewart tourer (£545), the Stanley Semi-Sports Four-Five Seater (£575) and the Sefton four-door, six-seat saloon (£725). All had British-built coachwork, and the standard specification included speedometer, clock, licence holder, spring gaiters and tyres. The engine had pump cooling and forced lubrication, while the gearbox, built in unit, housed three speeds. The brakes worked on the rear wheels and transmission only.

North Western Motors were obviously hedging their bets, for in 1923 they were also offering the Roamer, which was another car equipped with an imitation Rolls radiator. It also had a Continental engine, a 5-litre six, although earlier versions of this 'superb production' had used Duesenberg or Rutenber engines. Indeed, there was little to choose in styling or finish between Moon and Roamer, save that the Moon was cheaper! Both cars had curious suspension features, with the Moon possibly winning on points, for it had quarter-elliptic front springs and three-

quarter elliptics at the rear, while the Roamer was conventional at the front and double-cantilever sprung at the rear.

In 1924, the Moon acquired Lockheed external contracting brakes all round, and were thus, with Chrysler, one of the American pioneers of this kind of retardation. The car also featured detachable disc wheels with detachable rims, which seemed to be too much of a good thing. Price in Britain was down again to £375 for the St Louis four/five-seater and, by 1925, this price included automatic windscreen wiper, windscreen anti-dazzle device and, on the saloon, a rear-view mirror, an item of equipment notably lacking on most cars of the era. Two-tone paint was also available. The agent's publicity had an oddly up-to-date ring about it: 'While most announcements echo rising prices, the Moon gives you more quality, more distinction, more service and complete new features—at lower prices. It fairly bristles with new features that every motorist will be eager to read about —and see. It has the newest four-wheel hydraulic brakes, and genuine big, flexible balloon tyres. Also a new steering mechanism specially designed for greater leverage—an absolute necessity for balloon-tyre driving. Every mechanical unit in the Moon is the latest authority in engineering practice.'

Also in 1925, the Moon acquired a sister marque, the Diana, whose shouldered radiator shell was a rather pedestrian copy of the Belgian Minerva, and which

Above: the 1910 Moon 35 hp tourer. It was designed by Louis P. Mooers and featured a four-cylinder engine and shaft drive

bore on its cap a sculpture of Diana the moon goddess, with bow, arrow and dog (and not a stitch of clothing). It had a 4-litre straight-eight Continental engine with a Lanchester crankshaft vibration damper, and a chassis specification broadly similar to the Moon, except that it had wooden artillery wheels instead of discs. It could accelerate from 5 to 25 mph in 6.5 seconds, and had a top speed of over 70 mph. The two-seater roadster was in the fashionable 'sporty' idiom, with a golf-bag locker behind the seats; one variant offered a bronzed radiator shell with wire wheels plated to match.

Its makers called the Diana 'the easiest steering car in America' although, as it had the same Ross steering gear as its stablemate, this claim was a little suspect. However, the Diana only lasted from 1925 to 1928 before it was dropped, but the mock-Minerva radiator was also used on the 1927 Moon 6-60.

The old 23.6 hp model was dropped in 1926, after the British concessionaires had dropped prices in order to clear stocks. 'The most wonderful proposition ever made to the motoring public,' they called it, and then erupted in a riot of superlatives.

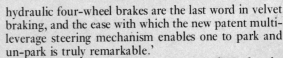

Below: the 20 hp Moon tourer of 1920 was powered by a six-cylinder Continental motor

'The Moon is a real luxury car that gives true motoring relaxation. Beautiful of line and engineering efficiency epitomised. It will register 50 to 60 miles an hour for as long as you desire, yet withal it is particularly easy to handle in traffic. The wonderful Lockheed hydraulic four-wheel brakes are the last word in velvet braking, and the ease with which the new patent multi-leverage steering mechanism enables one to park and un-park is truly remarkable.'

Prices were dropped from £375 to £295 for the tourer, from £395 to £315 for the roadster and from £495 to £395 for the four-door saloon, but were back up again for the new 6-60 at the end of the year. With a 19.8 hp Continental Red Seal engine of 2.8 litres (which had only pump and splash lubrication), it cost £395 in roadster guise, £375 as a tourer, £425 as a Coach and £465 as a Sedan.

At last the ubiquitous Moon Blue colour scheme had been dropped, and the standard finish was now in Pyroxyline cellulose (the earlier model had used Dupont cellulose), with a colour scheme of 'Cactus Grey below and between the belt and black above'; closed models were upholstered in Velour Plush with 'extra deep cushions'. The car's power unit was up-rated for 1928, to create a new model, the 6-72, which developed 66 bhp against the standard unit's 48; this was achieved by using a high-compression cylinder head. All Moon models now had a new design of radiator shell, this time very similar to that of the contemporary LaSalle, which was itself a crib of the Hispano-Suiza.

Moons were now apparently being exported to Britain in chassis form only, for North Western Motors were offering British-built coachwork with

Below: the Moon Motor Company produced cars from 1905 until 1930 and, during that time, established a reputation as makers of quality vehicles. Here a 1921 Moon six-cylinder tourer winds its way along a quiet English country road

British head, side and tail lamps. The range now consisted of a roadster, a coupé and a saloon, finished in Moon Blue Belco cellulose; prices ranged from £415 to £465.

With the dropping of the Diana, a straight-eight was marketed under the Moon name for the first time: this was the 1928 Aerotype 4.4-litre, which developed 85 bhp at 3100 rpm, using a high-compression side-valve power unit (again a Continental), with a twin-choke Stromberg Duplex carburetter. The Aerotype Saloon cost a cool £755, while the fixed-head coupé was priced at £725.

In describing the new model, the Moon publicity department reached new heights of hyperbole: 'The Continental 15-5-engined eight has a high-nickeled radiator, a cowl surcingle of which the cowl lamps are integral parts, and nickeled headlamps are connected by a monogrammed bracket. A cadet-type windshield visor, long sweeping full-crowned fenders and a deep running board give the cars a very low appearance . . . the body lines are of French-Spanish appearance.'

The six-cylinder model was rechristened Aerotype, too, and now had Bohnalite Invar strut aluminium pistons and a Lanchester vibration damper on the crankshaft; the saloon cost £575. Wire wheels were standardised throughout the range, and six-cylinder models had dampers on the front axle only, the eights having them front and rear.

In 1929, Moon announced a new version of the straight-eight, with a double-dropped chassis frame which lowered the floor line by seven inches, and a four-speed 'twin-top' gearbox in place of the three-speed units of its predecessors. The Lockheed brakes were now internally expanding, and the chassis had fully automatic pressure lubrication of the springs and shackle bolts. The new Moon was known as the White Prince of Windsor, in honour of the Prince of Wales, and its double-dropped chassis was also used on the six, which had adjusting rubber-type spring shackles. That year, Moon sold 2900 cars, but they also became embroiled with New Era Motors, Incorporated, in which they were united with Gardner, Kissel and Ruxton. The Gardner was a dullish vehicle whose slogan 'A Distinctively Different Motor Car' was about as far from reality as it was possible to get; the Kissel had been a sporting marque of some distinction and the Ruxton was a bizarre rarity. Ruxton's history was complex: it had been the brainchild of Archie M. Andrews, a financier who was on the board of Hupp

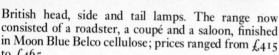

Above left: a 1923 Moon 6–58 Sport Phaeton. It was fitted with a 128 in wheelbase chassis

Above right: a Moon 6–60 de luxe roadster of 1927. It was powered by an in-line six-cylinder Continental engine which developed 47 bhp at 2600 rpm and gave the car a top speed of 80 mph

Motors. Andrews had named it after a friend, William V. C. Ruxton, who had shown enthusiasm for front-wheel drive, and who possibly seemed like a soft touch for a spot of extra capital.

The prototype Ruxton appeared in early 1929 and was hailed as being almost a foot lower than any other car of its day; it combined front-wheel drive with a rigid beam axle, and the power unit was a Continental straight-eight of 5.5 litres. Production began in mid 1930 in the Moon and Kissel factories and, although the Ruxton was sold as a high-priced luxury model, with prices ranging up to 5000 dollars, there was a curiously parsimonious look about the sedan versions. This was hardly surprising, for they were built by Budd using the same body dies as the British Wolseley. However, if these bodies were dull outside, they were well appointed inside, with colour schemes worked out by a leading stage designer named Joseph Urban, who even devised a livery of narrow horizontal rainbow bands for one car! The open bodies, on the other hand, were built by Raulang (who as Rauch & Lang had built electric cars from 1905 to 1908, latterly in the old Stevens-Duryea works at Chicopee Falls, Massachussets), and were strikingly handsome.

Twenty-five Ruxtons, which had such odd features as Woodlite parabolic headlamps and a gearlever projecting from the dashboard, were built in the Kissel factory (there was even talk of fitting one of the odd Elcar Lever engines into one of these Ruxtons, but it did not come to fruition). The rest—and production estimates of Ruxton output vary from 52 to 500 cars— were built by Moon, using Kissel-manufactured transmissions.

However, there were few sales for the Ruxton, and by 1931 New Era Motors was out of business, dragging Moon and Gardner down with it, while Kissel lingered on a couple of years longer, reorganised by George A. Kissel as Kissel Industries, attempting to market a Ruxton-inspired car with a Lever engine. The Lever engine and the Ruxton front-wheel drive were mechanically incompatible, though, and the venture quietly died.

As for Moon, the end was perhaps inevitable, for there was not really a place for low-volume quality cars in the American car market of the 1930s. But one wonders whether the St Louis firm could have kept going through the Depression if it had not been saddled with the other lame ducks of the New Era Group. Was it a case of 'Divided we stand, united we fall?' DBW

PURPOSE-BUILT TOWN CARS AND REBODIED FIATS

Moretti first built their own complete small cars, but began to concentrate on rebodied Fiats when things became difficult

THE MORETTI COMPANY is by no means one of the most famous car manufacturers to come from that ultra-productive area of Northern Italy around Turin and Milan. Indeed, with neighbours like Ferrari, Lamborghini, Maserati, Fiat, Alfa Romeo and Lancia, mostly marques that are surrounded by a mystical aura of speed and comfort combined with that unique stamp of Italian styling, the Moretti would have to be something very special to be realistic competition. Instead of attempting to compete with the luxury makers, Fabbrica Automobili Moretti SpA of Turin took the only other course available to them in the early 1960s: their maxim was: 'If you can't beat them, give up and start looking for a new area in which to sell'.

The little company, that had once taken great pains to build complete cars with 'home-made' engines, decided to divert into the manufacture of variations on the models of a larger marque, Fiat. In this field they had a better chance of survival for it would be cheaper for one man to indulge in his own designs of car body than to spend a large amount of money developing complete cars that had just a small chance of nibbling

Right: the first car produced by Giovanni Moretti, and separate from the actual Moretti company, was this two-seater, rear-engined convertible which he built in 1927

Below: the Moretti La Cita was built from 1945 until 1948. It was powered by a twin-cylinder 350 cc engine which developed 14 bhp and gave the car a top speed of 85 kph

at the cake of the then-thriving car-buying market. What better way to go about this than to shelter under the wing of Fiat, one of Europe's industrial giants, who would supply rolling chassis, complete with engines.

Moretti's own original cars were essentially of the mini type; the first, built in 1946, was called La Cita. This was powered by a front-mounted, 14 bhp, vertical-twin engine of 350 cc, which was obviously very economical. Based on a tubular frame, the car also featured hydraulic brakes and independent front suspension. The La Cita was originally available only as a saloon, but estate and coupé versions were later added to the catalogues, the latter having a claimed top speed of 60 mph and the ability to cover up to eighty miles on one gallon of petrol. Developed alongside the ohv twin-cylinder power unit was a four-cylinder

Above: towards the end of the 1960s, Moretti produced this neat 850 cc coupé. It used a rear-mounted Fiat engine driving the rear wheels

Below: Moretti's 750 coupé built during the early 1950s

twin-overhead-camshaft engine, which was later to be used in a Formula Three chassis. By 1950, the 350 cc La Cita was available in 600 and 750 cc forms, based on backbone chassis as opposed to the space-frame design used previously.

Still on the small-car theme, 27 bhp two-bearing single-cam and 51 bhp three-bearing twin-cam derivatives of the saloon's vertical twin were in production in that car by 1954. Moretti's Turin neighbours, Michelotti, did a styling exercise on a 1.2-litre Moretti chassis which was to retail in America at the high price of 2900 dollars. After experiments with that peculiarly Italian device, the small-engined commercial, as well as four-door versions of the saloon, the step was taken to build a new car based on the Fiat 500 Nuova; this was in 1957.

Although this transition to rebodied production cars had taken place, for a time, a large range of Moretti's own cars could still be purchased. They were as follows: in 750 cc form, there were two single-cam saloons, the 27 bhp and the 43 bhp, designated Super, there was a buzzy little twin-cam GT, an 820 cc estate, a 1-litre 50 bhp saloon and, by now, the Formula Junior rear-engined racer. The racer was built and driven by Aquilino Branca, who was later to build Formula Three cars under his own name, and had moderate if not outstanding success. Branca did not actually work with Moretti, but had an agreement that he would be able to use the company's advertising and marketing as long as Branca's cars, which were some of the first to feature mid-mounted engines, carried Moretti's badge. On the production front, there was also a neat little coupé called the Golden Arrow. It featured Dunlop disc brakes and, like all the other

Above: in 1962, Moretti marketed this attractive convertible named the 2500SS. It used the six-cylinder Fiat engine

Below: a 1963 Moretti 1500 coupé. Like most Morettis, it used Fiat engine parts

production cars, coil and wishbone suspension. As can be seen, the range was very large for a small company, but unfortunately only a hundred or so cars were actually sold in 1958, obviously nowhere near enough to warrant such a large selection which composed, primarily, mini cars for the ever-growing small-car market.

The company's name was changed to Moretti Fabbrica Automobili e Stabilimenti Carrozzeria SAS in 1962, this coinciding with the decision to concentrate on rebodied Fiats. A large step up market was taken with a convertible based on Fiat's six-cylinder 2300, the engine of which was enlarged to 2.5 litres to produce a very respectable 163 bhp. This stayed in production for but a year, from 1962 to '63.

Thereafter, with Moretti's own cars gone, the company built a range of cars on the Fiat 500 and 850 chassis. A large range of engines was available in both

saloon, coupé and estate-car bodies. These were of 500, 595 and 850 cc sizes. By 1970, Moretti had been taken under the Fiat umbrella, selling their cars through the organisation's large network. One of the most popular vehicles on the market at this time was the Midimaxi, a Citroën Mehari-type 'Jeep', based on Fiat 127 front-wheel-drive mechanical parts. Other cars to be seen were De-luxe and Sport versions of many popular Fiats, looking not too different, but just enough so for them to find a ready market. One interesting exercise was a 132 safety coupé which featured faired-in headlamps and rubber strips around the car's perimeter.

In early 1975 there were about 150 employees at Moretti's factory, in via Monginevro, Turin, producing cars of similar concept to the rival Giannini. The past had seen cars with G. and S. Moretti's design showing in engine, chassis body and running gear, the present saw their bodies gracing the chassis of Europe's biggest car manufacturer and the future, with fuel shortages and general lack of funds, would depend on whether there would still be people with that little extra money over the Fiat base price who would be willing to spend that money on the Morettis that were different from the crowd. If there was no market, Moretti would go the way of all flesh, if there was still a market, they would continue in their sector with which they were slowly but surely getting to grips. LJC

Right: built by Moretti and sold through the Fiat organisation's network was the Midimaxi of 1970. It used a Fiat 127 engine driving the front wheels

Below: the 1972 Moretti 132 'safety coupé'. It was powered by the four-cylinder Fiat 132 engine driving the rear wheels

AN AGELESS THOROUGHBRED

Morgan cars are built by motor enthusiasts for the enjoyment of other motor enthusiasts

Above: a photograph of an extremely rare Morgan. This is the experimental four-seat three-wheeler built by H. F. S. Morgan in 1912

Right: the three-wheeler Morgan Grand Prix of 1913. It was powered by a twin-cylinder JAP engine

Far right, top: a drawing of the 1908 Morgan 8 hp

Far right, centre: a poster depicting early Morgan motoring

Far right, bottom: the distinctive winged Morgan badge

THE MORGAN IS A MAKE OF A CAR which could hardly be more English—it has been made in the shadow of the Malvern Hills since before World War I—but which means different things to different generations of enthusiasts. To the older folk, the name implies a simple, even crude, three-wheeled cyclecar, whereby many motor cyclists graduated to the car world, either with the more staid family models or with some of the very sporting pre-war models. To a later generation, those who commenced motoring just before or soon after another World War, the Morgan name means an essentially sporting four-wheeler, still simple in conception, but offering very good performance and all the fun of open-car fresh-air driving. It is significant that the sliding-pillar, coil-sprung form of independent front suspension evolved by H. F. S. Morgan for his first three-wheeler was still in use in 1975 for the complete Morgan range.

It all began in 1884, that being the year in which Harry Morgan, the son of George Morgan, curate and later vicar of Stoke Lacy in Herefordshire, was born. After a short and unhappy time at Marlborough, Harry Morgan studied engineering at the Crystal Palace Engineering College. He left with a sound knowledge of drawing and designing and was encouraged by his ecclesiastical father to continue his studies with the GWR. This is interesting, because while it has been said that W. O. Bentley's fine cars sometimes resembled the locomotives he likewise worked on during his apprenticeship to engineering, the same can hardly be said of the motor vehicles turned out subsequently by H. F. S. Morgan!

Morgan left the railway to open a garage in 1906 at Malvern Link, near his home. Here he obtained agencies for Darracq and Wolseley cars and later branched out with a bus service between Malvern and Worcester, using a 10 hp Wolseley. This was not a success and was changed into a hire-car branch of the garage. Fame was to come to H.F.S. in his manufacturing rather than his transport activities. A keen cyclist, he soon decided to build himself a motor cycle. However, the country roads of *circa* 1910 were not very suitable for two-wheelers and the motor-car craze was expanding, causing the Trade to contemplate inexpensive vehicles that might be profitably sold in considerable numbers. Whether it was this thought that prompted Morgan to deflect from his idea of a motor cycle to that of a simple car, a cyclecar, is not known, but for keen Morganists it is fortunate that it was so. With assistance from the engineering master at nearby Malvern College, H. F. S. began his experiments. He had an engine, in the form of a 7 hp vee-twin Peugeot he had acquired for his motor-cycle project.

The first thing that this ingenious man did was to braze up a tubular frame, having a central tube or backbone, which was like that on which all subsequent Morgan three-wheeler chassis were based. It was a triumph of lightweight construction, achieved with a minimum of materials and labour. The engine was hung out in front on transverse tubes, the aforesaid coil-spring independent front suspension was contrived at the extremities of these cross-tubes, itself using more tubing, and the propeller shaft ran down inside the central backbone to a bevel box, from the transverse shaft of which emanated the simple two-speed dog-and-sprocket transmission. There was no reverse provided, but a Morgan was so light that it could be lifted up at the back by most owners when they wanted to turn it round! There were no gears to crunch and no expensive gearbox for Morgan to make or to have to buy out. The chains of this soon-to-become-famous two-speed transmission ran one on either side of the single back wheel. A band on either side of this rear wheel gave foot and hand braking and steering was by means of a side tiller.

Here then was the original Morgan three-wheeler. It was a single-seater, devoid of bodywork, and it emerged from the Morgan works in 1909. Morgan displayed his devotion to steel tubing by using the side members of the chassis as silencers for the air-cooled engine! It must be remembered that in those days motoring knew few comforts and the open single seat of this first Morgan did not deter people. Indeed, H.F.S. soon knew he was onto a good thing: the power-

on a programme of regular entries in competition events; backed by his father's financial help and interest, which included defending his son's product in the motor and motor-cycling papers, the Morgan became very popular. At this time, *The Light Car & Cyclecar*, which had a fine photographic front cover, was giving a cup for the light car or cyclecar which covered the greatest distance in an hour's run on Brooklands Track. In a narrow single-seater Morgan, H. F. S. set out to beat the holder, in 1912, watched by his grandfather in his top hat and clerical collar. The Morgan first covered 55 miles within the time limit, was beaten by Wood's friction-driven GWK by a narrow margin, and set off again in November, to cover nearly 60 miles in the hour. Harry Martin had already won the first cyclecar race to be held at Brooklands in a Morgan-Jap and, from that time on, the make was to

Below: the Morgan factory at Pickersleigh Road, Malvern Link, photographed during 1920. Morgans were entirely hand built in those days, a policy still pursued by the Morgan company to this day

to-weight ratio of his little vehicle was such that it had a very useful performance, on the hilly terrain round Malvern, leaving behind up the gradients much bigger and more elaborate cars.

With firm support from his father and his wife, H.F.S. lost little time in becoming a cyclecar manufacturer. He displayed a Morgan at Olympia in 1910, received a very good Press, and Harrod's, the great London store, became one of the first Morgan agencies. By the 1911 Motor Cycle Show the Morgan three-wheeler had blossomed out as a two-seater runabout. This two-seater, the engine of which was under a coal-scuttle-type bonnet, had a hood, a windscreen and wheel steering and met with immediate success. There was a hand starter and the least expensive of these three-wheelers sold in 1911 for only £65.

H. F. S. Morgan and his wife, Ruth, soon embarked

figure in every kind of competition with unqualified success, which helped very materially to sell the cars.

The following year, 1913, W. G. McMinnies entered a Morgan for the French Cyclecar Grand Prix and his carefully prepared machine won from a Bedelia and a Violet-Bogey, having averaged just under 42 mph for the 163 miles of the race. H.F.S. won a gold medal in the very tough 1913 ACU Six Days' Trial, his Morgan having to run in the side-car class, as three-wheelers had to do on many occasions. There followed many splendid performances by Morgans in the great MCC long-distance reliability trials, which still continued in 1975. All this put the Morgan from Malvern very much in the eye of the buying public and at the 1913 Motor Cycle Show the first of the Grand Prix models made its appearance. Records at Brooklands and victories in races and trial events caused

Opposite page, top: W. G. McMinnie and passenger F. Thomas pose in their 1913 GP for Cyclecars winning Morgan

Centre: the 1919 Morgan De Luxe three-wheeler

Bottom: a 1917 Morgan Grand Prix model

demand to be more than the small factory could meet and at this time no thought was given to making a full-scale motor car.

Indeed, when World War I was over, the Malvern works was very busy. A quickly detachable back wheel was a long-needed improvement and for 1921 the Popular model cost £150. It had an 8 hp JAP engine and the body was made from poplar wood. By 1923, the price of this aptly-named Popular Morgan was down to £128 (it had been renamed the Standard model, as it happens), and you could decide between a JAP or a Blackburne engine. The fast Grand Prix Morgan attracted the sporting youth who had £155 to spend, but the chap with young children went for the Family model which had two very tiny seats behind the front bench, divided by the arch which accommodated the single back wheel. This cost £148 with an air-cooled engine or £158 for the water-cooled model, which had its radiator behind the engine. The Aero Morgan had made its appearance, too, with an

Anzani engine and list price of £148. MAG engines were also available, so H.F.S. had little fear of power unit supplies drying up. He kept the two-speed chain-and-dog transmission, eventually agreed to gear-down the direct steering, and put all manner of extras in his catalogues, such as Impirvo puncture-proof fillings in the inner tubes of the tyres for 7/6d and a four-speed gear for £10 extra.

It must be remembered that in those far-away days the roads were comparatively free, and that three-wheelers, apart from being economical on petrol, tyres and insurance (not then compulsory), commanded an annual tax of but £4, compared to £8 a year for an Austin Seven. So Morgans were deservedly in great demand and rivals appeared every so often. None was as well liked in those days as the make from Malvern, where the works had to be expanded to meet the

Top: the Matchless-engined Super Sport of 1934

Above: Super Sport Morgans in action

Opposite page, top: the Darmont-Morgan, built in France under licence

Far right: a vee-twin 1096 cc JAP-engined Morgan

Bottom: a 1922 Morgan three-wheeler

dealers' requirements. In 1923 and again in 1924 Morgan won the top award in the Junior Car Club's General Efficiency Trial, so they cannot have been as crude as their economy of materials and construction suggested.

In 1924, there came a set back to H. F. S. Morgan's keen appreciation of competition work as a means of proving and popularising his products. In the fourth JCC 200-Mile Race at Brooklands E. B. Ware's Morgan-JAP overturned and its occupants were very badly hurt. Thereafter, the authorities banned three-wheelers from speed events. This was a great blow and these machines had to revert to motor-cycle status under the ACU regulations. They were still permitted in trials, however, but it was some years before they were again allowed to take part in car races. It took the formation of the New Cyclecar Club to achieve this

and it was perhaps poetic justice that in the first NCC event, a race with artificial corners, at Brooklands, it was a four-wheeler and not one of the tricar competitors that overturned!

For 1924, electric lighting was available, at a cost of £8 extra, and side valve and overhead valve, air-cooled and water-cooled, models were well established, while 75 mph was guaranteed from the single-seater Morgan-Blackburne. Many more competition victories were achieved before the speed ban of 1924 came into being, and in that year the 976 cc Popular Morgan sold for £110, the 1098 cc Aero Morgan for £148 and the single-seater for £160. The price of conventional cars was falling, however, and some elaborate three-wheeled rivals to the Morgan had appeared.

However, the light Morgans (three-wheelers had to weigh under 8 cwt to qualify for the tax reduction), which could give 45 or more mpg and run easily at 70 mph in 40 bhp form, went on selling. Moreover,

they were getting faster and faster in racing guise. Harold Beart built himself a very special water-cooled 1096 cc Blackburne vee-twin car with a 3.33 to 1 top gear and a streamlined body weighing only 43 lb, which put 91.48 miles into the hour on Brooklands (whereas in 1912 H.F.S. had not exceeded 60) and which was able to exceed 100 mph. In later years the Morgan team in the Light Car Club's relay race at the track were always the most exciting sight of the day and the only real challengers of the works Austin Seven team. They crackled round at the top of the steep bankings, the drivers keeping both hands on the steering wheels by locking the hand throttles open with rubber bands! Morgans, like motor cycles, relied on Bowden-wire controls and drip-feed lubricators.

Dynamo lighting had become standardised by 1925, by which year the Standard model was sold for £95, when an Austin Chummy cost £149. De luxe models made up the range and you could go courting a girl in an Aero if you could afford £130.

The following year, 1926, Eric Fernihough, the famous racing motor cyclist, set something of a vogue by installing a single-cylinder engine of 494 cc in a racing Morgan. For the 1927 season the bevel box was improved, grease-gun lubrication was introduced and front-wheel brakes were fitted to some of the Morgan range. You could even have an electric starter to turn the vee-twin engine if you paid an additional £10; dashboards were of mottled aluminium and the Standard model was quite a bargain at £89 with double-pane windscreen and electric hooter. All manner of successes were chalked up in trials and speed contests and the Morgan Club was re-formed in

1927. In the MCC London–Edinburgh Trial alone fourteen Morgan trikes brought home eleven gold medals and three silver medals. Before the year 1928 was ushered in, four pounds in price had been lopped-off the Standard two-seater and the first of the Super Sports models had made its appearance, priced at £155 with a tuned 10/40 overhead valve JAP high-compression engine. This same engine was fitted at the front of the Aero model, which was then priced at £132, but with an air-cooled JAP twin this spartan and sporting Morgan sold at £119. Family men could have the two-by-two Family model for £102, or for £112 if they preferred a water-cooled power plant. These were

Below: a 1939 Morgan 4/4. It used a water-cooled, four-cylinder 1122 cc engine. The price asked for a complete machine was 185 guineas

Left: a Morgan 4/4 negotiating the watersplash at the bottom of Darracott hill, Cornwall, during 1939

Opposite page, top: another view of the Morgan 4/4, this being a 1936 model Le Mans replica

Opposite page, bottom: a get together of Morgan Owners' Club members pictured at a race meeting at Silverstone

Far right: another Morgan three-wheeler was the F2 model. This used the famous Ford side-valve engine of 1172 cc

the 1928 prices that enabled H. F. S. Morgan to hold his own, in his little factory, with the prevailing small cars on four wheels, many of them now carrying saloon bodywork.

Minor improvements marked the 1929 Morgans, but the design was virtually unchanged from the original 1909 conception. Geared steering, still of a very high ratio, became standard instead of being offered as an extra, and greater stability was given to some of the more sporting models by using a wide-track front-end. H. F. S. Morgan continued to drive his cars in long and strenuous trials, that great Morgan exponent Clive Jones made his début and Malvern had a works driver in the factory store-keeper, C. T. Jay, who won the Cyclecar Grand Prix at Brooklands in 1929 at 64.7 mph in a 750 cc Morgan-JAP. By now both the Standard and the Family models were listed at a modest £87 10s, the Aero at £110 and the Super Sports, which was the sophisticated sports version, at £145. Morgans were inexpensive to buy and to run, they were enormous fun, and they could be looked after by anyone who had been used to servicing his own motor bike; nor could Morgans be called slow vehicles. In 1930, at the Paris track, a woman, Gwenda Stewart (later Hawkes), got 113 mph out of her racing version. However, time moves on and the wise and wily H. F. S. Morgan felt the need for some changes in his odd but excellent little cyclecars. So in 1930 the fool-proof two-speed transmission was replaced by a three-speed gearbox at the end of that enclosed propeller shaft, final drive being now by means of a single chain to the rear wheel. Two-speeders were made up to 1933, but only in small numbers, although

KUV 706

this transmission was retained for the Family model so that it could be sold for as little as £80. The M-type chassis featured a knock-out back wheel spindle and was much lowered. In fact, refinement was the watch-word; even the twin aero screens on the Aero model were replaced with a two-panel vee screen and the valve gear on the ohv engines was actually enclosed.

It was obvious that the best years of the vintage-type three-wheeler were running out, however. Small cars were becoming more and more efficient, with closed bodywork, four-speed gearboxes and effective brakes. They were also getting less and less expensive, with a number of one-hundred pound examples, culminating in the £100 Ford Popular saloon. H. F. S. Morgan countered this by putting in Ford four-cylinder water-cooled engines, first the Eight and then the Ten, along with his partner George Goodall, in 1935. However, the chain final drive and separate Morgan three-speed gearbox was retained. Nor was the two-cylinder engine entirely neglected. The Matchless vee-twin appeared in the last batch of such Morgans,

Above left: the 1958
Plus 4 Morgan

Left: the rare Plus-
Four-Plus, of which only
50 examples were built.
This glass fibre-bodied
car was a complete
departure from the
traditional vehicles
produced by the
Malvern Link company,
and did not go down too
well with the loyal
enthusiasts of the
marque. However, the
company did not take
long to get back to their
'traditional roots' with
the Plus 8

in air-cooled and water-cooled versions, and with side-by-side and overhead valves. These had a capacity of 990 cc and some of them, the very last of a long line of Morgan three-wheelers, were shipped to Australia after World War II. However, it is as the F-type Ford-powered model that the final range of three-wheelers is best remembered. There was the handsome Super Sports, with its spare wheel recessed in a barrel-tail, and the Family model, with more space for growing children than the first Morgan to carry this type-name, and with a dummy radiator-grill, adopted in 1933.

Although the Morgan works at Pickersleigh Road, Malvern Link, were about the smallest car-manufactury in the land, the company knew what was needed to keep open. Harry Morgan's father had died in 1937, but H.F.S. survived until 1959, dying at the age of 77, his cyclecar ambitions amply fulfilled. His son, Peter Morgan had joined the company in 1947 and was running it in 1975, very much as his father did before him. He was selling largely to the American market and while the tycoons of the Motor Industry were shouldering their considerable worries, Peter was enjoying his Ferrari and his very nice country home!

Chris Lawrence's Plus 4 which won its class in the 1962 Le Mans. This car, powered by a 128 bhp Triumph TR2 engine, was still being raced in early 1975

This is to anticipate, however. The unavoidable demise of the three-wheeler in pre-war times was countered at Malvern by the introduction of a very sporting four-wheeler in 1935. It was a low-hung, compact, and distinctly good-looking little car, making good use of the three-wheeler Morgan's independent front suspension and separate gearbox, but having a conventional back axle. It was in some ways a rival of the MG Midget from Abingdon and was the salvation of the long-established company, when three-wheeler sales had been flagging in this country.

For an engine for the new four-wheeler, which was called the Morgan 4/4, a 1122 cc Coventry Climax was used, giving 34 bhp at 4500 rpm. This was an overhead-inlet, side-exhaust-valve engine, which enabled the little car to do 70 mph. The new 4/4 cost 185 gns in 1936 and was to become very popular and also to carry on the great Morgan competition reputation. The chassis was very low, being underslung beneath the back axle; the original 4/4s were two-seaters, but in 1937 a four-seater was added, which in no way departed from the car's sporting flavour. So, although the famous three-wheelers did not fade out until war intervened, the Morgan 4/4 was growing ever more popular and a neat drophead coupé was announced in 1938, costing £236. When supplies of the Coventry Climax engine dried up, a Standard Ten specially modified for the Morgan Motor Company was substituted. This was of 1267 cc and developed a useful 39 bhp at 4800 rpm. These 4/4s gained awards in the RAC Rally and one ran in the Le Mans 24-hour race in 1938, entered by a Miss Fawcett. This latter event led to the introduction of a Le Mans Replica model, with fold-flat windscreen, cycle-type front mudguards, a slightly smaller engine swept volume to put the car in the 1100 cc class, and one instead of the Morgan's traditional twin rear-mounted spare wheels. It cost £250 and could exceed 80 mph.

Morgan never departed from the sports-car image so well exemplified by the 4/4. After the war a change to the 2-litre Standard Vanguard engine put it into a larger and more exciting category, the chassis merely being strengthened and enlarged to make this possible. The new model was called the Plus-Four and cost originally £625 as a two-seater and £723 as a coupé.

Above: the 184 bhp Plus 8 put the Morgan company into the ranks of the ultra-high-performance car manufacturers

Below: a 1965 4/4 Series II

Increased performance was then gained by installing the Triumph TR2 and TR3 power units, in 1954 and 1956, respectively; Morgan re-entered the smaller sports-car field with the Series II 4/4 with side-valve Ford Ten engine, brought out at the 1955 Motor Show. These cars maintained the great competition background of the make and along with a Plus-Four-Plus glass-fibre coupé, led to the 1975 Morgan models: the £3000+ 3½-litre Plus Eight, which was using the light-alloy Rover V8 engine and gearbox, and the ohv Ford-powered 1600 4/4s. For a long time, exposed headlamps and a non-adjustable driving-seat, along with wooden floorboards, were a Morgan hallmark. Recessed headlamps were eventually adopted and the Rover power unit sounded the death-knell of the separate gearbox. Otherwise the Morgan was largely unchanged, in specification, in hand construction under the control of old-style craftsmen, and in its purely sporting demeanour. The Plus-8 had a very high performance in respect of top pace and pick-up, and the sporting successes have continued, including a class win at Le Mans in 1962.   WB

PLUS 8

The name Morgan is synonymous with the traditional British sports car; the type of car that gave the expression 'hairy' a new meaning. In fact, when, in the mid sixties, the Malvern Link, Worcester, company diverted from tradition to build a closed glassfibre car, the Plus-Four-Plus, there was such an outcry from the loyal band of Morgan enthusiasts that the company stopped production after a mere fifty cars had been built.

However, the next major step taken by the company was greeted with approval from all sides, when 1968 saw the introduction of the Plus 8, looking like any other 'Moggy' from the outside. When the centre-hinged bonnet was raised, one could see a break from tradition, though: no more the docile four-cylinder unit; now there was a big, powerful V8 in the compartment, ready to ooze power with the slightest encouragement from the driver.

The Plus 8 uses the Rover/Buick 3528 cc unit which produces 184 bhp and 226 lb ft of torque. Due to the poor aerodynamics of the car, the top speed is not as great as it could be, but 125 mph should be fast enough for most people, especially with the hood down. Acceleration is electric—0–60 mph in a mere 6.7 secs—and eighteen miles are returned for every gallon of fuel.

Morgans also use, or suffer from, sliding-pillar front suspension and a rigid rear set up that transmit every irregularity and change of surface to the seat of the driver's pants. Originally, a Moss gearbox, separate from the engine, was used, but Rover's own box was utilised from 1973.

The only outward changes in appearance from the Plus 8's slower brothers are the 15 in light-alloy wheels clad in 185-section Dunlop Aquajet tyres and that cloud of blue rubber smoke and the diminishing blur

of a car heading for the horizon if it is accelerated in anger!

ENGINE Front-mounted, water-cooled 90° V8. 89 mm (3.50 in) bore × 71 mm (2.80 in) stroke = 3528 cc (215.3 cu in). Maximum power (DIN) 184 bhp at 5200 rpm; maximum torque (DIN) 226 lb ft at 3000 rpm. Light-alloy cylinder block and heads. Compression ratio 10.5:1. 5 main bearings. 2 valves per cylinder operated, via push-rods and rockers, by a single camshaft at the centre of the V. 2 SU carbutettors.

TRANSMISSION Single-dry-plate clutch and four-speed manual gearbox. Ratios 1st 3.619, 2nd 2.127, 3rd 1.379, 4th 1, rev 3.419:1. Hypoid-bevel final drive with limited-slip differential. Ratio 3.310:1.

CHASSIS Ladder frame.

SUSPENSION Front—independent by vertical sliding pillars,

coil springs and telescopic dampers. Rear—non independent with a rigid axle, semi-elliptic leaf springs and telescopic dampers.

STEERING Cam and peg. Turns from lock to lock 2.25.

BRAKES Front discs and rear drums, servo assisted.

WHEELS $5\frac{1}{2}$ in × 15 light alloy.

TYRES 185 × 15.

DIMENSIONS AND WEIGHT Wheelbase 98 in; track—front and rear 50 in; length 146 in; width 59 in; height 52 in; ground clearance 7 in; dry weight 1876 lb; turning circle between walls 38 ft; fuel tank capacity 13.5 gals.

BODY 2-door, 2-seater roadster.

PERFORMANCE Maximum speed 125 mph. Acceleration 0–60 mph 6.7 secs. Fuel consumption approximately 18 mpg.

MARINA

With the merging of the British Motor Company and Leyland, the many car companies caught up in the mix were separated and put under their respective headings as quantity-produced advanced cars, quantity-produced conventional cars and specialist cars, like the Rover and Jaguar. Morris had, for many years, been building 'badge variations' of the Austin, but under this new scheme Morris were gradually to phase out their advanced front-wheel-drive cars to concentrate on conventional vehicles like the Marina, introduced in 1971.

The idea behind the Marina was to have a range of cars, replacing the Minor and Oxford, that would be easily serviceable and cheap to run, as well as being attractive to fleet buyers.

Power units for the car were the 1.3-litre A-series unit and the 1.8-litre B-series engine, available in single and twin-carburettor forms. A two-door coupé and a four-door saloon were the first models marketed, with a four-door 1.8-litre estate following later in 1973.

One of the main criticisms of the Marina when it first appeared was levelled at the suspension department, the car having handling and road-holding that inspired the driver with little confidence. This failing was due, more than anything, to the car's concept: uncomplicated systems for ease of servicing. The front layout was ex-Minor, with wishbones, lower trailing links, longitudinal torsion bars and lever dampers acting as upper arms. The rear was non-independent with a rigid axle, semi-elliptic leaf springs and telescopic dampers.

ENGINE Front-mounted water-cooled straight-four. 70.6 mm (2.78 in) bore × 81.3 mm (3.20 in) stroke = 1275 cc (77.8 cu in) (1.3), or 80.3 mm (3.16 in) bore × 88.9 mm (3.50 in) stroke = 1798 cc (109.7 cu in) (1.8 and 1.8TC). Maximum power 60 bhp at 5500 rpm (1.3), 82.5 bhp at 5100 rpm (1.8), or 93.5 bhp at 5500 rpm (1.8TC); maximum torque 69.7 lb ft at 2450 rpm (1.3), 99.4 lb ft at 2900 rpm (1.8), or 106.3 lb ft at 2600 rpm (1.8TC). Cast-iron cylinder block and head; compression ratio 8.1:1 (1.3), or 9:1 (1.8 versions); 3 main bearings (1.3), or 5 main bearings (1.8 versions). 2 valves per cylinder operated, via pushrods and rockers, by a single camshaft, side. 1 SU carburettor (1.3 and 1.8), or 2 SU carburettors (1.8 TC).

TRANSMISSION Single-dry-plate clutch and four-speed manual gearbox, or torque converter and three-speed automatic. Ratios for manual versions of 1.3 (1.8 versions in brackets) 1st 3.412 (3.110), 2nd 2.112 (1.926), 3rd 1.433 (1.307), 4th 1 (1), rev 3.753:1 (3.422:1). Ratios for automatics 1st 2.293, 2nd 1.450, 3rd 1, rev 2.094:1. Hypoid-bevel final drive. Ratio 4.110:1 (3.636:1).

CHASSIS Integral.

SUSPENSION Front—independent by wishbones, lower trailing links, longitudinal torsion bars and lever dampers acting as upper arms. Rear—non-independent by a rigid axle, semi-elliptic leaf springs and telescopic dampers.

STEERING Rack and pinion. Turns from lock to lock 4.

WHEELS 4.5 in steel.

TYRES 145SR × 13 (1.3 and 1.8), 155SR × 13 (1.8 estate), or 165SR × 13 (1.8TC).

DIMENSIONS AND WEIGHT Wheelbase 96 in; track—front 52.38 in (1.3), or 52 in (1.8), rear—52 in all models; length 166.12 in (saloons), 163.12 in (coupés), or 167.54 in (estate); width approximately 64.2 in; height 56.12 in (saloon), 55.35 in (coupé), or 56.54 in (estate); ground clearance 5.75 in (coupé and saloon), or 5.52 in (estate); dry weight 1914 lb (1.3 coupé), 1940 lb (1.3 saloon), 2040 lb (1.8 coupé), 2061 lb (1.8 saloon), 2172 lb (1.8 estate), 2072 lb (1.8TC coupé), or 2131 lb (1.8TC saloon); turning circle between walls 31 ft; fuel tank capacity 11.5 gals.

BODY 2-door, 4–5-seat coupé, 4-door, 5-seat saloon, or 5-door, 5-seat estate.

PERFORMANCE Maximum speed 82 mph (1.3 versions), 95 mph (1.8 versions), or 100 mph (1.8 TC versions). Fuel consumption 30 mpg (1.3 versions), 26 mpg (1.8 versions), or 24 mpg (1.8 TC versions).

PURPOSE BUILT FOR THE MASSES

William Morris left school at 15½. When he died in 1963 he left behind him one of the biggest and most famous companies in the history of British motoring

WILLIAM RICHARD MORRIS, who became the first Viscount Nuffield, was a short, stocky, chain-smoking hypochondriac who made a vast fortune out of motor-car manufacture, and gave nearly £30 million of it to charitable trusts. He was born in 1877, in a small terraced house in Comer Gardens, Worcester, the son of a wayward character who flitted from job to job, and who had even been a stagecoach driver in North America before his son's birth. During his stay in America, William's father had also lived with a tribe of Red Indians for some time and had been adopted as a full member of the tribe. By the time young William was old enough to go to school, the family had moved yet again, to a house in James Street, Cowley, then a small village on the outskirts of Oxford.

William Morris was educated at the St James Church of England School in Cowley, and began work at the age of 15½, in the shop of an Oxford cycle agent named Parker. The foreman, Dupper, was supposed to teach the boy the trade; young Morris was evidently a fast learner, for within nine months he was demanding a wage rise of sixpence a week on top of the

Right: William Richard Morris was eighteen when this photograph was taken in 1895. By this time he had left school and was working in the bicycle industry. In 1901, he built himself a motorised cycle and so began the legend of Morris

Below: the first car ever offered for sale by Morris was the Oxford model of 1913. It was fitted with a four-cylinder engine of 1018 cc

four shillings he was already earning. Parker turned the claim down, and Morris resigned to set up in business on his own, repairing cycles in his father's garden shed. From there it was only a short step to the manufacture of complete machines from bought-in components, and Morris received his first order from the local vicar, a tall man who demanded a larger-than-usual mount

with a 28-inch frame to suit his unusually large body.

The successful completion of this commission brought Morris further orders, but the fledgling cycle manufacturer didn't just rely on word-of-mouth publicity for his products: he also raced them, to such good effect that at one time he was champion of three counties—Oxfordshire, Berkshire and Buckinghamshire—over distances ranging from one to fifty miles. However, he wasn't infallible, as F. G. Hunt (the mechanic who in 1913 built the first Aston Martin) recalled nearly three-quarters of a century later:

'In '97—Diamond Jubilee Year—Bill Morris had a little cycle shop in Oxford. During the celebrations, Colonel Porter of Fairford Park allowed a cycle race on his land. Bill Caldicott, the Fairford postmaster's son, said to me: "Thee knows how to ride a bike, Frank—why don't thee go in for the race?"

'So I enters, riding an old Star with dropped handlebars—heaviest machine of the lot! It was on inch-and-a-half Warwick road tyres while the other riders were using proper path-racing tyres. There was Bill Morris and a pal of his, a chap named Mitchell from Oxford and Arthur Griffiths, champion of the NCU at that time . . .

'My mother breaks two eggs into a glass with a decent drop o' brandy. " 'Ere, me boy," her says, "that'll stay thee wind!"

'Of course, they all shoots away from me at the start, but sure enough I gets me second wind and catches them up. Morris and his pal were lying third and fourth—but I slips between them and comes in third!'

But minor setbacks like this didn't impede the teen-aged Morris's progress. He had originally used his father's front parlour and garden to display his bicycles; soon he was successful enough to rent a shop at 48 High Street, Oxford, as well as repair premises in Queens Lane.

Morris built himself a motor bicycle in 1901,

Top: the two-seater Morris Oxford runabout of 1913. It proved very popular with press and public alike, in spite of its limited seating space

Centre: successor to the Oxford was the Cowley model, introduced in 1915. It was fitted with a four-cylinder motor of 1548 cc

Bottom: a family group photograph taken in 1919. Centre of attraction is a Morris Cowley tourer

machining the engine from proprietory components (though like most of its contemporaries it was doubtless a pirated de Dion Bouton design) and thought that this type of machine had sufficient sales potential to warrant quantity production. However, he lacked the capital for such a venture, and was forced to go into partnership with a local cycle dealer named Joseph Cooper. They built a couple of motor cycles in 1902 before Cooper had cold feet over this rash scheme and backed out of the partnership. Morris was forced to cast about for other backers, and before long was one of three partners in the 'Oxford Automobile and Cycle Agency Limited', which boasted premises at 16 George Street, Oxford, as well as Morris's leasehold shop in the High Street.

At the November 1903 Stanley Cycle & Motor Show in the Royal Agricultural Hall, Islington, the company showed four Morris motor cycles. One was a belt-driven machine fitted with a $2\frac{3}{4}$ hp MMC air-cooled engine while the other three were chain-driven. Two of these were bicycles, one with a $3\frac{1}{2}$ hp de Dion water-cooled power unit and one with a $2\frac{3}{4}$ hp air-cooled de Dion, while the third was a $2\frac{3}{4}$ hp de Dion-powered tricycle fitted with a forecarriage.

The company had also moved into the motor car business, and were offering 'the Speedwell Light Motor Car, two seats, fitted with de Dion engine of 6 hp, gear drive'. Speedwell were also UK agents for the Serpollet Steam Car, which was also marketed by the Morris company.

But while Morris was working fourteen hours a day in the garage, one of his partners, an undergraduate, was burning up the company's profits with a com-

Top: another version of the Morris Cowley; this is the open tourer of 1923

Above: a fleet of 1913 Morris Oxfords stands ready for inspection prior to being delivered to various new owners

bination of extravagant entertaining and over-generous discounts: and the Oxford Motor Agency was soon bankrupt. Morris had to borrow £50 and stand in the pouring rain at the auction where the partnership's assets were sold off to buy back his own tool kit, which had been seized to help pay off the debts.

On his own again, he retained the High Street shop, plus converted livery stables in Longwall, where there were a few machine tools downstairs, and an office upstairs where Morris's old father kept the accounts. This time, the business was a success, and in 1908 Morris disposed of the cycle agency, the High Street lease and the design rights of the motor cycle, to a friend named Armstead.

As well as operating a taxi and hire-car service, Morris had replaced the antiquated tram service in Oxford with a considerable fleet of 'ugly red motor-buses', and was agent for Arrol-Johnston, Belsize, Humber, Hupmobile, Singer, Standard, and Wolseley cars; for a time he retained a couple of motor-cycle agencies.

By 1910 he had sufficient capital for expansion: the Longwall premises were torn down and completely rebuilt in best Edwardian Classic style, earning the local nickname 'The Oxford Motor Palace'. In addition, further premises were acquired in 1910 at Cross Street and in 1913 in the old Queen's Hotel.

William Morris was now in a position to realise a long-standing ambition—to become a motor manufacturer. He planned to manufacture a quality light car, to sell at a modest price; but he would assemble it from the best proprietory engine, gearbox and chassis components available. In that way, he would be able to produce in quantity without spending any of his precious capital on development or tooling. Additionally, the use of components made by companies who were acknowledged experts in their fields would guarantee a reliable end product.

He had begun investigating the supply of components in 1910, but found that he would need additional capital; in 1911 William Morris once again plunged into partnership. This time, however, he had found the ideal backer, Lord Macclesfield, a wealthy motor enthusiast who was prepared to invest some £25,000 in Morris's proposed manufacturing venture, without interfering too much in how the company was run.

In August 1912, WRM Motors Limited was founded, with Macclesfield as president and Morris as managing director. Morris had already contracted for the supply of components for his new car: the engine/gearbox units would be supplied by White & Poppe Ltd, a Coventry-based partnership between a British and a Norwegian engineer, E. G. Wrigley & Company would provide the worm-drive rear axles (though that irascible genius Fred Lanchester had once claimed that the only use for a Wrigley worm was as fishing bait) as well as the front axles and steering mechanism, while a local coachbuilder, Raworth, would supply the bodies.

For his factory, Morris had acquired the former Military Training College at Temple Cowley, once the grammar school where Mr Morris senior had been educated. It wasn't sentiment which prompted his son to take over the building, however, but the low price at which it was available, the result of its having stood empty for twenty years.

Though Morris now had a motor works, he was unable to produce cars, for White & Poppe had failed to produce engines on time. Apparently Willans & Robinson of Rugby, who were supplying the castings for this power unit, had supplied the first set at half the correct size, due to a dimensioning error in the White

& Poppe drawing office. The delay meant that Morris couldn't exhibit at the November 1912 Motor Show at Olympia as he had planned, but he didn't waste his railway ticket, for he took a set of blueprints up to London, and on the strength of these persuaded Gordon Stewart, of the London motor agents Stewart & Ardern, to place an order for 400 Morris-Oxfords rather than the Marshall-Arter cyclecars that he planned to buy. Incidentally, Stewart was the active member of Stewart & Ardern—Ardern being very much a sleeping partner, a shadowy figure that few people connected with the company could ever recall having seen.

Following the Motor Show fiasco, the car's first public appearance was scheduled to be the North of England Motor Show at the Exhibition Buildings, Rusholme, Manchester, held from 14–22 February 1913, where the catalogue promised the presence of a chassis and a complete Morris Oxford two-seater. The two-seater *did* appear: but it wasn't quite what it claimed to be, for the cylinder blocks still hadn't come through, and the engine was a wooden dummy!

The first roadworthy Morris Oxford wasn't ready for Stewart to collect until the end of March 1913. He drove off confidently, only to come to a halt in the midst of mechanical chaos a few yards further on with a shattered universal joint in the transmission. Poppe had specified that this joint should be made of cast iron for durability, but his factory had used an inferior grade of iron which shattered under stress. After Stewart had again come to grief with a second universal failure on the road to London, Morris demanded that all universals should henceforth be cast from bronze instead of the naturally brittle iron.

There was another major drawback to the Morris

Oxford that was not realised by either Morris or Stewart: they were both little men, who assumed that as the standard two-seater body would take the pair of them without discomfort, it would be spacious enough for anyone. In fact, even for a couple of normal stature, the Morris Oxford was distinctly tight under the armpits, and for a tall driver it was well-nigh impossible to carry a passenger as well.

The motoring press, however, took kindly to the little car, which was one of the liveliest in its class. *The Cyclecar* found that its 1018cc engine could achieve 38 mph in second gear—equivalent to a dizzy 3800 rpm—and that top speed was around 55 mph. At that speed, however, the lightness of the car proved a handicap, for the suspension took over, and the little Morris bounded along the road like a hare and became virtually uncontrollable.

The price of such performance was a touch of temperament, for though the engine was generally willing and lively, it was very particular about sparking plugs, only running reliably on German Bosch units. And it tended to run very hot: on one occasion a miserable B. H. Davies of *The Autocar* had to ladle water out of a puddle with his sou-wester to replenish the handsome (but inefficient) round-nosed brass radiator of his Morris Oxford.

It must have been an equally soggy journalist who wrote barbedly in *The Cyclecar* that the car's hood 'served to keep off the major portion of the rain'!

But such minor failings couldn't conceal that the Morris Oxford was, at £175, remarkably good value, and, during the first nine months of production (March–December 1913) output totalled 393 cars; the following year, this figure soared to 909. This happy state of affairs, however, was to be quickly upset by the outbreak of war, and production was curtailed so that

Above: a splendidly restored and maintained 1926 Morris Cowley, pictured at a vintage and veteran car meeting

Right: the in-line, side-valve, four-cylinder Continental motor as used in the Cowley

Opposite page, top: a four-door Morris Cowley saloon of 1923

Centre: a 1922 Morris Cowley sports fitted with two-seater boat-tailed coachwork by Compton and Hermon Ltd

Bottom: a 1926 Morris Oxford tourer. By this time the capacity of the side-valve engine had grown to 1802 cc

the Cowley factory could be devoted to the production of munitions. Morris lobbied the corridors of power in Whitehall so effectively that he received contract after contract for supplying the Navy with minesinkers. Morris Oxford production was progressively cut back; only 180 were built in 1915, 13 in 1916 and one in 1917, assembled from parts produced before the war.

In any case, the Morris Oxford had already served its purpose by proving to Morris that he could be a success as a car manufacturer. Now he planned to challenge the giants of the motor industry on their own terms. He realised that a lively two-seater like the Morris Oxford was limited in its appeal, and that the future lay with the low-cost, reliable, family four-seater, a type which was at that period almost exclusively the province of American manufacturers. Morris had already projected a four-seater version of the Morris Oxford in 1913, only to find that it would be uneconomically expensive to build.

He therefore determined to find out for himself how the Americans could manage to produce four-seaters so cheaply, and, accompanied by Hans Landstad, the chief draughtsman of White & Poppe, he spent a month in the United States at the end of 1913.

This fact-finding trip proved invaluable: Morris was also to obtain quotes from a number of American component suppliers which proved to him that it would be cheaper to buy parts in America and have them shipped across the Atlantic than to obtain them from English manufacturers. He asked White & Poppe to quote for a 1500 cc engine/gearbox unit for the car he was planning, but they couldn't bring the cost down under £50, which was virtually twice what the Continental Motor Manufacturing Company of Detroit was asking.

His new-found role as a manufacturer of munitions didn't prevent Morris returning to the United States on 18 August 1914, again accompanied by Landstad. Even then, the design of the new car hadn't been finalised, for Morris and the seasick Landstad used the voyage to lay down the outline of a four-seater car designed round the American components for which they had received quotes after their previous visit.

Despite the outbreak of war, Morris contracted for 3000 engine/gearbox units from Continental, and then returned home, while Landstad stayed on to gain first-hand experience of American mass-production methods, working with Continental by day, finalising the design of the new Morris at night and spending what time remained visiting other motor manufacturers including, inevitably, Ford, where he obviously learned a great deal.

Once the first Continental Red Seal engine intended for the new Morris was running successfully, Landstad returned home to Coventry. But it was little surprise that he joined WRM Motors soon afterwards, about the time that development of the new model began. By April 1915 the prototype was running. Its name gave *The Autocar* food for thought: 'I wonder why the new car is called the Morris Cowley? Does the name conceal a horrid threat that Cowley will ultimately swamp Oxford?'

In Morris terms, that is exactly what happened, for the Cowley in two-seater form undercut the cheapest Oxford: cost was 158 guineas against £168, a small difference that seemed the larger when one car was compared with the other. The Cowley could carry a genuine four-seater body, and had an engine of 1495 cc. Furthermore, its design was far more up-to-date, for the engine featured such Yankee conceits as a detachable cylinder head and a dipstick; dynamo lighting replaced the oil/acetylene system of the Oxford and the rear axle had helical gearing for quiet running.

But an even greater advantage of the new model was that supplies of components were assured (until the German U-Boats became a menace) at a time when the British components makers were devoting their factories to war work. Maybe Morris saw his factory's output of minesinkers as insurance against loss of components: even so, half the 3000 Continental engines shipped over during the war were sent to the bottom of the Atlantic by the enemy.

Nevertheless, Morris was able to maintain production of the Cowley throughout the war, while most of his contemporaries were forced to cease assembly around 1916. Peak year of the Continental-engined Cowley was 1916; 684 were sold, against 161 in the last three months of 1915, 125 during the whole of 1917 and 198 in 1918. The year 1919 saw 281 Cowleys produced; the following year just one Continental Cowley left the works.

Two unforeseen events had combined to upset Morris's carefully laid plans to dominate the United Kingdom market with Cowleys built from American

components: firstly, in September 1915, the Chancellor of the Exchequer, Reginald McKenna, imposed a duty of 33⅓ per cent on imported cars and accessories, which meant that the price of the cheapest Cowley rose to 185 guineas just as the model became generally available. And then, in March 1916, the Government placed a total ban on the importation of American cars or parts (except those used to manufacture commercial vehicles). Hardly surprisingly, Morris added a delivery van to the Cowley range in November 1916 . . .

A fresh problem came with the Armistice and the lifting of the ban on American imports, for the Continental Motor Company decided that there

Top: the Morris 8 saloon was introduced in 1935; it used a four-cylinder 918 cc engine

Centre: a flat-radiatored 1928 Morris Cowley

Bottom: a Morris 8 tourer of 1938. This model had a top speed of 60 mph—quite impressive at the time

wasn't enough demand to warrant resuming production of the 1496cc engine used in the Cowley. So Morris, limping along on what remained of his wartime stock of parts, had to cast about for British suppliers once again. White & Poppe were unwilling to co-operate, the Dorman Engine Company inconveniently wanted a £40,000 deposit as evidence of good faith, and the New Pick Motor Company of Stamford, Lincolnshire, had insufficient production capacity.

But now that the dogs of war had ceased barking, the munitions factory set up at the beginning of hostilities by French motor and armament company, Hotchkiss & Cie in Coventry was sadly unemployed. Their works manager, H. M. Ainsworth, had plenty of pre-war experience in the company's car plant at St-Denis and lost no time in calling his directors over from France for a conference with Morris. It was agreed that Hotchkiss would produce an engine to Morris's specification, would hopefully be able to reach Morris's price target as production rose, and would not need a deposit on the order. By September 1919 the Hotchkiss engine, a pretty faithful copy of the Continental Red Seal, to which Morris had acquired the design rights, was being fitted into cars, and manufacture, which had slowed almost to a standstill, began to gather momentum: from 5 in September 1919, it rose to 10 the next month and to 35 in November. However, the component shortages meant that Morris had missed out on the post-war car sales boom. And just as the Cowley factory had got back into its stride in 1920, disturbing reports came from America of a sudden and vicious recession in car sales—even Ford had had to close down his factory temporarily. By the end of the year, the slump had hit Britain.

Morris sales plummeted from 276 in September 1920 to 92 in December and 68 the following month. As the old WRM Motors company had been dissolved in mid 1919 and a new company, Morris Motors

Limited, formed with a nominal capital of £150,000 to exploit the anticipated vastly increased Morris sales to the maximum by getting rid of the old North of England and South of England agents and appointing a new dealer force, the drop in sales was particularly embarrassing to William Morris.

One can imagine Morris sitting in the old headmaster's room in the Cowley factory which was his office for nearly half a century, belching with the stomach wind which perpetually bothered him, and perhaps sipping on a glass of Sanatogen or bicarbonate of soda—his two panaceas—to try to quell his internal disquiet. How to get sales moving once again? The idea, when it came to him, wasn't original, but it had already worked for Henry Ford. And the key to it was that newly appointed network of agents.

He would cut the prices of his cars—and the agents' profit margins—in an attempt to clear his unsold stocks and maintain production. The most popular model, the Cowley four-seater, was reduced by the greatest amount, £100, from £525 to £425; the two-seater shed £90, bringing the price to £375. In late 1919 the Oxford name had been revived for a de luxe version of the Cowley: the Oxfords now lost £25 from their purchase price, which became £510 for the two-seater and £565 for the four-seater, while the more sybaritic coupé was now £80 cheaper at £595.

It was a good scheme, and a similar venture had saved Ford; but the British firm of Bean had already tried it with a total lack of success. Morris, however, had timed his reductions impeccably: sales rose to 244 in February, 377 in March, and showed a total of 3077 for the year, compared with 1932 models sold in 1920. Even Morris was taken aback at the success of the price cuts: their effectiveness was measured in increased profits, and Morris suddenly became a major force in the British motor industry. Other manufacturers belatedly followed his lead at the Motor Show and cut prices by an average of 17 per cent—but Morris reduced his prices even more. The four-seater

Below: the Minor is a model name synonymous with Morris. The first Minors were built in 1928 and used four-cylinder, overhead-camshaft, 847 cc engines. At a price of £125, the Minor proved tremendously popular

Cowley dropped from £375 to £299, the four-seater Oxford from £425 to £341. In the space of nine months, the price of the former model had been cut by 35 per cent and that of the latter by 21 per cent.

Paradoxically, the increased motor taxation imposed by the 1920 Road Traffic Act was another beneficial factor in the Morris success story. In 1920, Ford had over 40 per cent of the British market: but the new Act charged the motorist £1 per horsepower (RAC rating) instead of the maximum of £6 6s that had previously prevailed, and the Ford was now taxed at £22 annually. The Morris cost £150 more than the Ford to buy, but its annual tax was only £12; and to the parsimonious mind of the average motorist this annual saving was more important than the cheaper first cost of the Ford, and before long the Morris-Cowley was challenging the Model T on the home market.

The 1922 season was doubly successful: a total of 6937 cars was sold, while Morris reduced his selling prices still further, to the point where they seriously embarrassed his less affluent rivals, many of whom went under in their efforts to compete.

Now Morris decided to play the autocrat: and the first result of this policy was a parting of the ways between Morris and the man who had originally provided his financial backing, Lord Macclesfield.

Top left: a 1938 Morris 8 Series II four-door saloon

Top right: the Morris Six Series MS saloon was produced from 1948 until 1954. It was powered by a six-cylinder, overhead-camshaft engine of 2215 cc. Pictured is a 1951 model

Bottom: the distinctively styled Morris 10 cwt station wagon of 1949

With £25,000 invested in the company, Macclesfield was naturally interested in how it was being run, and was quite likely to make unannounced visits to Cowley and wander round the production lines chatting to the workmen; he also annoyed Morris by asking questions about company policy at board meetings. These were curious affairs, for Morris was not very good at conventional ways of doing business, and conducted the meetings with a grasshopper inconsistency which his naturally inarticulate manner did little to alleviate.

Morris resented what he regarded as Macclesfield's interference in the way he ran his company, and decided to buy him out; the peer was surprised to receive a cheque representing the face value of his shareholdings, which had a far greater potential worth, but took the hint gracefully and severed his connection with the firm for £25,000.

Now William Morris was in sole command, and aiming to create a completely self-sufficient car-producing empire which, like that of his American exemplar, Henry Ford, would have no need to rely on outside suppliers. Already several companies were almost entirely dependent on Morris business for their continued survival, and it followed with logical inevitability that William Morris should take them over. One by one he acquired Osberton Radiators Limited, Hollick & Pratt, the bodybuilders (whose

factory had just burned down, and whose director, Lancelot Pratt, became Morris's second-in-command, but died aged 44 in 1924), and—the biggest coup of all —the Hotchkiss factory at Coventry.

Hotchkiss fought hard to maintain their independence, but Morris eventually overcame their resistance with an offer of almost £350,000 for their share capital, and Ainsworth departed for the main Hotchkiss factory at St-Denis, where he remained in charge of car production until the Germans marched into France. The Hotchkiss works became Morris Engines Limited, and output soared as the factory's unrealised potential was exploited.

The ailing Wrigley company was also acquired—it later became Morris Commercial Cars—and Morris managed to obtain extended credit from Dunlop, who supplied all his tyres, and Lucas, who provided all the electrical equipment. As he had asked his bank for twice as much credit as he needed, and as he insisted on cash payment for all cars before they left the factory, William Morris was in the happy position of running his factory on the money of those who depended upon his products for their livelihood.

He was also still in the garage business, but since 1919 had entrusted the running of the Morris Garages to a general manager, Edward Armstead, the friend who had bought the design rights to the motor cycle

Top: in 1954, Morris revived the Cowley model name and gave it to this medium-sized saloon. The car was powered by a four-cylinder, 1200 cc engine. In 1956, the capacity was increased to 1489 cc

Above: one of the most famous and popular models ever produced by Morris was the Minor 1000 model. This is a 1957 version

in 1908. Three years later, Armstead gassed himself in mysterious circumstances, and his sales manager, Cecil Kimber, took over. Hence, shortly afterwards, the first MGs. . . .

Morris was empire-building almost by instinct, and occasionally he over-reached himself. He bought a coal forest from one of the Free Miners of the Forest of Dean in the fond hope of supplying his factories' needs to fire the furnaces and provide heating. But the mine-workings were flooded, and the scheme came to nothing.

So, too, did his acquisition, in December 1924, of the Léon Bollée factory at Le Mans. This attempt to produce a car for the French masses resulted in a loss of £150,000 in four years and several unsaleable models before production was stopped in 1928.

Another fiasco was Morris's attempt to build a car for the colonies, where American makes had long been dominant. The Empire Oxford was built by Morris's truck factory, Morris Commercial Cars Limited, and had a 15.9 hp engine coupled to a four-speed gearbox. It seemed a well built car in the best Morris tradition—but it just didn't sell. Indeed, the Australians sent most of theirs back to Cowley in disgust!

This must have been a bitter rebuff to Morris, who had a great liking for Australia, and was already cultivating the habit of taking a cruise there each year.

However, on the home market, Morris had little cause for complaint. His 'bullnosed' Cowleys and Oxfords were selling in phenomenal numbers, with sales soaring from 6,937 in 1922 to 20,024 in 1923, to 32,939 in 1924, and peaking at 54,151 in 1925, the last full year that the old model was produced.

The Bullnose, which was produced in 11.9 hp form as the Cowley (and Oxford pre 1924) and as the 13.9 hp Oxford from 1923 on, had a certain homely charm, plus some distinctive features like its permanently engaged Lucas Dynamotor, which combined lighting and starting functions, giving the side effect of uncannily silent engine starting without the whir and clash of the Bendix pinion. This, however, was completely nullified by the Bullnose's three-speed gearbox, on which first emitted a mellow moan and second an agonised shriek like a buzz-saw ripping through timber which could be heard for half a mile on a still day.

At the end of 1926, the restless tide of progress claimed the Bullnose, and a new model appeared, with a fashionably square-cut radiator which was claimed to give 60 per cent greater cooling capacity than the older pattern (which was, coincidentally, more expensive to produce).

The new model was the result of a visit to America by William Morris in September 1925. The fact that while there he had turned down an offer of £11 million for Morris Motors was irrelevant: what mattered was that he had met Edward G. Budd of Philadelphia and his fast-talking vice-president in charge of sales, Hugh Leander Adams.

They had given Morris the full hospitality treatment, and convinced him of the merits of the Budd all-metal body construction, with the result that Morris Motors joined with the Budd Company in setting up a factory in England to produce Budd bodies under licence: it was named the Pressed Steel Company. With this novel form of body construction (which was not the first all-metal coachbuilding to be seen in England, however) fitted on a redesigned chassis of greater torsional rigidity, Morris seemed to have the answer to the problems of producing bodies in vast quantity to match his production of chassis. But there were many teething problems, not least of which was the total inexperience of the Pressed Steel Company. The dies were untried, and the methods of working totally alien to the workforce. When the first all-steel bodies were fitted to Morris Oxford chassis, it was evident that the standards of finish were far below those of even the cheapest coachbuilt bodies—and the dies were reputed to have cost £120,000 before a single panel had been produced!

The panelling was wavy, door and window apertures were out of true and the windscreen leaked—'It ought to be sold as an all-weather body,' remarked a director when the car was shown to the Morris management for the first time, 'it lets all the weather through . . .'

The problems were solved, but it took time. Morris was displaying all his characteristic worry signs, scratching the nape of his neck, sitting cross-legged and wagging his foot up and down . . . and to cap it all he had contracted a painful bout of sciatica after slipping on the concrete floor of his garage, which acted as a sharp spur to his latent hypochondria, and encouraged him to contribute towards the extension of the Wingfield Orthopaedic Hospital.

It must have been a trying time for his wife, who was intensely jealous of his work—as well as being probably more parsimonious in small things than her husband. He had married quite late in life, and his wife, the former Elizabeth Maud Anstey, was a first-class cyclist—'a jolly good powerhouse on the back of a tandem' was how one of Morris's executives irreverently described her. The couple's idea of a relaxing weekend was a tandem trip from Oxford to Aberystwyth and back, but when William Morris became too involved in his work, his wife retreated into her resentment of his work, and refused to have any children. Consequently, as Morris grew older, so he began to lose interest in his empire, for he had no heir to pass it down to, and he began to take refuge in his lengthy trips to Australia, leaving others to take the helm in his absence.

His last great act of empire-building came in 1927 when, against determined bidding from Sir Herbert Austin, Morris bought the moribund Wolseley company, formerly part of Sir Basil Zaharoff's Vickers group, for £730,000. Wolseley had been ruined by an ill-conceived model called the 'Silent Six', but their name still carried an aura of prestige.

Furthermore, the Wolseley acquisition also brought Morris an engine design which had the promise of greatness about it. This was the single-overhead-camshaft layout which Wolseley had cribbed from the Hispano-Suiza aero-engines they had built, reputedly without licence, during World War I. Under Wolseley's aegis, however, this had proved a power unit of singular gutlessness, with its hidden reserves shown only by Sir Alastair Millar's Wolseley Moths at Brooklands.

This was the design of engine chosen to power the new light car which Morris was planning, though it first appeared on the 2½-litre Morris Six of 1928, which was developed into the 1930 Isis. News of the Morris light car appeared in a controlled leak in May 1928, prompting Morris's rival, Clyno, to bankrupt themselves in an attempt to produce a £100 version of their 9 hp Century model. The 8 hp Morris Minor was introduced for the 1929 season, benefitting nicely from the move to smaller cars caused by the reintroduction of the petrol tax after a seven years' hiatus. The first year's production of the new model totalled 12,500; altogether 39,000 overhead camshaft Minors were built before production ceased in 1932.

In 1929, William Morris was created a baronet; in

1934 he became Baron Nuffield, taking his title from an Oxfordshire village. Between those dates, his attitude to the company he had founded took a fundamental change. He had made history with the first full size £100 car, a side-valve Minor two-seater available only in grey with black radiator and lamps. This was announced as the clock struck midnight at the Stewart & Ardern New Year's Party which celebrated the arrival of 1931, and, having achieved this qualified success (for the car didn't sell particularly well), seemed gradually to lose interest. His trips to Australia became even more protracted, and he was

Top: the Mini Minor was introduced in 1959 and was still being made in 1975

Centre: the Morris Oxford of 1967

Bottom: the Morris 1100 of 1962

Left: the Morris 18–22 series model was introduced in 1975. Engines used were the 1800 cc four-cylinder B-series and the 2200 cc six-cylinder E-series

Below: Lord Nuffield, then in his 85th year, pictured with the 1962 Morris 1100

content to leave the running of his company in the hands of delegates like Leonard Lord, who had come to Morris from Hotchkiss, and who had become one of Britain's leading authorities on mass production techniques—and a ruthless organiser. In 1936 Nuffield refused to give Lord a share in the profits—and Lord stormed out to join Austin, vowing that in the fullness of time he would be back to take Cowley apart 'brick by bloody brick'. Which is almost precisely what happened when Sir Leonard Lord masterminded the formation of the British Motor Corporation in 1952, a shotgun wedding of almost incompatible partners.

Nuffield's lack of interest was evident in the company's products during the 1930s; initially, these had a solidly traditional air, with only minimal nods in the direction of progress, such as the adoption of the 'Eddyfree' windscreen, big-hub wire wheels and fully-valanced mudwings (and, less successfully, direction indicators in the shape of the Wilcot Robot, midget traffic lights fixed to either side of the car, and so confusing in use that they were quietly junked at a loss of £50,000). Then, in 1934, came the Minor's successor, the Morris Eight, whose styling was a blatant crib of the contemporary Model Y Ford—and which sold over 50,000 in nine months, 250,000 in its four-year life, before it was replaced by the streamlined Series E.

Nuffield, who put 25 per cent of his stockholding in Morris Motors on the market in 1936, had thereby created a vast fortune for himself, as the 5s shares were selling for around £2. In order to put his wealth beyond the reach of the taxman, Nuffield began endowing charities in earnest; by 1938 he had donated £11,500,000 to research, education and charity. Over £3 million of this had gone to Oxford University (in spite of his long-seated mistrust for the students, who had always been slow settling their accounts in the cycle-building days, and his feud with the University authorities, who resented the encroachment of the Morris industrial empire on the City of Dreaming Spires): in 1937 he endowed Nuffield College, where post-graduate students could study social, economic and political problems. Hand-in-hand with this went his involvement with Sir Oswald Mosley's Fascist movement, for at that period Nuffield was a firm believer in government by benevolent dictatorship. Despite his sympathies for the Blackshirts, he was created Viscount Nuffield in 1938.

By now his role in the Nuffield Organisation was largely negative, as a bearer of destructive criticism, and his hypochondria was becoming an open embarrassment to his executives. Nuffield had convinced himself that he had diabetes, and had contracted the habit of giving himself urine tests in the office. One day during the war, one of his directors took a £6 million Ministry of Supply contract to Nuffield for signature. The great man, glancing at the clock, apologised, crept into a corner of the room, and returned bearing a full test-tube, to which he added a pinch of copper sulphate, heating the noxious mixture over a spirit lamp. Unfortunately, the tube shattered, and the contract was deluged with Nuffield's sample...

After the war, Nuffield was instrumental in founding an Australian factory for the Nuffield Organisation in a second attempt to break into the Antipodean market with a purpose-built product. This venture eventually cost the British Motor Corporation a great deal of money, and was expensively shut down in 1974.

Following the creation of British Motor Corporation, Nuffield became no more than a figurehead. Though the company's two greatest post-war designs, the Minor and the Mini, were produced during his chairmanship, it is doubtful whether he had any say in their format at all.

And certainly when Nuffield died in 1963, it was as a philanthropist and not as a motor engineer that he was remembered. However, his memory of recent events had been clouded by his last illness, and, perhaps kindly, during his final months, Nuffield was living in spirit in the great days of the pre-1930 era. PD

MORS IS THE LATIN WORD FOR DEATH, a coincidence which did not escape the notice of a motorphobe Member of Parliament at the turn of the century, who claimed that the name implied that Mors drivers had the licence to kill anyone who crossed the path of their cars. Nor was the situation alleviated by the fact that the company was apt to use the Latin tag *Mors ianua vitae* in their advertising.

It is, however, difficult to see a deathshead in the hirsute and rubicund features of Emile Mors, the marque's progenitor, who in Victorian days had risen to become one of France's leading electrical engineers, heading one of the country's biggest telegraph, telephone and electrical-equipment factories. In the late 1880s, Mors became aware of Léon Serpollet's experiments with steam vehicles, and built a light three-wheeled steam carriage which was the first of its kind to have an oil-fired boiler (Serpollet was still using coke as a fuel); eighteen vertical fire-tubes were arranged over a similar number of wicks which could be raised or lowered to regulate the generation of steam. The steam was superheated in a copper coil before being passed to the vertical rear-mounted engine, which drove directly from crankshaft to rear wheels. The car, which had rack-and-pinion tiller steering, was shown at the 1889 Paris Exposition and again at the 1900 retrospective exhibition. Seven or eight of these vehicles were built, and in 1904 one was still in regular use by an enthusiast in Vendôme for travelling between his house and the local railway station—a good achievement for that time.

However, Mors realised the limitations of this design and, for the time being, devoted himself to the development of petrol motor trucks for portable railways,

THE GATEWAY TO LIFE

The Mors motto was 'Mors ianua vitae', which means 'death is the gateway to life'

several of which were built in 1892–3 to a patent taken out in England.

In 1895, he built his first petrol car, with a rear-mounted V4 air-cooled engine (which had, however, water-cooled cylinder heads) designed to minimise vibration. In the interests of simplicity and reliability, belt drive was adopted; ignition—of course—was electric, by coil and dynamo, with a battery used to boost the dynamo for starting. Once the car was running, the dynamo supplied all the ignition current, the surplus being used to recharge the battery. Two years later, the marque made its first appearance in competition, when Emile Mors himself drove a two-seater 5 hp Mors to seventh place in the 106.2-mile Paris–Dieppe Race on 24 July 1897, averaging 19.6 mph; two four-seater Mors driven by Mouter and Viard were sixth and seventh in their class, although their average speeds of 12.2 and 11.9 mph were hardly spectacular by more modern standards.

Top: the 6 hp four-cylinder, four-seater Mors of 1899

Above left: this is an 1897 two-seater version of the 6 hp Mors

Above right: by 1901, Mors cars had begun to look less like carriages and more like the modern motor car

The following season saw the end of Emile Mors's brief career as a racing driver: he was lying third in the Paris–Bordeaux race when he collided with a cart near Angoulême. Mors and his co-driver, Toussaint, were thrown from the wreck, and their team-mate, Levegh (the *nom de course* used by the rich and consumptive Alfred Velghe), gave up his chances of winning by stopping to give first aid to Mors, who had broken his collarbone. That year's racing Mors cars were belt-driven, with the V4 engine at the rear. The next year saw the company's first true racing cars, designed by Mors' new chief engineer Henri Brasier. These followed the contemporary Panhard layout, with front-mounted vertical in-line four-cylinder engines of 4.2 litres. Then, commented the Parisian *Motor Review*, 'there began a struggle for supremacy that forms the most brilliant page in automobile history . . . the new Mors, built purely for speed, eclipsed everything in that year by winning the events

good to automobilism, and the struggle itself had the still more important result in compelling the makers to surpass each other in the building of speedy vehicles'.

Just to show that the company had not entirely forgotten its origins, however, Emile Mors built an experimental petrol-electric car, one of the very first of its type, around this time; he also experimented with a magnetic clutch a year or so later. On the touring front, a new flat-twin light-car was available from 1899, although it had low-tension-magneto ignition in place of the ingenious dynamo.

The marque's racing successes obviously sold cars: when the firm began production on a serious scale, in 1898, the works employed 200 workmen. Six years later, the total had risen to 1200, and two cars per day were being turned out in the immense factory in the Rue de Théâtre.

By 1901, the touring Mors had in-line power units like the racers (although they retained the old air-cooled cylinder layout until 1902), chain drive and a primitive form of multi-choke carburettor also forming part of the specification.

The company's racing prestige had suffered a

in which it took part, and raised the record in long distance races to 37 miles an hour'. That record was made in the last race of the old century, the 163-mile Bordeaux–Biarritz, won by Levegh; his car attracted attention by its distinctive appearance, with its wedge-shaped bonnet, unlike any other racing car.

'Panhard and Mors,' continued the *Motor Review*, 'now fought a valiant battle for supremacy, M Mors coming out in 1900 with 20 hp cars piloted by men like Levegh and Fournier. The public interest in the rivalry between the two firms was so intense that the popularity thus given to racing did a vast amount of

Top: a drawing of a 6 hp Mors of 1898

Above: the brutal-looking Mors 60 hp racer, as used on the 1901 Paris–Bordeaux race

wounding blow when, despite convincing performances, Mors had failed to be selected for the French team for the 1900 Gordon Bennett. So, Levegh, in one of the new 7.3-litre Mors racers, followed the contestants in a 'freelance' capacity, and would have come second had he been officially taking part. Just to show it had not been a fluke, Levegh won the 837-mile Paris–Toulouse–Paris race against tough opposition, finishing well on elapsed time ahead of his nearest rival, Pinson, in a Panhard, although the Panhards of Pinson and Voight arrived at the finish actually in front of the Mors.

Below: this superbly restored machine is the 1902 Mors Paris–Vienna racer. It used a 9.2-litre engine and was chain driven. The car pictured is registered for the road and has taken part regularly in the annual London to Brighton run

Officially, the racing Mors for the 1901 season were rated at 28 hp, although their drivers reckoned that 60 hp would have been nearer the mark. Proof positive that Emile Mors' policy of 'build bigger . . . build faster' was the right one for that stage of automotive technology came with Fournier's victories in the Paris–Bordeaux and Paris–Berlin races that year. Mark you, a cyclist nearly changed the course of motor-

Below: a tile drawing of a 1903 Mors competing in the Paris–Madrid race. The drawing can also be seen on the Michelin building in London

PARIS-MADRID 1903   GABRIEL sur MORS

ing history when he dropped his paraffin lamp into a pool of petrol lying under the Mors just before the start of Paris–Bordeaux, but the flames were extinguished before more than superficial damage occurred.

Had Mors bothered to enter Fournier rather than Levegh for the Gordon Bennett, organised concurrently with Paris–Bordeaux, they would have won it, for the highest-placed GB contestant, Girardot (Panhard), was only ninth in the main event. Unfortunately, Levegh was eliminated by gear troubles near Tours.

Fournier won Paris–Berlin in convincing style, arriving half-an-hour ahead of Léonce Girardot, 'the eternal second', who was driving a Panhard. De Knyff (Panhard) was third, while Mr Designer Brasier was fourth, at the wheel of one of his own creations. Just how big a part luck played in motor racing was amply proved when Fournier started up his car for a triumphal drive through Berlin after the race —and the driving chain broke!

Despite the introduction of the 1000 kg weight limitation for 1902, Mors once again increased the engine capacity of their racers. These also featured a new design of four-speed transmission, which gave direct drive on top gear, plus a pioneering use of dampers, the first real attempt to deal scientifically with the bounding and leaping of the racing-car when at high speeds, a fruitful source of power loss. Two hydraulic dampers were fitted to the front axle, four to the back, and the Mors cars did indeed prove very fast; but trouble with the new gearbox eliminated Fournier from Paris–Vienna after he had *averaged* 71 mph from Paris to Provins, and then passed an express train as if it was standing still. Indeed, the Mors mortality rate in this race was alarmingly high, though it was said that 'the Mors prestige was not in the least decreased by their failure in Paris–Vienna'.

Indeed, 1902 wasn't really a Mors year, for Brasier left to join Georges Richard. Then their leading driver, Henri Fournier, transferred his allegiance to the new Hotchkiss company, which then added insult to injury

by enticing Brasier's colleague, Terrasse, to join them as designer; he then created a racing Hotchkiss that was more Mors than the genuine article.

A third member of their drawing office was to resign a year or so later; he was Charles Schmidt, who emigrated to America to design Continental-style cars for Packard.

Meanwhile the Mors company's racing career had reached a glorious peak with Gabriel's victory in the notorious Paris–Madrid; the car with which he averaged 65.3 mph from Paris to the race's abandonment in Bordeaux was one of the new Mors Dauphins. The company built 13 Dauphins in all, and their design represented a considerable technical advance over anything Mors had done before. They had pressed-steel chassis and an inlet-over-exhaust engine with all valves mechanically operated from a single camshaft, and, most strikingly, bodywork 'of the best racing design, quite smooth from radiator to back axle, in shape not unlike an upturned boat'.

But this wind-cheating shape was abandoned in 1904, when the company's racing cars acquired the new 'shouldered' pattern of honeycomb radiator that had just been introduced on the touring Mors models (and which, almost certainly, was the inspiration for the classic Packard radiator shape, which appeared after Schmidt had joined the American company).

These 110 hp, 13.6-litre cars were fast—one of them recorded a speed of 108.5 mph during 1904—but Emile Mors anticipated even larger, faster racing cars. However, the days of brute force were passing, and so

Above: a 1906 Mors with coachwork by Barker. Mors cars of this era had a reputation for quality and class

were the days of Mors and Panhard supremacy. Mors did not even bother with the 1905 Gordon Bennett, raced not at all in 1906 and made only token appearances in 1907 and 1908, culminating, if that is the word, in a failure-strewn attempt on the 1908 Grand Prix which even the presence of Camille Jenatzy in the team failed to enliven.

The company's touring cars followed the fortunes of the racers: when Levegh and Fournier were dominating the lists, Mors private cars were in wide demand, rivalling Mercedes as the *dernier cri* in motoring fashion.

But when the company gave up competition, the touring cars went into a gentle decline. Not that there was anything cheap or shoddy about the latter-day Mors; on the contrary, they tended to bristle with technical ingenuities like M Mors' compressed-air

Above: after the Mors company gave up competition, the touring cars went into a gentle decline. They were nevertheless still very impressive motor cars. This is the four-cylinder, two-seater Mors tourer of 1908

Right: a 1904 Mors tourer competing in the 1974 London to Brighton run

starter, which appeared around 1906, the same time that the company offered that ingenious form of windscreen known as the *Pare-Brise Huiller* after its inventor, a Mors director who was perhaps more famous under his *nom de course* of Gilles Hourgières.

There was, too, the Mors clutch: 'By the action of the clutch spring a cone is pressed forward between two levers, which tightens two bands lined with cast-iron segments round a steel band fitted to the flywheel. A very gradual engagement is obtained by this device, which has the merit of imposing no end thrust on the crank shaft'. And 'this device' was to remain a feature of all Mors cars over the next 20 years.

Another technical innovation of pre-Great War days was the herringbone-pattern final-drive gearing that was the obsession of the company's new manager, André Citroën, and which he would adopt, in stylised form, as the symbol of his own company in later years.

Citroën took over the running of Mors after the company had all but collapsed in the 1908 depression, and under his influence sales began to pick up, aided, no doubt, by the decision of the British agents (Jarrott & Letts, of Great Marlborough Street) to take the entire output of the 10/15 light car introduced at the end of 1909.

But even the activities of *le Petit Juif* couldn't reverse the process of decay. The first signs that the recovery had only been temporary came in 1912, when the company began to supplement its own power units with Silver Knight sleeve-valve engines supplied by Minerva of Antwerp (whose London agent, Danny Citroën, was related to André of that ilk); two years later Mors was totally beknighted save for the smallest model and a new side-valve 17/20 hp sporting car of handsome appearance.

After the war, it was nothing but decay and sleeve-valves: Citroën took over the Mors factory to produce

his Type A, though the older marque continued a sort of existence for a few more years.

Indeed, the Mors SSS (*Sans Soupapes Silencieuse*) was a rather fine car, with a radiator similar to the contemporary Bentley and four-wheel-braking from 1921. Minerva engines of 3.6-litres (plus, from 1922, a 2-litre unit) were used, but by 1926 production of Mors cars had just petered out.

The name was revived briefly during the war for a range of electric cars, though these were about as relevant to the company's history as the modern electric golf carts built in America under the Chadwick name are to that marque's supercharged Great Chadwick Six of 1908.

Perhaps the same veil that should be drawn over the wartime electric Mors should also cover the last vehicles to bear the name, for these were depressing motor scooters called, optimistically, Speed, built in the early 1950s before the marque finally succumbed to the *rigor mortis* that had been threatening for almost half a century.   DBW

THE SON OF MOSCOW

Moskvich is the second-oldest motor manufacturer in Russia.
The company specialises in medium-sized, low-priced saloons

TAKEN LITERALLY, THE NAME MOSKVICH means 'Son of Moscow' and it was in Moscow in 1947 that the Moskovskii Zavod Malitrajnikh Automobilie factory was established to manufacture passenger cars. Although it was relatively late in the development of the motor car, the Moscow factory is the second oldest car production facility in Russia, the first being the Gorky factory which produces Volga cars.

The first car which the factory produced was, in fact, manufactured from the dies which the Russians obtained from the German Adam Opel AG factory when the end of World War II brought about the enforced dismantling of the Russelsheim factory during 1945.

Called the Moskvich 400, this model was consequently identical to the pre-war Opel Kadett. Powered by a four-cylinder engine, which produced 23 bph, it was uprated in 1954 by three horsepower to become the Moskvich 401.

Two years later, the body was restyled to give birth

Below: the Moskvich 412 saloon of 1973. It was powered by a four-stroke, four-cylinder, 1478 cc engine, developing 80 bhp at 5800 rpm. It was also available with a 1760 cc Perkins diesel engine

to the Moskvich 402 and the engine power was increased to give 35 bhp at 4200 rpm. At the same time, a four-wheel-drive 410 version was introduced.

In 1958, the Russian factory produced the 45 bhp 407 range which had, as well as the saloon, station-wagon, ambulance, taxi, delivery-van and four-wheel-drive derivatives. Five years later, with the 407 still in production, a new model, the 403 saloon, was introduced and it too had delivery-van and station-wagon derivatives, although from a stylistic point of view the differences to the previous model were largely in the trim rather than anywhere else.

In 1966, the more radically changed 408 models were launched. A five seater, the saloon version was powered by a four-cylinder, 1.4-litre, overhead-valve engine, which produced 60 bhp. Suspension was independent at the front, while the rear was mounted via conventional leaf springs. Transmission was through a four-speed, fully synchromeshed gearbox. Station-wagon and delivery-van versions were produced and

VME 603M

Above: although Moskvich cars are not generally considered as sporting vehicles, they have nevertheless gained some impressive sporting results. Here two Moskvich 408s pass through an Afghan village during the 1968 London to Sydney Marathon, an event in which the cars performed very creditably

for the first time the cars were offered with optional extras such as twin headlamps, sun visors and electric windscreen wipers.

Early 1968 saw the announcement of the 412 series, powered by a 1480cc, overhead-camshaft engine, which produced 80 bhp and which still constituted the basic model of the 1975 range of cars.

The Moskvich 1500 range, introduced in May 1974, was an improved version of the original 412, with a new radiator grill, new fascia and an improved braking system. With estate and delivery-van derivatives, the car was still powered by the four-cylinder, 1478cc, overhead-camshaft, in-line, five-bearing-crankshaft unit which produced 80 bhp (SAE) at 5800 rpm. With a top speed of 90 mph, the engine had a compression ratio of 8.8:1 and a twin-choke down-draught carburettor. Transmission was through a centrally

mounted, four-speed, all-synchromesh gearbox and a single-plate diaphragm clutch. Servo-assisted drum brakes were fitted all round. Steering was by globoid worm and roller.

Standard features of the car included heater, two-speed wipers, fully reclining front seats, burst-proof locks and a cigar lighter. All models featured laminated windscreens, collapsible steering columns, dished steering wheels and padded dashboards.

The Moskvich 1500 five-door estate was powered by the same engine as the saloon, which give it the slightly slower top speed of 85 mph. The Moskvich 1500 three-door delivery-van had identical performance and technical characteristics to the estate.

Diesel-engined versions of the 412 were first assembled in Belgium by Sobimpex and called the Scaldia. They were powered by the English Perkins

Left: a Moskvich 400 of 1951. This was the first model that Moskvich produced and was based on the pre-war Opel Kadett

Left: the Moskvich Scaldia was built in Belgium and used the 1760 cc Perkins diesel engine, which produced 62 bhp at 4000 rpm

1760 cc diesel engine, which produced 62 bhp (SAE) at 4000 rpm and had a compression ratio of 22:1, giving the car a top speed of 75 mph. This diesel engine was also available in the estate version.

In the competition field Moskvich entries performed very creditably in the London to Sydney Marathon in 1968, while three Moskvich saloons finished the gruelling, 16000-mile World Cup Rally of 1970. In 1972, a Moskvich driven by Tony Lanfranchi was entered in Group One of the British Saloon Car Racing Championship and performed so well that the car won both the Castrol and Britax sections of the Championship before the season was complete, as well as all the class prizes that year. This success was repeated again in 1973.

In the Avon Motor Tour of Great Britain in July 1973, Moskvich entries took first, second, third and fourth places in their class.

Moskvich vehicles were first imported into Britain in the middle of 1970 by Satra Motors Ltd, a subsidiary of the New York-based Satra Corporation. Satra is an abbreviation of Soviet-American trading and the company was set up to promote trade between East and West.

Satra had bought out in June 1970 the previous company handling Soviet car imports in Britain, Thompson and Taylor (Russian Cars) Ltd, which had been formed in March 1960. Sales of Moskvich cars rose, as a consequence, from 300 units in 1969 to 14,500 in 1973.

In September 1974, Satra Motors opened a new car importation and preparation centre in Bridlington, Yorkshire, which was capable of handling up to 120 cars per day.   BJ

Above: 1968 saw the introduction of the Moskvich 412 model range. This car was powered by an overhead camshaft, 80 bhp, 1478 cc engine. It was also available in estate-car and delivery-van versions

Moskovski Zavod Malitrajnikh Automobilei introduced the Moskvich 412 in 1968. It was powered by a 1478 cc, 70 bhp, hemi-head engine that could take the four-door saloon to 90 mph. The car was still being produced in 1975, although the company was now titled Avtomobilny Zavod Imeni Leninskogo Komsomola.

Priced on the British market at £745 in early 1975, the 412 was probably the best value for money car available, the estate version costing a mere £104 more.

Suspension for the Moskvich is of the independent front type, using wishbones, coil springs, an anti-roll bar and telescopic dampers, while the rear is rigid with semi-elliptic leaf springs and telescopic dampers. Unfortunately, the car has a high centre of gravity which makes for dramatic cornering, not helped by the not-too-sophisticated suspension. A worm-and-double-roller steering, with 3.5 turns from lock to lock, does not ease matters when one is trying to steer out of sticky situations. However, it must be said that in the first full year of Group One racing in Britain during 1973, Tony Lanfranchi, driving a 412, walked away with the National Championship with consummate ease.

For the basic price, the buyer gets probably the most comprehensive tool kit as standard equipment on any car. The 23-piece set comprises, among the basics, a starting handle, a grease gun, a hand pump, tyre levers, a spare fan belt, a tyre-pressure gauge and an under-bonnet inspection lamp that plugs into the fuse box.

ENGINE Front-mounted, water-cooled straight-four. 82 mm (3.23 in) bore × 70 mm (2.76 in) stroke = 1478 cc (90.2 cu in). Maximum power 70 bhp at 5800 rpm; maximum torque 76 lb ft at 3000 rpm. Light-alloy cylinder block and head with wet liners. Compression ratio 8.8:1. 5 main bearings. 2 valves per cylinder operated, via rockers, by a single overhead camshaft. 1 downdraught twin-barrel carburettor.

TRANSMISSION Single-dry-plate clutch and four-speed manual gearbox. Ratios 1st 3.490, 2nd 2.040, 3rd 1.330, 4th 1, rev 3.390:1. Hypoid-bevel final drive. Ratio 4.220 (saloon), or 4.550:1 (estate).

CHASSIS Integral.

SUSPENSION Front—independent by wishbones, coil springs, an anti-roll bar and telescopic dampers. Rear — non-independent by a rigid axle and semi-elliptic leaf springs.

STEERING Worm and double roller. 3.50 turns from lock to lock.

BRAKES Servo-assisted drums all round.

WHEELS 4½in × 13.

TYRES 165 × 13 (saloon), or 175 × 13 (estate).

DIMENSIONS AND WEIGHT Wheelbase 94.49 in; track—front 48.70 in, rear—48.31 in; length 161.02 in; width 61.02 in; height 58.27 in (saloon), or 60.04 in (estate); ground clearance 7.28 in; dry weight 2205 lb (saloon), or 2271 lb (estate); turning circle between walls 32.8 ft; tank capacity 10 gals.

ELECTRICAL EQUIPMENT 12-volt, 42Ah battery. Two headlamps.

BODY 4-door, 5-seater saloon, or 5-door, 5-seater estate.

PERFORMANCE Maximum speed 90 mph. Acceleration 0—50 mph 10 secs. Fuel consumption 27 mpg.

This magnificent four-color encyclopedia is brought to you by Columbia House

in cooperation with Orbis Publishing Ltd., one of Great Britain's most enterprising publishers.

Rather than change any of the encylopedia's authoritative international automotive text, we have

included a glossary of terms that will give you immediate American equivalents, a conversion table

for the international metric system, and a conversion table for equivalent monetary values.

Glossary

BRITISH	AMERICAN
Aerial	Antenna
Aluminium	Aluminum
Apron	Skirt
Big-end	Rod (conrod) bearing
Blower *(colloquial)*	Supercharger
Bonnet	Hood
Boot	Trunk
Brake servo	Power brake
Bulkhead	Firewall
Capacity	Displacement
Carburetter; carburettor	Carburetor
Check strap	Door stop
Clutch release bearing	Clutch throwout bearing
Control box	Voltage regulator
Crown wheel and pinion	Ring gear and pinion
Cylinder block	Cylinder crankcase
Dip switch	Dimmer switch
Door pillar	Door post
Drop arm	Pitman arm
Drop-head	Convertible
Dynamo	Generator
Epicylic gearbox	Planetary gearbox
Exhaust silencer	Muffler
Facia panel	Dashboard
Gear lever	Gear shift lever
Gearbox	Transmission
Gearbox housing	Transmission casing
Gearchange	Gearshift
Glassfibre	Fiberglass
Grease nipple	Grease fitting
Gudgeon pin	Piston or wrist pin
Half shaft	Axle shaft
Handbrake	Parking brake
Hose clip	Hose clamp
Ignition harness	Ignition set
Kerb	Curb
Layshaft	Counter shaft
Main shaft	Output shaft
Marque	Brand, make

BRITISH	AMERICAN
Motor	Engine
Number plate	License plate
Overrider	Bumper guard
Paraffin	Kerosene
Parking brake	Parking lock
Petrol	Gasoline, "gas"
Petrol pump	Gasoline or fuel pump
Production car	Stock car
Propellor shaft	Drive shaft
Quarter light	Door vent
Rear lamp	Tail light
Rear seat squab	Rear setback or backrest
Reverse lamp	Back up light
Roof lamp	Dome light
Saloon	Sedan
Scuttle	Cowl
Selector rod	Shift bar
Servo-assisted	Power assisted
Side lamp	Parking light
Side member	Side rail
Spanner	Wrench
Sparking plug	Spark plug
Starting handle	Crank handle
Steering column	Steering post
Steering relay	Steering idler
Stub axle	Steering knuckle
Sump	Pan
Swivel pin	King pin
Toe board	Toe pan
Track	Tread
Track rod	Tie bar or track bar
Two-stroke	Two-cycle
Tyre	Tire
Valance	Rocker panel
Wheel arch	Wheelhouse or housing
Wheel brace	Wheel wrench
Windscreen	Windshield
Wing	Fender
Wishbone	A-arm; Control arm
Works	Plant, factory

Metric Equivalents
(Based on National Bureau of Standards)

Length

Centimeter (Cm.)	= 0.3937 in.	In.	= 2.5400 cm.
Meter (M.)	= 3.2808 ft.	Ft.	= 0.3048 m.
Meter	= 1.0936 yd.	Yd.	= 0.9144 m.
Kilometer (Km.)	= 0.6214 mile	Mile	= 1.6093 km.

Area

Sq. cm.	= 0.1550 sq. in.	Sq. in.	= 6.4516 sq. cm.
Sq. m.	= 10.7639 sq. ft.	Sq. ft.	= 0.0929 sq. m.
Sq. m.	= 1.1960 sq. yd.	Sq. yd.	= 0.8361 sq. m.
Hectare	= 2.4710 acres	Acre	= 0.4047 hectar
Sq. km.	= 0.3861 sq. mile	Sq. mile	= 2.5900 sq. km.

Volume

Cu. cm.	= 0.0610 cu. in.	Cu. in.	= 16.3872 cu. cm.
Cu. m.	= 35.3145 cu. ft.	Cu. ft.	= 0.0283 cu. m.
Cu. m.	= 1.3079 cu. yd.	Cu. yd.	= 0.7646 cu. m.

Capacity

Liter	= 61.0250 cu. in.	Cu. in.	= 0.0164 liter
Liter	= 0.0353 cu. ft.	Cu. ft.	= 28.3162 liters
Liter	= 0.2642 gal. (U.S.)	Gal.	= 3.7853 liters
Liter	= 0.0284 bu. (U.S.)	Bu.	= 35.2383 liters

$$\text{Liter} = \begin{cases} 1000.027 \text{ cu. cm.} \\ 1.0567 \text{ qt. (liquid) or } 0.9081 \text{ qt. (dry)} \\ 2.2046 \text{ lb. of pure water at } 4\ C = 1 \text{ kg.} \end{cases}$$

Weight

Gram. (Gm.)	= 15.4324 grains	Grain	= 0.0648 gm.
Gram	= 0.0353 oz.	Oz.	= 28.3495 gm.
Kilogram (Kg.)	= 2.2046 lb.	Lb.	= 0.4536 kg.
Kg.	= 0.0011 ton (sht.)	Ton (sht.)	= 907.1848 kg.
Ton (met.)	= 1.1023 ton (sht.)	Ton (sht.)	= 0.9072 ton (met.)
Ton (met.)	= 0.9842 ton (lg.)	Ton (lg.)	= 1.0160 ton (met.)

Pressure

1 kg. per sq. cm.	= 14.223 lb. per sq. in.
1 lb. per sq. in.	= 0.0703 kg. per sq. cm.
1 kg. per sq. m.	= 0.2048 lb. per sq. ft.
1 lb. per sq. ft.	= 4.8824 kg. per sq. m.
1 kg. per sq. cm.	= 0.9678 normal atmosphere

$$1 \text{ normal atmosphere} = \begin{cases} 1.0332 \text{ kg. per sq. cm.} \\ 1.0133 \text{ bars} \\ 14.696 \text{ lb. per sq. in.} \end{cases}$$

Approximate Values of the Pound (£)
in terms of U.S. Dollars ($)

1914-1919	$4.76
1935	4.90
1936	4.97
1937	4.94
1938	4.89
1939	4.46
1940-1949	4.03
1950-1967	2.80
1968-1970	2.40
1971-1972	$2.40/2.60
1972-Present	2.60/2.10